Charles Wordsworth

The Outlines of the Christian Ministry

Delineated and Brought to the Test of Reason, Holy Scripture, History...

Charles Wordsworth

The Outlines of the Christian Ministry
Delineated and Brought to the Test of Reason, Holy Scripture, History...

ISBN/EAN: 9783337141479

Printed in Europe, USA, Canada, Australia, Japan

Cover: Foto ©Lupo / pixelio.de

More available books at **www.hansebooks.com**

THE OUTLINES

OF THE

CHRISTIAN MINISTRY

DELINEATED

AND BROUGHT TO THE TEST OF REASON, HOLY SCRIPTURE, HISTORY,
AND EXPERIENCE; WITH A VIEW TO THE RECONCILIATION OF
EXISTING DIFFERENCES CONCERNING IT, ESPECIALLY
BETWEEN PRESBYTERIANS AND EPISCOPALIANS.

BY

CHARLES WORDSWORTH, D.C.L.

BISHOP OF S. ANDREWS,

FELLOW OF WINCHESTER COLLEGE.

LONDON:

LONGMANS, GREEN, AND CO.

1872.

PREFACE.

THE FOLLOWING LECTURES were written as they now appear, about three years ago; and they were intended to have been delivered in the principal cities and towns of Scotland, especially at the seats of our four universities—Edinburgh, Glasgow, Aberdeen, and St. Andrews. Several reasons, both of a public and private nature, concurred at the time to prevent the accomplishment of this design; and it is not improbable that the publication would have been indefinitely postponed, or even abandoned altogether, had not the perusal of Professor Lightfoot's masterly dissertation[1] on 'the Christian Ministry,' (which, though it came out first in 1868, I did not happen to see till quite recently), revived my interest in the subject, and confirmed me in the conclusions at which I had arrived. My first impulse, on reading that

[1] Appended to his edition of St. Paul's Epistle to the Philippians.

essay, was to apply to the Professor with a request
that he would allow it to be reprinted apart from the
volume to which it belongs, with the view to its being
used as a text-book by students of presbyterian
denominations, as well as by ourselves; not as
though I concurred—or expected Presbyterians to
concur—in the representation of every particular
point exactly as it there stands, but because I regarded it—and ventured to hope that their learned
divines and theological professors[1] would also regard it—as, on the whole, an admirably competent
and fair discussion of the important subject with
which it deals. In short, I entertained the idea that
the critical and, so to speak, scientific spirit of the Professor's essay—entirely in harmony, as it is, with the

[1] When the above was written, I
had not read Principal Tulloch's
article in the 'Contemporary Review' for the present month (January 1872), 'On the English and
Scotch Churches,' nor was I aware
that he had spoken of Professor
Lightfoot's Dissertation in terms
virtually the same as I have used.
It gives me sincere pleasure to be
able to anticipate his concurrence in
the recommendation of it which I
have expressed above. And when
he admits, as he does in that same
article, that now 'there are few wise
Presbyterians who do not see weak-
nesses in their own system arising
from the disuse of episcopacy,' p.
236, I hail the statement as affording
the very basis we require for a
mutual understanding; and I re-
ciprocate it by expressing my own
belief, that there are few wise Episcopalians who do not see elements
of strength in the presbyterian system
which are wanting to their own. See
also the statement of Dr. P. C.
Campbell, Principal of the University of Aberdeen, quoted below, p.
92, note.

most advanced scholarship of the present day—its
thoroughly accurate and profound research, its calm
judicial tone, and above all, its transparent impar-
tiality—leading the writer to distrust conclusions in
favour of his own clerical position, rather than the
contrary—would suffice to recommend it to all who
desire to find some common ground, upon which the
advocates of episcopacy and presbyterianism may
look for the reconciliation of their mutual differences.

This, as I have said, was my first impression ; but
when I turned to my own MS. and began to compare
it with the dissertation in question, without any
undue predilection, I trust, for my own performance, I
could not but see that, however inferior the latter
might be in many respects, the more popular form
into which it had been cast, as necessary for 'Lectures' to a miscellaneous audience, and still more its
comprehensive practical character, leading me to
speak of many most important matters with which
the Professor had no call to deal, might tend to
render its publication now not the less, but rather
the more desirable, as a separate and independent
witness in favour of conclusions which are *substantially* identical and common to us both. At the same
time, I have not failed to give my reader the benefit of constant references to Dr. Lightfoot's work,

wherever we traverse the same ground ; and I have carefully pointed out, I believe, every instance in which I have found that the view which I had taken is different from his.

And now it may be expedient to state shortly in this place what has been my intention and aim in these Lectures.

Their main purpose is, by a succinct but exact and exhaustive method, *first*, to enquire what may be presumed to be—and *next*, to show what has actually been—the probable will and design of God in regard to the constitution of the Christian Ministry.

In executing this purpose, there has been no desire to challenge the validity of ordinances administered otherwise than according to that constitution. It is not denied—on the contrary, it is most freely and joyfully admitted—that spiritual benefits may be— and have been—derived to those duly qualified to receive them under other systems. But, on the other hand, it is maintained, nevertheless, that, the Church being God's Institution, and God being, as the Scripture teaches, a God 'not of confusion but of peace,' in His Church no less than in His World, a conscientious and enlightened sense of duty should induce the true servants of God to conform themselves to the arrangements which He appears to have made with the view to that result. More particularly, it is argued that the preservation and enjoyment of peace and order among Christians, (greatly as we all must regret their loss, and desire their return), *are not to be expected*, so long as a portion of the Church's organisation, which is so deeply rooted, as the Threefold or Episcopal ministry can be shown to be, in the history of the past, and which runs up so clearly, without any other form of ministry actually discernible, into apostolic times and into Scripture itself, is set aside and disallowed.

The author, therefore, has no wish to impose the conclusion which he has reached, as necessary or binding upon the conscience ; except so far as whatever is thought, upon sufficient grounds, to be subservient to the cause of peace and order in religion, and to be agreeable to reason, and to indications of a divine intention, fairly gathered from Scriptural rules and examples, and from the general practice of the universal Church, may justly be considered necessary and binding upon the conscience of those *who so think* ; though not of those who, upon the like, or, as they may suppose, better information, have been led to think otherwise. Only it is earnestly entreated, for the love of God and man, that 'the like or better information' may not be assumed without proof ; but may be brought openly to the light of day, and submitted to the same close inspection which the writer challenges for his own argument. If indeed I had not, on my own part, sifted the whole question to the bottom with the utmost accuracy and conscientiousness of which I am capable—as in a matter of the gravest and most solemn importance to us all, socially, politically, and religiously—I could not have ventured to come forward as I do with such an appeal. For though I may appear to speak boldly and confidently, it must not be supposed that I am not keenly sensible of the extreme delicacy and difficulty of the task which I undertake, when I invite, for the most part, those whom I address to do that from which we are all of us naturally averse—viz. to reconsider the grounds of the position in which they find themselves (it may be, from accidental circumstances, or from inherited necessity, rather than from deliberate choice), and which they have hitherto perhaps been accustomed to regard with satisfaction, if not with confidence. As it is, there are two large classes of Christians in particular, who, I cannot but hope, will be inclined to look with some interest on this appeal, and endeavour to promote the end at which it aims. I mean, first, all who desire to maintain the public profession of our National Christianity throughout Great Britain ; which is becoming daily more and more weakened through the continuance of our separations, especially the separation between our two National Church establishments : and, secondly, all who appreciate the necessity and the benefits of the Reformation in the sixteenth century ; the maintenance of which has also become imperilled through the same cause. A third, and I fear a rapidly increasing class, who point to our separations as an excuse for their distrust and practical rejection of all religion, may be expected, on the other hand, to regard the whole discussion with indifference, if not with scorn.

There is one other point upon which it seems necessary to speak before I conclude this Preface.

It has too often been the practice, on the part of the opponents of the threefold ministry, to press the advocates of it to conclusions which are as undesirable as they are unnecessary. Because we hold that such a ministry is, and, in view of the past history of the Church, must ever be, expedient, if not essential to unity and good order among Christians, it does not, therefore, follow that we insist upon it as 'of divine right' in the highest sense in which that phrase may be understood, or in the same sense in which the two great sacraments of the Gospel are of 'divine right.' The latter are imperative in consequence of the express and direct command of Christ Himself, while the former rests for its immediate sanction upon no such command, but upon the duty of order and unity in the Christian body—not in this or that portion of the body, but in the whole—as it has existed from the beginning and will continue to exist till the end of time. For my own part, on the one hand, I accept Professor Lightfoot's conclusions as amply sufficient and satisfactory when he writes as follows :—

'If the preceding investigation be substantially correct, the threefold ministry can be traced to apostolic direction, and, short of an express statement, we can possess no better assurance of a divine appointment, or at least a divine sanction.'—Page 265. And again: 'The form of the ministry has been handed down from apostolic times, and may well be presumed to have a divine sanction.'—Page 266.

On the other hand, I also agree with him that 'the facts do not allow us '—certainly do not require us—'to unchurch other Christian communities differently organised ': though I cannot forbear adding, that *the co-existence* of such different organisations, equally claiming to be 'Churches,' *in the same place*, has not come up in the course of the Professor's investigation, and appears to rest upon no sufficient human, as it certainly rests upon no divine authority. And further,

—though I do not believe that a single well-authenticated instance of merely presbyterian ordination is
to be found in the records of the ancient Church,[1]
—I agree with Dr. Lightfoot that 'the general
rule' (p. 231, comp. p. 224) upon that point is all
that we ought to plead for, and that sufficient
grounds are to be discovered (without descending to
post-Reformation times) in the nature of the early
evidence itself—and I would add in the spirit which
appears to have guided the primitive Church in dealing
with the reconciliation of old and wide-spread differences—to induce us to suspend, so far as may be necessary, the obligation of the rule, if by so doing we can
open a way for return to that unity which it was one
great object of the rule to accomplish and secure. In
a word, if we are to extricate ourselves out of our present position (which no earnest Christian can approve
of, or feel to be satisfactory), we must look to the
broad principles of the Gospel, and to its spirit of
charity and brotherly love, which should suffice to remind us that God 'will have mercy and not sacrifice,'
whenever sacrifice interferes with that higher law;

[1] On the other hand, it has to be *assumed*, on our part, that a distinct form of ordination was required from the beginning for each of the three orders; which cannot, I believe, be *proved* till we come to the third and fourth centuries.

which is above *all* ordinances; and certainly, therefore, above such as cannot claim the obligation of
an express command; which sacrifice could claim when
the prophet Hosea was inspired to write those words.
I am fully persuaded that if the bishops and councils
of the primitive Church had been called upon to consider a case similar to that of presbyterian Scotland
at the present day—a case of inveterate and widely-
spread divergence from catholic usage—but a divergence accompanied all the while with most unquestionable exhibitions of true Christian character, and a
most conscientious fervent desire to do honour to the
written Word of God, they would have taken their
stand upon those broad principles and that charitable
spirit; provided they had reason to hope that such a
course would serve to heal the separation, and would
also tend to the better and more extensive observance
of the suspended usage for the time to come. Upon
this point I shall be prepared to speak more at length,
and more definitely, if the proper season and occasion
for my doing so should ever arrive. In the meantime
let me recommend to the consideration of all my
readers, both episcopalian and presbyterian, the following words of Antony Faringdon, which it would
have been well for the Church of England if she

had taken for her guide at the time of the Restoration :—

'The rules of discretion and spiritual prudence will teach us that thriving lesson—to lose something that we may gain the more ; to yield that we may overcome ; not to be overjust to ourselves that others may be won at the last to do us the more right; not to stand upon credit and reputation when we plead for peace.'—Serm. lxxxi. (preached A.D. 1654), vol. iii. p. 400.

It was my endeavour to make each of the three Lectures complete, as far as possible, in itself, in consideration of the different persons who might be present on different occasions among the audience ; and it is possible that this may have given rise to somewhat more of repetition, or redundancy in the treatment of the subject, than would otherwise have been the case. Should the reader be conscious of such an objection, I must ask for his kind indulgence to forgive it.

Having now reached the twentieth anniversary of my consecration to the episcopal office, I feel that I am committing to the press what may not improbably prove my last legacy to my fellow-Christians ; and I earnestly pray that the Divine Blessing may

attend it, in proportion to the singleness of purpose
with which I have laboured to make it not altogether
unworthy to promote the great and all-important
object at which it aims.

PERTH, *January* 25, 1872.
        (*Conversion of St. Paul.*)

ANALYTICAL VIEW

OF

CONTENTS OF THE THREE LECTURES.

———•◦•———

LECTURE I.

a 2

II. Second main Argument—from Holy Scripture and from History.

LECTURE II.

Second main Argument—*continued*.

Author's former standing-point, at the close of the first century, resumed, and the historical evidence traced *downwards* through the earliest post-apostolic age (A.D. 100–233), and, more generally, into subsequent times :—

OBJECTIONS TO FOREGOING EVIDENCE CONSIDERED
AND ANSWERED.

LECTURE III.

III. Third main Argument—ex consequente;

OUTLINES

OF THE

CHRISTIAN MINISTRY.

—◆◇◆—

LECTURE I.

IT WAS OBSERVED not long ago, by a writer in one of our leading journals, that 'the few and feeble attempts which have been made to effect a union of Christians have almost all proceeded upon the assumption that there is some one Church which is destined to assimilate and absorb all the others;' and it was added, 'As long as this belief prevails our very endeavours after union will only tend to exasperate the spirit of division.' Concurring as I do in the truth and justice of that remark, I desire, first of all, to disown and repudiate, on my own part, any such assumption.

I shall not indeed deny that one of my objects in these Lectures is to induce you to think less unfavourably of Bishops than many, I know, have been taught and are wont to think of them. I wish to be allowed to show you that there is much—very much—to be said, I do not mean for ourselves

B

personally, but for our office ; and that, not as it may be found
in any special development, not as it exists or has existed
in any one particular Church, but *in itself.* I wish, more
particularly, to plead that, whatever may have been the delinquencies of our forefathers, either before or since the Reformation ; whatever may have been their delinquencies—and
I am not here to extenuate them—they were no necessary
part of the system itself ; and that we, their descendants,
having been disestablished and disendowed for nearly two
centuries, have now suffered enough on their account. But
why do I wish, why do I come forward, to attempt this ?
Not certainly with a selfish or contracted view to our own
interests ; not certainly because I desire merely to uphold
Prelacy, still less to assail or disparage Presbyterianism ; nor
simply because, as a bishop of the Church, I am bound, so
far as I may be able, to vindicate and promote what appears
to me to be the truth : no ; but because the truth which
I would seek to recommend is, I am persuaded, no less
desirable for others than for ourselves ; or, to speak more
plainly, because it is, in my opinion, of the utmost importance to the interests of us all—to our moral, social, political
and religious interests, and, I will add, to the interests of the
Gospel throughout the world—that the differences between
Episcopacy and Presbyterianism should be reconsidered with
a view to their removal, or adjustment upon sound principles ;
in order to place religion in a stronger position against irreligion, and, at the same time, to place reformed Christianity
in a stronger position against that which is still unreformed.

These, and no less than these, are the great objects which
I have in view. And am I mistaken when I say that the
circumstances, both of the country and of the time in which
we live, are more than commonly suited to encourage us to
make such an attempt?

Scotland is the only country in Christendom in which an
independent national Presbyterianism and an independent
national Reformed Episcopacy are so intermingled that they
can look upon each other face to face. Both in turn have
been once and again in a position of State Establishment.
Neither hitherto has been so fully and so permanently successful in that position, but it must have felt that it might,
with benefit to itself, have borrowed something from the
other. When the one has been weak the other has been
strong, and in that which the one has most lacked the other
has most abounded. Such is the advantage which we possess in comparison, for instance, with any of the countries
upon the continent of Europe, in none of which a Reformed
Episcopate is to be found, however much it may be desired
by many; though Episcopacy unreformed is to be found in
all of them. And in regard to the advantage of the present
time, we have recently been told upon high authority, that
'the age in which we live is one of searching enquiry after
truth.' What, then, can be more suitable than that we
should set ourselves to apply such an enquiry to the subject
upon which our main difference has turned; not as desiring
to prove that one party has been in the right, and the other
in the wrong, but as frankly admitting that there have been

*Advantages
of Scotland
and of the
present time.*

faults on both sides, and as simply desiring to ascertain the truth, in order that the truth, which alone *can*, through the blessing of God, may now at length reconcile our differences and reunite us to each other.

Necessity of
Union.

It is nothing more than a truism to say, that division among the adherents of any cause is a certain source of weakness to that cause, and a hindrance to its success. Now, I trust, we are all adherents of Christianity, and most of us, if not all, adherents of Reformed or Protestant Christianity. As adherents of Christianity we require greater union, for its own sake, because unity among His disciples is prescribed by the Divine Author of our religion. As adherents of Reformed Christianity we require the same, in order that, presenting a united front upon true principles, we may be able to maintain and advance our position against the unabated aggressions of the Church of Rome, which, because it is ostensibly united, though upon false principles, is still found, in spite of its errors, to possess for many minds an attraction which, on account of our differences and divisions, we cannot boast.[1]

[1] The following words were spoken by the Pope, March 20, 1869, in answer to an Address from a deputation of English Romanists : 'We must cultivate in a most especial manner the spirit of unity ; for *in that lies our strength, and its want is the weakness of our adversaries.*' He repeated, 'Protestants are disunited ; and our strength in the difficulties we have to encounter lies in perfect union.' Compare with the above a recent statement of the Bishop of Ely : 'Union is vital to Christianity now ; and if Rome alone in Western Christendom exhibits an united front, it will draw a much larger host of earnest hearts into it than it has ever drawn yet.'

And let us not be told that the truth which may lead to such a blessed and important result is either immaterial in itself or impossible to be ascertained. There are, I know, many, too many, who are inclined to hold one or both of these positions. For my own part, I cannot allow that anything whatever which tends, practically and directly, to create disunion between fellow-Christians and fellow-countrymen, and thereby to dishonour God by disobedience to His plain commands, and to give advantage to the enemies of true religion, can properly be regarded as of little or no importance. Neither can I admit that the difficulty of ascertaining the truth upon the subject before us is by any means so great or insurmountable as some would lead us to suppose,[1] if only we will undertake the enquiry in a proper spirit. We have all accepted the settlement of a question which in itself is far more difficult, far more impossible for any but men of learning and laborious research,—I mean, in regard to the books which constitute the canon or authentic volume of Holy Scripture,[2] a subject upon which all the Reformed Churches are agreed among themselves, but are not agreed with the Church of Rome. In like

The question important, an not incapable of solution.

---

[1] Take, for example, these words of Mr. Hallam, writing of Scotland in the seventeenth century : ' The main controversy between the Episcopal and Presbyterian Churches was one . . . . little more interesting than those about the Roman Senate or the Saxon Wittenagemot, nor per- haps more capable of decisive solution ; it was at least one as to which the bulk of mankind are absolutely incapable of forming a rational judgment for themselves.'—*Const. Hist.*, iii. p. 443.

[2] See below, Lecture ii.

manner I am persuaded that the question of the right constitution of the Christian ministry is fully capable of solution,
and of solution in a way far more plain and obvious to men
of ordinary understanding.   Originally, indeed, there was no
difficulty about it at all.   No learning, no investigation was
required ; men had only to follow the plain teaching of
God's Word, which bade them, on the one hand, not to
separate themselves, and, on the other, to obey those who,
in spiritual matters, had legitimately the rule over them
(Heb. xiii. 17 ; see also 7–9).   They would easily see that
observance of these precepts was quite inconsistent with the
notion of a variety of ministries in the same Christian community, or even in the Church at large; unless it could be
proved that the apostles themselves had authorised such
variety in different localities—a supposition inconsistent with
the fact that all, or nearly all the historical evidence which
we possess goes to prove the direct contrary, showing, as it
does most conclusively, that the primitive Churches, when
fully organised, exhibited everywhere one and the same
system.[1]

How the
question has
become
difficult.

There was, then, I say, under the Divine guidance, no
difficulty at all about this question in the first instance. And

[1] Upon this point the following
words of the historian, Gibbon,
afford a testimony which is all-
sufficient. Speaking of the Church
in the second century, he writes :
'*No Church without a bishop* was
(then) *a fact* as well as *a maxim.*
As soon as we have passed the difficulties of the first century, we find
Episcopacy *everywhere established,*
until it was disturbed by the republican genius of the Swiss and German Reformers.' See also below,
p. 31 sq.

although afterwards, when usurpation and misgovernment had provoked a spirit of insubordination, and when a spirit of insubordination led men to divisions, and when all such divisions [1] were attended more or less with deviations from the original model; although, I say, when the question had become thus perplexed, difficulties undoubtedly arose— difficulties which do now require learning and research to master them—yet I cannot believe they are insurmountable. I cannot bring myself to think that God would have required, as we see in Scripture that He does, united and harmonious action on the part of His Church—which united action we know by experience to be impossible without a substantial unity and uniformity in its constitution, more especially its clerical constitution—I cannot bring myself to think that He would have required this unless He had designed to mark out sufficiently what was to be the form of that constitution, and had also provided evidence which (though obscured more or less, in proportion to men's disobedience) should never cease to be accessible, to enable us to discover it. Moreover, we know the evils—the hindrances to the healthy and effectual working of the Church—which are caused by sectarianism, and especially ministerial sectarianism; and is it to be supposed that we are for ever to be condemned to this state of things because the only sufficient remedy is

---

[1] I am speaking of those subsequent to the Reformation. In the earlier times the hold of the threefold ministry was so strong upon the consciences of Christians of all kinds, that it was retained even by those bodies who separated from the Church.

unattainable? It is true that ministerial division is often only the index and representative of a divergence in other respects; but it is also true that the greatest separation, the most melancholy and most extensive feud which has ever arisen among fellow Christians in this country, has arisen *mainly* out of disagreement in regard to this single point, the true constitution of the Church's ministry; and to this day the same single point forms the distinctive ground of that most unbrotherly discordance between the northern and southern portions of Great Britain, which, whether as Englishmen or Scotchmen, we have all most occasion to deplore. Once more: it can be shown that elements of identity underlie the principal diversities of system which actually exist, and that the diversities themselves can all be traced historically to one and the same common origin.

For these, among other reasons, I cannot but conclude that there ought to be discoverable what I may venture to call emphatically the right constitution of the Christian ministry, and that the fault must lie with ourselves if we fail to discover it, and to agree upon its acceptance.

So far I have explained the general scope and grounds of the enquiry, upon which I would invite you now to enter, and the principal object which it has in view. I have next to state, that I propose to divide the treatment of it into three main heads or lines of argument.

Threefold Division of Subject.

1. The argument *à priori*, or from what was rationally to have been expected beforehand under the circumstances of the case.

2. The *Scriptural* and *historical* argument, which will contain the formal and direct proof, and therefore will require to be treated most fully.

3. The argument *ex consequente*, or from the results which tend directly or indirectly to confirm the conclusions before arrived at.

Such is to be the course of our proposed investigation. I have already admitted that the enquiry cannot now be conducted so as to lead to any sound or trustworthy conclusion without study and research. For this reason I have announced that I address my appeal more especially to the learned professors and students of our universities. But I address it, in the next degree, to all those who are responsible in the sight of God for the right guidance of the mass of the humbler and less-instructed of their fellow Christians and fellow countrymen ; to the ministers of religion, to the members of the Legislature, to the better educated of the laity of all ranks, to the leaders of public opinion in all departments. At the same time, I shall endeavour to make all that I have to say perfectly intelligible, and I hope not altogether uninteresting to any miscellaneous audience who may favour me with their attention ; and while I shall avoid, as far as possible, all appearance of controversial disputation, I promise you that I shall omit to notice no argument of importance which has been alleged upon *either* side, and I shall produce no testimony or quotation of any kind which I have not myself drawn directly from its original source.

Persons more particularly addressed.

I now begin with the first main argument—the argument *à priori*, or from rational anticipation.

The Church a visible organisation.

1. When we see the Church spoken of in Holy Scripture as a body, as a kingdom, as a house and household, as a sheep-fold, as a tree or plant, we seem in these comparisons to be referred at once to the idea of a constitutional unity. And this idea is strengthened when we further read, still in connection with the same comparisons, that there must be no schism, no disjointure, in the body ; no rebellion, no insubordination, in the kingdom ; no division, no dissension in the house ; no alienation, no wandering from the fold; no splitting, no dissevering of the branches from the parent tree. Nor will it suffice to understand these requirements, as though they could be satisfied with fulfilment only in a spiritual sense. Doubtless their fulfilment in that sense is essential.[1] Doubtless, whatever else the Church may be, it is above all things (to take the foremost of these typical comparisons) a body spiritual, a body mystical. But, as militant in this world, it is, and must be also a body visible ; a body having form and constitution ; no less than an army is visible, and has a form and constitution as such, over and above the immortal souls of the men of whom it is composed. We cannot, therefore, escape from the conclusion, that there

---

[1] See the admirable remarks of the Bishop of Salisbury in his ' Bampton Lectures,' pp. 198–200. And Professor Lightfoot has well pointed out (p. 237) how the extravagance of hierarchical pretensions, as exhibited, for instance, in parts of the Ignatian Epistles, and in the Clementine Homilies, naturally led to the spiritual reaction of Montanism.

is a constitution, a right constitution, of the Church and of its ministry, which is to be sought for and maintained, if we would pay due attention to the laws which Christ Himself has prescribed, and the means which He has provided for the life, the welfare, and the extension of the Body of which He is the Head. He alone, I need scarcely say, is the sole original source, as of all power in the world, so of all government and administration in His Church; and without authority from Him, as the Head, as the High Priest of our profession, as the one only supreme Bishop and Shepherd of our souls, nothing is, or can be, lawfully done, that is done, in *any* constitution of the Christian ministry.

2. Again: the analogy of what we may observe in the external world would lead us to the same conclusion. It is true that the utmost variety abounds everywhere in Nature; but only such variety as is regulated by strict regard to the principle of *order*, and to the due fulfilment of the functions which each portion of creation is expected to discharge. We are expressly told in the New Testament that God is 'a God not of confusion,[1] but of peace' and order in His Church, no less than in His world; and we know from experience, that the prescribed functions of the Church are not only imperfectly performed, but grievously impaired and hindered in consequence of the diversity of ecclesiastical organisations which now exists. In a word, 'Order is God's first law:

Analogy from order of Nature.

---

[1] 1 Cor. xiv. 33. 'Confusion'; 'want of a settled constitution.' in the original ἀκαταστασίας, literally

is it, then, to exist everywhere save in the ministry of the Christian Church?

Correspond-
ence be-
tween the
Jewish and
Christian
Ministry.
3. Again: the evident relation which we discern between the Law and the Gospel, the Jewish and the Christian Church; a relation which exhibits the latter as the continuation and completion of the former;[1] a relation which is exemplified in the correspondence between the two great Jewish ordinances of Circumcision and the Passover, and the two great Christian sacraments of Baptism and the Lord's Supper; between the Jewish Sabbath and the Christian Lord's Day; between the public and private worship enjoined upon the Jew, and the public and private worship[2] enjoined upon the Christian; between the Jewish covenant of infant circumcision and the Christian covenant of infant baptism; between the form and substance of the inspired teaching of the Jewish Scriptures, and the form and substance of the inspired teaching of the Christian Scriptures; between the foundation of the Jewish Church upon the twelve patriarchs, and the foundation of the Christian Church upon the twelve apostles; Christ Himself being in both revealed to faith as the Head Corner Stone.[3]   This correspondence,

---

[1] See Bishop of Lincoln on Jeremiah xxxiii. 18–22.

[2] The ritual of the Tabernacle and Temple is consummated and spiritualised in the Christian Church. See Bishop of Lincoln on Isaiah lx. 7. See also the prophecy of Amos ix. 11, 12, as quoted by St. James in the Council at Jerusalem, Acts xv. 15-17.

[3] It might have been added between the observance of the Jewish festivals, such as the Feast of Tabernacles, Passover, and Pentecost, and the observance of the Christian festivals, such as Christmas, Easter,

I say, when traced in its details, would naturally lead us to
look for some tokens of a similar correspondence between
the constitution of the Jewish and the constitution of the
Christian Church; in other words, would lead us to look not
only for a definite organisation, but for an organisation of a
peculiar form.[1]   And the reasonableness of this expectation
is confirmed when we consider that it is one duty of the
Christian Church and ministry, as it was of the Jewish, to
act as guardian of Holy Scripture—and not only of the same,
but a greatly enlarged volume of the Scriptures; and to
teach not only the same, but a much more extensive and
more mysterious system of revealed truth.   Now in the
Jewish Church we find not only a body of men solemnly
called and set apart for the ministerial office, but a gradation
of orders in that body; consequently in the Christian Church
we look for the same in both respects: we expect to find a
graduated ministry—a ministry of three orders, corresponding
(so far as the different circumstances[2] admit) with the threefold ministry of the high priest, priests, and Levites among
the Jews.   Such a correspondence, moreover, appears to
have been predicted by the prophets of the Old Testament,[3]

and Whitsuntide. See Zechariah
xiv. 16-19; John vii. 2; Acts xviii.
21; xx. 16.

  [1] See below, Lecture ii.

  [2] That the correspondence does
not extend to the sacerdotal character of the Jewish ministry is shown
by Professor Lightfoot (pp. 184,

243-262); though, perhaps, he has
stated the negative somewhat too
broadly.

  [3] See Isaiah lxvi. 21; Jeremiah
xxxiii. 20-22; Mal. iii. 3, 4. The
word 'priest' in the singular is constantly used in the Old Testament
to *designate* the 'high priest,' and in

and, as we shall see hereafter, was plainly recognised by the ancient Fathers.[1]

Objections
answered.
Nor has this argument, so far as I can judge, been really invalidated by any of the objections which have been brought against it.[2] If it be alleged that because Christ is the only true Head of the Christian ministry, therefore there is no room in it for a superior order, like that of bishops, we reply that to the faithful Jew He was also the only true head of the Jewish ministry; and that as the high priests were His types and ministers in the latter, so the apostles and their prelatical successors are His *representatives* and ministers in the former.   If it be objected that because there was only one high priest, therefore the supposed corre- spondence gives an advantage to Popery, we reply that the remark is founded on a misconception.   The Jewish ministry was not, and was not intended to be, Catholic, as the Chris- tian is; and the resemblance is to be looked for in an ex- tensive diocese under a single bishop; with its cathedral, like the temple, for the centre of its worship, rather than in the entire body of the Christian Church.[3]   Once more.   It

the plural, so as to include him. The 'sons of Levi' would comprehend the three orders.   See below, Lecture ii.   In 2 Kings xxiii. 4, we read of 'Hilkiah the *high priest*, and the priests of *the second order.*'

[1] See below, Lecture ii.

[2] Stillingfleet's 'Irenicum' ad- mits that 'the Jewish pattern' is sufficient to *justify* 'superiority and subordination of one order to another in the Christian ministry,' p. 174, sq.

[3] See Dr. Crawford's 'Presby- terianism Defended,' p. 8, sq., compared with the author's Synodal Address for 1864, p. 21, sq.; Sadler's 'Church Doctrine—Bible Truth,' p. 199, sq.; and the Bishop of Lin- coln on Jeremiah xxxiii. 18-22.

has been attempted to break the force of the argument derived from the analogy between the three-fold ministry of
the Law, and the three-fold ministry of the Gospel, by looking for the type of the latter in the organisation of the
Jewish synagogues.[1]   But to this we reply that the institution of the Synagogues, though recognised by our Lord and
His apostles, was not, so far as appears in Scripture, a
divine ordinance ; and certainly it has no claim like that of
the priesthood, to be put upon a footing of comparison with
the ministry ordained by Christ Himself.

There is, then, we maintain, in this comparison a strong
à priori ground in favour of a graduated or three-fold
ministry in the Christian Church.   And this being so, I
cannot refrain from pointing out further in relation to the
Jewish priesthood, how carefully the succession of high
priests, priests, and Levites, was continued, notwithstanding
all the confusion of political revolutions.   On the return
from the Babylonish captivity no one was allowed to exe-
cute any sacred office who could not prove his Levitical
descent.   And this rule, we are told on the authority of
Josephus, was never relaxed.[2]   In like manner the prophetical passages of the Old Testament before referred to
would lead us to conclude that a similar continuity was intended to be maintained in the Christian ministry, amid all
the revolutions to which the Church might be subjected in

(margin: Succession of Jewish Ministry carefully preserved.)

---

[1] See Stillingfleet's ' Irenicum,'   Chron. vi., preliminary note. Also
pp. 239, 253, 265, 268, 285.   ibid. note on ix. 20.
[2] See Bishop of Lincoln on 1

different countries from time to time. For example, we read in Jeremiah : ' Thus saith the Lord, David (i.e. Christ) shall never want a man to sit upon the throne of the House of Israel; Neither shall the priests, the Levites,[1] want a man before me to offer burnt offerings . . . and to do sacrifice continually.' And He goes on to compare this His divine covenant with David and with Levi to His natural covenant with the day and with the night, protesting that as the latter is indissoluble, so also is the former (Jerem. xxxiii. 17–22).

I have no wish to press the passage of St. Jude's Epistle, ver. 11, further than it will justly bear, but it certainly seems to imply that 'gainsaying' or opposition, like that of Core, which was directed not only against Moses, the civil governor, but against Aaron, the high priest, had been already committed in the Christian Church, by those who withstood the prelatical authority even of the apostles, as Diotrephes, we know, withstood St. John.[2]

Analogy from the object of Christian worship.

4. Again: the frequent occurrence of mystical analogies in Holy Scripture tends to confirm us in the same argument, leading us, as it does, to expect that the worship of God, as revealed in the Three Persons of the ever-blessed Trinity, would be consigned to a ministry, of which the form and constitution, being itself threefold, might serve to remind us

[1] In the history of Barnabas, *a Levite,* bringing the price of his land, and laying it at the feet of the apostles, we see an image of the subordination of the Levitical priesthood to the Christian, and of the absorption of the former into the latter.' — Bishop of Lincoln on Isaiah lxi. 6.

[2] See Hammond's 'Dissert.' 1., c. xii. p. 39, sq.; c. xiii. pp. 43–47.

of the Triune Being whom the Scriptures have taught us to confess and to adore. Yes, I venture to think it is something more than an idle fancy when we recognise the fitness of this divine economy; when we seem to discover the unspeakable mystery of Father, Son, and Holy Ghost shadowed forth and typified in *a father of the flock* sending forth chosen and ordained ministers of salvation to all his people; in an *everlasting priesthood* sent by him to preach and to offer reconciliation through the One atoning sacrifice; and in the multiplied succession of *the seven* 'men of honest report,' full of the sevenfold gifts of the Holy Ghost, who complete the ministry and dispense its grace, not only the alms and offerings cast into the treasury, but the comfort and the guidance of the Spirit of truth and love.

5. Again: as all human society is imperfect without some form of civil government, and as the best form of government has been proved by experience to be that of a constitutional monarchy, balanced by inferior degrees of rank and power, so in the Church it is reasonable to look for a corresponding form, and, I may add, for *no other*; because, however deflections from the highest standard—deflections involving much variety—may be admissible in civil polity, it was to be expected that only the best organisation would be admissible in ecclesiastical polity; this, I say, was to be expected as a consequence of God's greater care for His Church, designed, as it is, to promote, not transitory and temporal, but permanent and eternal interests. Nor is this all. God has expressly revealed His will that the Church

Analogy from Civil Government —how far admissible.

C

should be constituted as a Catholic or universal whole; in other words, as ' one body,' a body so united as not to be divisible without sin, and subject to the same code of laws (i.e. the Holy Scripture) and the same fundamental ordinances.[1] But He has not revealed this in either respect as regards the states and nations of this world; rather He has indicated the contrary, both by His Word and by His providence. Consequently, we find, that whereas a diversity of government among nations does not prevent them from maintaining all those friendly relations which their circumstances may require for their mutual good, it is not so in the case of ecclesiastical communities. On the contrary, experience teaches us that religious intercourse and co-operation do not, and cannot, take place between them for their

[1] It is the neglect of this consideration which misled young Edward Stillingfleet when he wrote in his ' Irenicum,' p. 153 : ' There can be no necessity (for uniformity of Church government) but either by way of *means to an end,* or *by way of divine command.* I know *none will say* that any particular form of government is necessary absolutely by way of means to an end ; for certainly, supposing no obligation from Scripture, government by an equality of power in the officers of the Church, or by superiority of one order above another, are indifferent in order to the general ends of government, and not one more necessary than another.' This may, perhaps, be truly said with regard to political government, but certainly it is not true of ecclesiastical—for the reasons mentioned in the text ; and so far from ' no one' saying that a general uniformity of Church ministry is ' necessary as a means to an end,' I am persuaded that *everyone* will say so who has sufficiently considered that union and communion (an end certainly prescribed in Scripture) between different Churches is unattainable without an essential agreement upon, and acceptance of, the same ministry as well as the same Scriptures and the same sacraments.

common benefit—no, not even when the individuals of whom they are composed are neighbours, friends, or relations, and their interests, as such, *compel them to associate*—unless their form of Church government (together with their form of Christian doctrine) be substantially the same.[1]

It has been a favourite argument with those who deny the obligation of uniformity in the Christian ministry to point to the dissimilarity of political governments, and to infer that there is no more ground for uniformity in the one case than in the other.[2] But it will be evident from the remarks now made that this analogy, however plausible, is not a just one. Its fallacy would, I believe, have been more apparent if the question of the ministry or clerical executive of the Church had been kept more distinct from the question of its polity or government, which, though inclusive of the ministry, is not identical, and ought not to be confounded with it. Whatever we may think of ecclesiastical polity as a whole, it is certain that the ministry of the Church is an ordinance of Christ Himself in a way far more definite than can be pleaded in behalf of any civil executive.

6. Once more : the interests that are at stake, and depend in no small degree upon the due discharge of the functions, especially the higher functions, of the Christian ministry, are of such a kind, so inestimably precious, so unspeakably mo-

The great ends of the Ministry would lead us to expect graduation.

---

[1] See the author's Synodal Address for 1864, p. 72 sqq.

[2] Stillingfleet's 'Irenicum,' pp. 192 sq. 402 sq., where he quotes the opinions of Bochart, Grotius, Lord Bacon, and others, to tha effect.

mentous, that we should naturally expect to find, not only a body of men set apart for their performance—which confessedly we do find—but an order of rank in that body, with stages of promotion fixed and regulated, so that intervals of time and service must elapse, sufficient at once to afford experience to each individual and to test his character, before he can be commonly admitted to its most important duties. This precaution of graduated advancement is observed in other callings and professions, such as those of the law, of the army and navy, of the civil service; and how much more reasonably may it be looked for and required in the organisation of the Christian ministry, with its far more weighty and more solemn responsibilities. Moreover, the same principle is confirmed very strongly by the fact that the apostles themselves were not fully consecrated and installed in the great office which they were to exercise after Christ's departure until they had received, at suitable intervals of time, a thrice-repeated call and mission from their divine Master.[1]

Such, then, in brief, is an outline of the argument, as it presents itself to us in its *à priori* form, the form in which (as it seems to me) the question we have to consider may be best approached.

Argument from Holy Scripture. I now proceed, in the second place, to the Scriptural and historical argument; in other words, we have now to ascertain whether the facts of the case, as found in Scripture and

[1] See Luke vi. 13, ix. 1; John xx. 21.

in the history of the Church, do actually exhibit such results as our preceding line of argument has led us to expect.

First, then, I observe that the facts recorded in the Gospels respecting our Lord's appointment of the twelve apostles, and the distinct position and operation which He assigned to them, would seem to afford conclusive proof that, in the system of the Gospel, *ministerial agency* and *authority* was from the first, and was to continue to be, a leading principle. Moreover, I remark, that the authoritative action of each apostle did not depend upon his acting in concurrence with, or in dependence upon, his apostolic brethren, (except in cases of more than ordinary importance, such as occurred in the Council of Jerusalem,) but was personal and individual ; in other words, was complete and independent in itself. And further, the fact that the apostles were not chosen by the Church, but by Christ, before the Church was in existence, may be regarded as a sufficient indication that the Church itself, through its members, is not the source of ecclesiastical power and ministration, but that these are derived to it from its divine Head, through the apostles whom He ordained.[1] And the subsequent mission of St. Paul, to be the apostle of the Gentiles, by a direct call from Christ in Heaven, and his fuller and more formal ordination, with Barnabas, eleven years afterwards, by express command of the Holy Ghost, are additional evidences to the same effect. Nor can I omit to add, that the distinction and preeminence which were given by our Lord Himself in His own

Preliminary assumptions.

---

[1] See Wheatly 'On Common Prayer,' ch. ii. lect. iii. sect. 1, p. 84 sqq.

ministry to 'the twelve' above 'the seventy,' must be allowed
to afford a presumption that in the ministry of the Church
the system to be observed would be one not of equality but
of subordination.

These propositions being assumed, let us investigate carefully what was the particular form of ministry which the
twelve apostles, with Paul and Barnabas, who had been put,
as I have said, into the same peculiar and distinct position,
did, by the aid and guidance of the Holy Spirit, actually
institute.

Starting-
point of en-
quiry—end
of first
century.

For this purpose, let us begin by taking up our stand at
the close of the first century ; that is, upon the confines of
the apostolic and post-apostolic age, which will also be the
confines of inspired and uninspired testimony.

Why chosen.

I choose this particular position, in the first instance,
because it affords a starting-point which is neither too early
nor too late in the course of our investigation. On the one
hand, in occupying it, we may feel assured that we are not
so far from the first beginnings of the Church but that we
are still upon safe and certain ground. On the other hand,
it was not to have been expected that the ministry of the
Church would be able to assume what was eventually to be
its full and perfect organisation during the earlier stages of
its existence. This, I say, was not to have been expected,
on several accounts. First, the men to be admitted into the
ministry would require, for the most part, to go through a
course of preparatory training, more or less prolonged ;
especially such as were of heathen parentage, and had lived

only in heathen lands.[1]   **Many years** after the Church had
been founded by St. Paul at Ephesus, he felt it necessary to
admonish Timothy **not to** ordain 'a novice.' (1 Tim. iii. 6.)[2]
Next, the inhuman treatment with which the first disciples
were constantly assailed, and the command **which** they had
received, **that** when persecuted in one city they should flee
into another, may remind us that the settled establishment
of diocesan episcopacy was a thing not easily to be accomplished, nor speedily to be looked for under such circumstances.   And if at Rome, towards the close of his life, St.
Paul himself had **occasion** to complain that Demas, formerly
his fellow-labourer, **had** 'forsaken' him, through 'love of
this present world ; ' and—still worse—that at his first being
brought to **trial** 'all men forsook him ; ' he would see cause
enough to be slow and cautious in appointing any **to prelatical power.**   Again : before the Christian ministry could
be fully instituted and openly displayed, it was necessary, in

---

[1] Epiphanius **has justly remarked**
that 'the apostles **were not able to**
establish all things immediately at
first. . . . In the infancy of the
Church it was necessary to adapt
the arrangements of the ministry, in
some degree, to the fitness of the
men who offered themselves, and to
the circumstances of each particular
case.' And he adds : 'No system
in the world was ever completed
and brought to perfection except by
degrees.'—Vol. i. p. 908.   Comp.
'Irenicum,' pp. 180, 328 sq.; Bilson,

ch. xii. p. 287 ; Smalridge, serm. i.
p. 192 ; Beveridge, 'Cod. Canon,'
lib. ii. c. xi. p. 313.

[2] Comp. the second canon of the
first General Council (of Nicæa,
A.D. 325), where this text is quoted,
with a strict injunction that it should
be still observed in regard to every
candidate for the ministry : 'Nam
et tempore opus est ut sit catechu-
menus, et post baptismum multâ
probatione indiget.' See Labb.
Concil., ii. pp. 45, 238.

the order of God's providence, that the Jewish ministry, as having been also of divine institution, should disappear.[1] But that disappearance, we know, was not immediate upon the commencement of the Christian Church. On the contrary, it did not take place till after the deaths of the far greater number of the apostles, including St. Peter and St. Paul. This interval extended over nearly forty years, during all which time it was manifestly the will of God that the Jewish priesthood, though doomed, and 'ready to vanish away,' should be treated by Christians with all due respect.[2] It is upon this ground, probably, that we nowhere read in the Acts of any formal institution of either a bishop or of presbyters at Jerusalem ; just as we nowhere read of any formal abolition of the Jewish Sabbath, or formal institution of the Christian Lord's Day. And the truth is, that for some time both of those days, our Saturday and Sunday, were almost equally observed by the primitive Christians. Lastly, for the causes and under the circumstances now explained, it seemed good to the divine Head of the Christian Church, during the first period of its existence, to make large use, especially in heathen lands, of miraculous gifts and offices,

---

[1] Comp. the author's Synodal Addresses for 1864, pp. 26, 38, and for 1866, p. 25.

[2] See Acts xxiii. 5. (The date of that incident is A.D. 60.) Stillingfleet's 'Iren.,' p. 255. Bishop of Lincoln on 1 Chron. xiv. 'During that interval of near forty years the apostles and other faithful Christians communicated in the services of the Temple as well as in those of the Church.' Also on Acts xi. 46, and 2 Chron. v. 5. The bishops of Jerusalem were all ' of the circumcision' down to A.D. 136. See Euseb. H. E., iv. 5.

which for a time occupied the place, and performed the part of ordinary ministration, to a considerable extent, and, as may be supposed, with far greater effect.

For these reasons, we shall, as I have said, commence our investigation from the time at which St. John, the last of the apostles, closed his ministry; and, advancing upwards from that point, proceed to take a retrospective survey of the scriptural and apostolic age.

First, then, St. John himself, shortly before his death,[1] which occurred at Ephesus, about A.D. 100, composed the book of Revelation (A.D. 95) while he was an exile in the island of Patmos. In that book he is directed by Christ Himself to write seven letters to the Seven Churches of the Lesser, or rather Lydian, Asia. And to whom, in each case, by Christ's own order, does he address them? To a presbytery? To a synod? To a general assembly? No— but to an individual whom He calls the 'Angelus' of each Church. And who is this individual? Might not he be the temporary president or 'moderator' of a presbytery or synod or general assembly? In order to answer this question, let us first consider the name of the individual, and then the duties which he is required to perform. We know what the

Testimony of St. John.

Angels of the Seven Churches.

---

[1] Milman, agreeing with Lücke, boldly asserts that 'the Revelation of St. John belongs to an earlier period of his life, before the destruction of Jerusalem.'—*Hist. of Christianity*, vol. i. p. 388. If there were *sufficient* authority for this assertion, the argument above would not be weakened, but rather confirmed. Professor Lightfoot also seems inclined to adopt the later date of the Apocalypse, 'with,' as he says, 'most recent writers,' p. 198.

name 'moderator' means. It means one who sits as chairman, and moderates in the business of a meeting for the time being, with no permanent office, no superiority but that which it is necessary for him to use as president, and who, in all other respects, is simply an equal among equals.

Meaning of the name 'Angel.'
The name 'Angelus' means one who is *sent* with a message. It is applied to John the Baptist as the 'messenger' of Christ (Matt. xi. 10; Mark i. 2; Luke vii. 27). It is so similar in meaning to the name Apostolus—which signifies one who is *sent out*—that this latter word is also translated 'messenger' in two places of St. Paul's Epistles, viz. 2 Cor. viii. 23; Phil. ii. 25. From this, and from its ordinary use, to indicate an 'angel' of God,[1] we might reasonably infer that Christ, in these letters, intends it as a title of eminence in the person to whom it is applied, as it certainly was when applied to John the Baptist; and that He chose it designedly, rather than the name 'apostle' both on other accounts, and because these angeli of the seven churches were not 'sent out,' but stationary 'messengers,' and yet with so much of the missionary character, in the infancy of the Church, that the name would still be more appropriate as an official de-

---

[1] That, as used by St. John in the epistles to the Seven Churches, it cannot mean heavenly or holy angels, see Archbishop Trench on those epistles, p. 53 sq. On the other hand, however, Professor Lightfoot is not satisfied with the interpretation given above, and pre-fers to understand either 'an actual person—the celestian guardian of the Church—or only a personification—the idea or spirit of the Church,' p. 198. He does not appear to have considered the sense of the Greek name, otherwise than in its English signification.

signation[1] than that of *episcopus*, or settled *overseer*, which soon after prevailed, to denote diocesan superintendence. But to pass from the name to that which is more important, and more conclusive—the office itself. I think it would greatly surprise anyone who happened to be, at the time, either the in-coming or out-going moderator of a presbyterian presbytery, or synod, or general assembly, to find himself not only regarded as the representative [2] of his Church, but made so entirely responsible for its good government, as is implied in these letters of Christ addressed severally to the angels of the Seven Churches. Read the letters, and see what they contain. They contain no rebuke to the prelates of those Churches for arrogating to themselves a pre-eminence which was contrary to the design of Christ. No—but they condemn them, so far as they are condemned, for not exercising with sufficient zeal and fidelity the authority which, as holding that pre-eminence, they were bound to use. It is true, the names of the several individuals are not recorded,[3] and with good reason, because, as the Seven Churches themselves were typical and exemplary, so these addresses (we

---

[1] Archbishop Trench justly remarks: 'I am far from affirming that bishops were commonly called "angels" in the primitive Church; or called so at all, except with a more or less conscious reference to this use of the word in the Apocalypse, . . . The term belongs to the enigmatic, symbolic character of the book, elevated in its language throughout above the level of daily life.'—Page 56.

[2] Stillingfleet, 'Irenicum,' p. 298, suggests that 'in the prophetical style an unity may be set down by way of representation of a multitude.'

[3] See Dr. Crawford's 'Presbyterianism Defended,' p. 20.

may be sure) were designed to be universally applicable, for warning and instruction, in all ages of the Church.[1]

Ministry of the Seven Churches prelatical. For warning and instruction both in other respects, and not least in regard to the right constitution of the Christian ministry. For it is, I think, impossible [2] to put any satisfactory interpretation upon these ' angeli,' except by understanding them to mean individual officers, holding singly the highest and most responsible position in their respective Churches—a position which excludes the notion of a parity of many such in the same ministry within the same Church. I say of ' many such,' because at Ephesus, for example, one of those Seven Churches, which had its ' angel,' we know, from the Acts of the Apostles (ch. xx.), there had been a body of presbyters nearly forty years before; [3] and we also know

---

[1] On the political importance of the cities of the Seven Churches, see **Usher**, vol. vii. p. 61.

[2] **This** Mosheim admits in the **plainest terms,** ' De Rebus Christ.,' p. 133 ; and he goes on to add that, even if this proof of the antiquity of bishops could be ' overthrown '— which he declares it ' never ' **can** be—'ipsa tamen rerum veterum Christianarum consideratio nos eò *facile* ducet ut ipso civitatis Christianæ exordio haud multum juniores Episcopos esse statuamus.' Archbishop Trench declares : ' I again repeat my conviction that **in** these angeli we are to recognise the bishops of the several Churches. **So**

many difficulties, embarrassments, improbabilities, attend every other solution, all disappearing with the adoption of this, while no other rise in their room, that, were not other interests, often, no doubt unconsciously, at work, this assuredly is the conclusion to which all interpreters must have come.'—Page 58. I have already stated, however, that Professor Lightfoot is not of this opinion.

[3] In A.D. 58, ' the Church of Ephesus, which in the Acts is represented by its elders (presbyters), in the Revelation is represented by its angel or bishop.'—Milman, ' Hist. Christ.,' ii. p. 16. Archbishop

that thirty years before, Timothy had been placed there by
St. Paul in a prelatical position, with authority and instruction to ordain more presbyters, and also to ordain deacons
in a lower grade (1 Tim. iii. 13). So that here, in these
chapters of the Apocalypse, we see before the departure of
the last apostle, the diocesan and prelatical system fully
developed, not only with its 'angel,' having presbyters and
deacons under him, but with St. John himself as its archbishop or metropolitan. Moreover, all this we see not only
upon Scriptural and apostolic authority, but upon the direct
sanction and direction of Christ Himself.[1]

Uninspired testimony, contemporaneous, or nearly so, to
the same effect, also exists, and can readily be produced.
Such are the facts universally recognised in ecclesiastical
history, that Polycarp, bishop of Smyrna, and Papias, bishop
of Hierapolis, a city not far from Laodicea, were both
disciples of St. John. Such is the express statement made
by Clement of Alexandria,[2] in a narrative which he represents as carefully preserved and handed down to his own
time in the third century, that St. John, when (after leaving
Patmos) he had come to reside at Ephesus, was in the habit

Uninspired testimony to the same effect.

Clement of Alexandria.

Trench remarks : 'numerous as by
this time the presbyters must have
been, there is only one angel in each
of these Churches. What can he
be but a bishop? a bishop too *with
the prerogatives which we ascribe to
one.* His pre-eminence cannot be
explained away.'—Page 55.

[1] See Archbishop Usher on Original of Bishops and Metropolitans.
Works, vol. vii. pp. 45 sq., 56, 59,
69.

[2] 'Quis Dives,' &c., c. xli., vol. ii.
p. 959. Also in Euseb. H. E.,
lib. iii. c. xxiii. p. 82.

of going forth, upon invitation, to the neighbouring countries
of the Gentiles : in some to appoint bishops ; in others to
constitute or set in order whole Churches ; and in others
again to ordain into the number of the clergy (which seems
to imply priests and deacons[1]), this or that individual from
among those who were pointed out by the Holy Ghost.

Tertullian. Again : Tertullian, the contemporary of St. Clement, writing
about one hundred years after the apostle's death, speaks of
the foster Churches of St. John, and with allusion especially
to those of the Apocalypse, says that the order of their
bishops (and in the time of Tertullian we know that the title
of bishop meant a prelatical bishop and nothing else) is to
be traced to him.[2]   Once more : it is interesting to add that
St. Ignatius. in the Epistles of Ignatius, written only seven years after
St. John's death, we find the name of Onesimus as bishop of
Ephesus (c. i.), the name of Damas as bishop of Magnesia
(c. ii.), the name of Polybius as bishop of Tralles (c. i.) ; both
places not far from Ephesus ; and then descending to the
time of the first General Council—the Council of Nicæa—
in A.D. 325, we find among the names of the 318 prelates
who signed the acts of that Council, not only Menophanes,
bishop of Ephesus (in succession from Onesimus and from
Timothy), but Eutychius, bishop of Smyrna (in succession

---

[1] See Sclater's 'Original Draught,'
p. 235 sq. ; Usher, vol. vii. p. 58.
  [2] Contr. Marcion., lib. iv. c. v. ;
vol. ii. p. 366. The words are, ' in
Joannem stabit auctorem ; ' which,
in regard to Ephesus at least, must
be understood with some qualifica-
tion.   St. Jerome mentions that
St. John wrote his Gospel 'at the
request of the bishops of Asia.'—*De
Vir. Illust.,* vol. ii. p. 263.

from Polycarp), Artemidorus, bishop of Sardis (in succession from Melito, mentioned by Eusebius, and by Jerome, as occupying that see in the second century [1]) ; Soron, bishop of Thyatira, Ethymasius, bishop of Philadelphia, Nunechius, bishop of Laodicea ; so that, on that list, we find episcopal successors of six of the angels assigned to the Seven Churches in the book of Revelation ; and in the list of the bishops who subscribed at the fourth General Council—the Council of Chalcedon—we find a successor of the seventh, viz. Eutropius, the bishop of Pergamos.[2]

Such is the evidence, inspired and uninspired, upon the question before us, which we obtain, more or less directly, from the Scriptural teaching and apostolic authority of the Beloved Disciple. It is manifestly of such weight that it may be said to be conclusive, so far as it goes. Accordingly, the historian Gibbon (who, I need not say, had no bias in favour of the Christian hierarchy, prejudiced as he was against Christianity itself) has declared, mainly upon the strength of this evidence, that 'the Episcopal form of Church government' (which he describes as 'an honourable and perpetual magistracy') 'appears to have been introduced before the end of the first century.' And it is plain, he held that government to be Scriptural, because he refers to the introductory chapters of Revelation in proof that ' bishops

Importance of this evidence generally acknowledged.

---

[1] See Euseb. H. E., iv. 26, Jerome, ' De Vir. Illustr.,' c. xxiv.
[2] See Labbé's Concil., vol. ii. p. 52 sq. ; and vol. iv. p. 605. Eutropius was absent, but his metropolitan, Stephanus, bishop of Ephesus, subscribed for him.

under the name of angels were already instituted in the seven
cities of Asia.'[1]   The force of the same evidence has been
also felt and acknowledged by learned Presbyterians of the
Continent ; such as Grotius,[2] Scultetus,[3] Mosheim, the ecclesiastical historian,[4] and more recently by Röthe, the author
of a work on 'The Beginnings of the Christian Church;'
while among ourselves a distinguished Principal and theological professor not long since published a lecture, which
contained a statement in these words :—

'Episcopacy, as an order distinct from presbyters, has
continued in the Church since the later age of St. John.
This is simply matter of history, which no candid enquirer
can deny.'

Unfortunately there are many who are not candid or
impartial enquirers[5] in this matter; and many more, who

---

[1] Gibbon's 'Hist.,' c. xv. See also
above, p. 6. Hooker, 'Ec. Pol.,'
book vii. c. v. 2.

[2] Grotius goes so far as to say
that the Apocalypse affords an irre-
fragable argument that episcopacy
was approved by divine right—
'divino jure approbatum,' because
it was Christ Himself who, by St.
John, wrote to the seven 'angels.'
'De Imperio circum sacra.' Works,
vol. iv. p. 272.

[3] In Ep. ad Tit. In this instance I have not been able to verify
the quotation. But his words, I
believe, are : 'Angelos septem doc-
tissimi quique Interpretes interpre-

tantur septem Ecclesiarum Episcopos ; neque vero aliter possunt,
nisi textui vim facere velint.'

[4] See above, p. 28, and below, p. 76.

[5] I am sorry to observe that Dr.
Cunningham, whom I should be
unwilling to think *uncandid*, in his
Church History appears to place
the distinction between bishops and
presbyters a whole century later.
He writes: 'The *second* century
had not expired before we discover
traces of a distinction between
them,' vol. i. p. 65; and he adds,
with still greater violation of historical truth : 'Even in the third
century every congregation had its

knowing little or nothing of ecclesiastical history, still are forward to pronounce an opinion at variance with the facts; and consequently the strife is prolonged, simply as strife, to the injury of all our best and highest interests, moral, social, political, and religious.

But it may be argued—and German theologians, in particular, finding themselves in the predicament of having no episcopal ministry, are not slow to argue in self-defence— that the practice and authority of St. John alone (although we have shown that this testimony rests upon the express direction of Christ Himself) are not sufficient, so as to involve the obligation of the universal acceptance of the same ministry; and, further, it may be, and is, alleged that we shall find it far more difficult, if not impossible, to prove a similar ministry from the practice and authority of the other apostles. And this we may suppose was felt and intended by the respected writer, to whom I just now referred, when he allowed his frank admission of the primitive existence of episcopacy to go no farther back into the first, that is, the Scriptural and apostolic century, than to the 'later age of

St. John's testimony confirmed by that of other apostles.

own bishop.' Moreover, he has ventured to say in a note, that 'this is substantially the account of the matter given, not only by Neander but by Mosheim, and by Gibbon.' Now what Gibbon states, we have seen above, p. 6 and p. 31. And Mosheim represents that, 'when the apostles were scattered abroad'— and therefore *still living*—an in-dividual was chosen to be 'set over' (not 'preside in' as Maclaine translates) the College of Presbyters, 'qui primùm *Angelus* (Apoc. ii., iii.), posteà *Episcopus* dicebatur;' and that this arrangement seems to have been introduced first *at Jerusalem*; that is, under St. James.'—Cent. I. part ii. ch. 2. See below, pp. 66 and 75.

St. John.' Let us then proceed, as I proposed, in our retrospective investigation, and leaving the standing-point which I first selected—the close of the first century—let us advance upwards from the date of St. John's death, A.D. 100, first to that of St. Peter and St. Paul, who were martyred at Rome A.D. 68; and afterwards to that of St. James, surnamed The Less, who was martyred at Jerusalem A.D. 62; and looking again at the facts around us—the Scriptural teaching and the apostolic practice—from those points of view, let us see again how this matter stands.[1]

Testimony of St. Peter.

Of St. Peter's history, after his miraculous escape from imprisonment at Jerusalem, A.D. 44 (Acts xiii. 17), we know very little; but that little has, almost all of it, a most important bearing upon the original constitution of the Christian ministry. We know that he was again at Jerusalem, about six years later, being present at the Council of which we read in Acts xv., comp. Gal. ii. 9; and that when he was in Antioch shortly after, St. Paul 'withstood him to the face'

---

[1] It is the weakness of Röthe's theory, that he draws too hard and broad a line between the organising work of the apostles, St. Peter, St. Paul, and St. James on the one hand, and of St. John—with perhaps St. Philip and St. Andrew—on the other; and that he makes the origin of episcopacy to rest upon a decree of a second apostolic Council, which he supposes to have been held for that purpose presently after the deaths of the three former, and after the destruction of Jerusalem. See Lightfoot, pp. 200, 203 sq.; who, however, though he avoids these errors of Röthe, appears, like him, to refer the development of episcopacy too exclusively to secondary causes—in his argument (see pp. 204, 232); though in his conclusion he claims for it 'a divine appointment, or at least a divine sanction,' p. 265.

(Gal. ii. 11–13)—a sufficient indication that he enjoyed no
supremacy over the other apostles, that no appeal was
allowed to his judgment as of greater weight than theirs,·
still less as infallible. From thenceforward to the time of
his death we lose sight of him altogether in the history of the
New Testament.[1] His first Epistle, in which he 'exhorts'
(v. 1) the presbyters of the dispersed Jewish converts to whom
it is addressed, purports to have been written from Babylon,
and its probable date is A.D. 64; while the date of the
second Epistle may be placed about three years later, or a
year before his martyrdom. That besides the more general
episcopate which he shared with the other apostles, he was
also in a more restricted sense bishop of Antioch first, and
afterwards of Rome, as having been closely connected with
the foundation of both those Churches—or, at least, that he
assisted and sanctioned with his apostolic authority the constitution of those bishoprics—no one, I think, will be inclined
to doubt who has sufficiently examined the early and abundant testimony[2] to that effect which we still possess, and the

---

[1] See the Bishop of Lincoln on
the General Epistles, p. 37. The
passage 1 Cor. i. 12 by no means
necessarily implies the personal presence of St. Peter at Corinth. See
Milman's 'History of Christianity,'
i. p. 464, note.

[2] See Irenæus, iii. 3; Tertullian 'de
Præscript. Hæret.,' c. xxxii.; Origen
in Luc. Hom. vi.; Cyprian Epist.
lv. c. xiv. et alib.; Eusebius H. E.,
iii. 21, 35, iv. 1; and Chronicon,
year A.D. 44; Epiphanius, Hær.
xxvii. c. vi. Optatus, i. 10, ii. 2, 3,
10; Jerome 'de Vir. Illustr.,' c. i. and
c. xvi.; in Epist. ad Gal. ii. 11; St.
Chrysost., Hom. in S. Ignat. vol.
ii. p. 712; Ruffinus, Præf. ad Re-
cognit. Clement. Patr. Apostol. i.
p. 492; Fulgentius de Trin. c. i. p.
498. See Lightfoot, p. 207 sq.,
respecting the testimony of the Cle-

general acceptance which has been given to it by ecclesiastical historians. But whether the facts, as commonly stated, be received or no, is comparatively unimportant in our present argument; because it is quite indisputable—if anything in the history of the world be so—that a veritable episcopal succession commenced in both those cities some years before the close of the apostolic age, and (we must conclude) with the sanction and by the appointment of one or more of the apostles themselves. This succession has

Episcopal
successions
at Rome,
Antioch, and
Alexandria
during the
first century.

obtained for itself a place in books which are merely of a secular character, having no ecclesiastical bias, and which record it simply as matter of undoubted fact; just as they record the succession of Roman consuls, or Roman emperors, or other matters of the same kind, with no more hesitation in regard to their credibility than is felt in accepting the demonstration of a mathematical problem. Such a book is the 'Fasti Romani' of the late Mr. Fynes Clinton; a work of the highest authority as a chronological repertory; a work which Professor Blackie has truly said no scholar should be without;[1] a work not by an ecclesiastic, but by a layman, who was for many years a member of the House of Commons, and who, though a man of genuine faith and

---

mentine writings, and p. 218 respecting the early date of episcopacy at Rome. 'Hegesippus, who visited Rome about the middle of the second century, has left it on record that he drew up a list of the Roman bishops to his own time.'—See Euseb. H. E.,

iv. 22.

[1] 'Mr. Clinton's solid and massive work on Greek [and Roman] Chronology is the vade mecum of every scholar.'—Professor Blackie, Introd. Lecture, 1862.

piety, certainly was not a high Churchman. Well, then, this thoroughly learned and trustworthy work represents to us first Linus (mentioned by St. Paul in the second Epistle to Timothy, iv. 21, written from Rome), next Anacletus, then Clement[1] (also not improbably the same who is mentioned by St. Paul, Phil. iv. 3), then Euarestus, as successively bishops of Rome; it represents, first, Euodius, and then Ignatius as successively bishops of Antioch; it represents first Annianus, then Abilius, then Cerdon as bishops of Alexandria (with which metropolis St. Peter was also connected, either personally or through St. Mark[2]); it represents, I say, all these as having been bishops respectively in Rome, Antioch, and Alexandria—at that time the three capital cities of Europe, Asia, and Africa—before the end of the *first* century, or, in other words, within the Scriptural and apostolic age. Are we inclined to dispute whether there were emperors of Rome during that time? Do we intend to maintain that Pagan Rome was at that time governed by a republican, and not a monarchical constitution? If so, then may we also dispute whether, during the same time, Rome

---

[1] 'The reason for supposing Clement to have been a bishop is as strong as the universal tradition of the next ages can make it.'—Lightfoot, p. 219. See also below, Lect. ii.

[2] St. Jerome (after Euseb., ii. 16) speaks of St. Mark as having founded the Church of Alexandria, ' De Vir. Illustr.,' c. viii., and traces the succession of its bishops from him. Epist. ad Evang., i. p. 1194. Upon what he further says, in this latter passage, respecting the appointment of the earlier bishops of that Church, see below, Lect. ii., also Lect. iii. On the early Alexandrian succession which is recorded only by Eusebius, see Appendix to Lecture ii., and Lightfoot, p. 223.

had bishops ; then may we also maintain that Christian Rome was, at the same time, administered under a presbyterian and not a prelatical constitution. But if we will venture upon no such vain attempt,[1] if we accept the former facts as historic truth, as well ascertained and unquestionable realities, then I know not how we can answer it to God and our own consciences, if (through a spirit of obstinate prejudice or unchristian strife) we refuse to accept the latter facts as no less true and certain and unquestionable ; seeing they are brought before us in the same way, and rest upon similar testimony of ancient authors, such as no scholar can reject.

Objections taken to those successions groundless. It has, indeed, been argued[2] that in those catalogues to which I have referred, there may have been a personal succession, such as that of the Archons Eponymi at Athens,

---

[1] The reader who wishes to see young Edward Stillingfleet's attempt to that effect (made when he was scarcely 24 years of age) may find it in ' Irenicum,' pp. 296 sq., 321 sq. He even doubts whether St. Ignatius was 'brought to Rome to suffer,' and avows that the story of his martyrdom 'doth not seem to be any of the most probable.' He observes that 'in none of the Churches most spoken of is the succession so clear as is necessary,' p. 301. But we appeal from the unripened sentiments of this able but youthful and self-confident controversialist, with a *thesis* to maintain, to the more sober judgment and profounder learning of the mature scholar and divine. See the same E. Stillingfleet's Preface to his Ordination Sermon, preached and published 25 years afterwards (before he was made bishop), viz. in 1685. Works, vol. I. p. 358. Also ' Unreasonableness of Separation,' Pref., p. lxxi. sq., lxxvi. ; and his first charge as bishop in 'Eccl. Cases,' i. pp. 5-9.

[2] See Blondel's ' Apologia,' Præf. p. 7. Stillingfleet's ' Irenicum,' p. 300. On the other side, see S. Parker's ' Church Government,' p. 69.

and yet no succession of prelatical power. But if so, it must be asked, at what time and under what circumstances did the transition from the former to the latter take place? For that the succession was a prelatical one when Eusebius, and even when Irenæus wrote, will not be questioned. And why—except for some unworthy purpose of gaining a controversial advantage—why are we to be so uncharitable as to suppose that these and other ancient writers were guilty of fraud?—for such it was if they have represented an episcopal succession as continuous throughout in substantially one and the same character, which in fact was continued in two characters, widely different from each other ; guilty, I say, of fraud, of which we find no hint whatever in any historical record, and which they could have had little or no temptation to practise at a time when no controversy existed, or had as yet been ever known to exist, respecting the constitution of the Christian ministry?

So much, then, for St. Peter's history from this point of view. I next proceed to the history of St. Paul, in which, while the testimony of ancient authors will remain equally clear, the teaching of Holy Scripture will become far more manifest to the same effect, in proportion as the inspired memorials which we have received of that apostle are more abundant. It is, indeed, a noticeable fact—and indicates, I suppose, the pre-eminence which was at hand for the Gentile Church—that while his own epistles form by far the largest portion of the sacred writings which relate to the foundation and first upgrowth of the Church, the only Scriptural narra-

Testimony of St. Paul.

tive which records the acts of the apostles during the same period, so far as it embraces their missionary undertakings, is devoted almost exclusively to the labours of St. Paul. Whatever, therefore, is the result to which we may be led by this part of our investigation, it is only reasonable to conclude that we should have reached the same if the New Testament had favoured us with equally full details respecting the operations of the other apostles.

For a considerable time, and during all the earlier stage of his apostleship, it is evident that St. Paul retained in his own hands the supreme authority over all the Churches which he had founded; and we may, I think, not unfairly suppose that other apostles did the same.[1] In his first Epistle to the Corinthians, A.D. 57, twelve years after his consecration—he writes, 'so ordain I in all the Churches' (vii. 17). Again : in his second Epistle, he speaks of 'the care of all the Churches coming upon him daily' (xi. 28). We must, therefore, look beyond the date of the epistles which he wrote during that earlier period, if we desire to ascertain what provision he proposed to make for the ministerial government of the said Churches when the prelatical oversight which he had hitherto exercised in his own person must necessarily expire. Accordingly, with this design, we take up one of the latest of his epistles, the first to Timothy, written A.D. 65, only three years before his martyrdom. In that epistle, the first passage to which I desire to draw your attention, is the following in chap. iii. ver. 13 :—

---

[1] See Professor Lightfoot, p. 196 sq.

'They that have used the office of a deacon well, purchase to themselves a good degree (βαθμόν) and great boldness (of speech) in the faith which is in Christ Jesus.'

That is, they are entitled, St. Paul writes to Timothy, to be promoted by you in the ministry, for the discharge of duties similar, but higher and more advanced, than those in which they have been before engaged. In this text, then, which even St. Jerome has interpreted [1] as relating to a third order of the clergy, we see not only the actual foundation, but the true *rationale* [2] of the Christian ministry. First the candidates for the said office are to be 'proved,' that is, as we now speak, examined. Then, having been found worthy and ordained, provided they acquit themselves well in that office, after a due period of service, they are to be raised to the next order of the ministry, the order of presbyters or priests. It is important to remark that the Greek word translated 'degree' in this passage, was ever afterwards employed in the language of the Church to express any one of the three Holy *orders* of the ministry—the order of bishops, the order of presbyters or priests, the order of deacons.[3] Now I am afraid it must be said that this funda-

---

[1] 'Epist. ad Heliod.,' vol. i. p. 352. See below, Lect. ii.

[2] The same *rationale* is evidenced in the case of Philip the deacon with relation to the Samaritans whom he had converted and baptized, but was not able to confirm. Acts viii. 5-17. That case plainly shows that a man may have a commission to perform *some* spiritual functions without authority to perform *all.*

[3] See Suicer's Lexicon, under the word βαθμός. But comp. one of the Westminster divines, Mr. Sympson, in Dr. John Lightfoot's Journal. Works, vol. xiii. p. 92.

mental rule of St. Paul is not attended to in the presbyterian system. On the one hand, deacons, as such, *never* ' purchase to themselves a good degree' in the sense which St. Paul intended, because they do not serve with the view of becoming preaching presbyters, or pastors, and in fact, I suppose, rarely, if ever, become such. On the other hand, the ' great boldness of speech ' which a ' minister ' or preaching presbyter uses, he uses (if it be so) without having ' purchased,' as St. Paul speaks, the right to use it, by passing through the lower grade of the ministry which is here prescribed.[1] It is true they may or must have been licentiates, or probationers, for a longer or shorter period, and as such will have been allowed to preach ; but this arrangement only shows the practical value and necessity of the very law which the system, by arrogating the entire clerical function to preaching presbyters or pastors only, does in fact disallow; for probationers have no substantive position in the ministry, being not ordained. I am aware of the discussion which the divines of the Westminster Assembly held upon the position to be assigned to deacons—a discussion prolonged during the sessions of five days ;[2] and nothing, in my opinion, could be more unsatisfactory, except as showing how even able men may blunder and become

Discussion on deacons held in the Westminster Assembly.

---

[1] The Presbyterian Mosheim represents the presbyters of the first century as having been chosen *chiefly* out of the deacons (ex diaconis potissimum). 'De Reb. Christ.,' p. 128.

[2] Between December 15 and 28, 1643. See Lightfoot's Journal, Works, vol. xiii. pp. 83–93 ; Gillespie's Notes, p. 5 ; Baillie's Letters, vol. ii. p. 117.

perplexed over the simplest matter, when, in their delibera-
tions upon such questions, they infringe upon a principle
which the Scripture has laid down for its own interpretation,[1]
by assuming themselves to be wiser than all who have gone
before them. After much disagreement they came to these
conclusions :—that 'the Scriptures do hold out deacons as
distinct officers in the Church,' from Phil. i. 1[2] and 1 Tim.
iii. 8, and that 'the office is perpetual ;' but they confined
its duty 'to taking care in distributing to the necessity of
the poor,' from Acts iv. 1-4, and denied[3] that it 'pertains
to the office of a deacon to preach the word, or administer
the sacraments '—a conclusion which is certainly at variance
with the universal practice of the Church, and which, taken
in its full extent, appears to contravene the teaching of
Scripture both elsewhere,[4] and especially in these words of
St. Paul, of which I have been speaking. For instance, let
any one read the directions given for deacons in verses 8-12
of 1 Tim. iii. and compare them with the directions given for

---

[1] Isaiah xxxviii. 19 ; Jerem. vi.
16 ; Ps. lxxviii. 5-7 ; Hebr. xiii. 7,
17.

[2] A very doubtful text for such a
purpose. See Lect. ii. and Synodal
Address for 1864, pp. 43, 105.

[3] 'This business held a long and
large debate ; but at last was put to
the question, "whether the deacon
be to assist the pastor in preaching
and administering the sacraments " :
and it was voted negatively ; but at

the vote I was absent.'—Lightfoot,
ibid. p. 91.

[4] 'The seven ' (deacons) in Acts
vi. 6 were ordained with imposition
of hands ; they were 'men full of
the Holy Ghost and wisdom.'
Philip, one of the seven, preached
and baptized, Acts viii. 5, 12. Another, St. Stephen, was much more
than an almoner, Acts vi. 12. See
Hughes' 2nd Dissert. in Hickes'
Treatises, vol. iii. p. 353.

presbyters (*episcopi*) in the preceding verses of the same chapter, and he will be persuaded, I think, that both relate to the same kind of ministration, though in different degrees.

But to proceed in our examination of this first Epistle to Timothy. We have seen from it that the fundamental principle of the Christian ministry is one not of parity but of gradation, with the diaconate for its base. We have next to see the same principle culminating in the office which Timothy is to hold. St. Paul has placed him in a position in which he requires him to do at Ephesus all that he himself had done till now for that Church. He was to act as a superior, as a governor, not only over deacons, but over presbyters.[1] He is to ordain them, not 'suddenly,' but when examined, and found to be duly qualified (iii. 8–13, v. 22). He is to rebuke the teachers of unsound doctrine (i. 3), and accusations that may be brought against a presbyter he is to receive and try, but only under proper precautions (v. 19). He is himself to teach and exhort (vi. 2). In short, he is directed to do the very same that a modern bishop does in the administration of his diocese.[2] Now we desire to know what was the meaning of all this, if presbyters alone were the proper persons to do these things, or even were to be allowed to do them? No one can reasonably doubt that there was now, and had been for some time past, a sufficient number

---

[1] See Bilson, p. 299 sq.

[2] 'What is there which Timothy used to do in the Church of Ephesus, that bishops are not in all Churches both obliged and accustomed to do?' —Hughes' 2nd Dissert. See Hickes' Treatises, vol. iii. p. 326.

of presbyters at Ephesus. That city was the capital of Presbyters
at Ephesus Lydian Asia, and upon this and other accounts, it formed a most important post for the preaching of the Gospel. Accordingly, the great apostle had laboured in it continuously for three years—a longer period than he devoted (so far as we know) to any other of the Churches which he founded. That was between A.D. 54 and 57 (Acts xix. 8–10, xx. 31), about ten years before this appointment of Timothy. During his ministry of those three years it is certain he had ordained presbyters : as we are expressly informed that he did in every church upon his first apostolic journey (Acts xiv. 23).[1] This, I say, may be considered certain, because, a year or two later (A.D. 58 or 59) upon his return from Greece, he sent to Ephesus for 'the presbyters of the church' (xx. 17) to come to him at Miletus, in order that he might deliver to them, as their father in Christ, that most solemn and most affectionate episcopal charge which we read in the twentieth chapter of the Acts. And the testimony of that historical narrative is the more valuable, because in St. Paul's own Epistle to the Ephesians—written while he was a prisoner at Rome in A.D. 62, (that is, about three years after the delivery of that charge, and three years *before* Timothy's appointment,) there is nothing from which we can discover the then condition of the Ephesian ministry ;[2] only there

---

[1] Not, however, in any case, on his *first* visit to the Churches, but when he visited them a second time on his return homewards. This

observation confirms what is said above, p. 23.

[2] The only passages in that Epistle which touch upon the subject

are indications that it might soon require the care of a more effectual superintendence than the apostle himself in his absence, and now a prisoner, with the prospect of his approaching end, would be able to bestow.[1]

Timothy's relations to them.

It may then, I repeat, be regarded as certain from the narrative of the Acts, that there was already—and had been for some years—a body of ordained presbyters at Ephesus when St. Paul besought Timothy to abide there (1 Tim. i. 3) and shortly afterwards sent to him these written directions. And I ask again, what did these directions mean? Why was this slight to be put upon those presbyters?[2] Why were they to be superseded, or their office invaded by the appointment of Timothy, if they themselves were competent to perform the same functions? Why, for instance, was Timothy to be instructed to ordain presbyters and deacons at Ephesus, if their ordination could be rightly and lawfully performed by the presbytery which was already there? Is this the way that the wise master-builder is to build up the Church—to pull down what (as some would tell us) he has already perfected? No! the structure was not yet perfect, and he was now only adding to it what it still required—a resident[3] Chief Pastor. And a successor of this resident chief is to be

of the ministry are of a general character: viz. iii. 5, where 'apostles and prophets' are mentioned, and iv. 11, where, besides 'apostles' and 'prophets,' are enumerated 'evangelists,' and 'pastors and teachers,' as given to the Church for minis-

terial purposes. See below, p. 80, note 1.

[1] See ch. iv. 3, 14, compared with Acts xx. 29.

[2] See Bilson, p. 293.

[3] But comp. Lightfoot, quoted below, p. 56.

found (as we have seen) still in Scripture—in what St. John wrote at the dictation of Christ Himself—more than thirty years afterwards—to the angel of the same Church, the Church of Ephesus.

But before I can expect you to feel assured that the representation now made of these circumstances is the only true and just representation, I must invite you to do full justice to the arguments which have been urged against it from the presbyterian point of view. First, then, our attention is drawn to a matter of verbal criticism, which, strictly speaking, however, has little or nothing to do with the *facts* of the case. We know that our name 'bishop' is derived from the Greek word ἐπίσκοπος (episcopus), meaning overseer ; and further, we know that this same Greek word is applied to the Ephesian elders, (or presbyters,) in the Acts, xx. 17, and again, in reference, apparently, to those elders (or presbyters) whom Timothy and Titus were to ordain : i. Tim. iii. 2 ; Titus i. 5, 7. I shall have a better occasion to enter fully into this matter in my next lecture, when I come to take up *seriatim* the various objections that have been raised against our view of the Scriptural and historical argument. For the present, it may suffice to observe that a very little knowledge of the use of language, and especially of etymology, should be enough to guard us against the inference that because our word *bishop* is derived from the Greek word *episcopus*, therefore the signification of the former must be the same, or co-extensive with that of the latter. The truth is, they are not identical ; any more than

Objections taken to foregoing view—

1. From the clerical nomenclature in New Testament.

our word deacon, which is derived from the Greek διάκονος (diaconus), is in meaning co-extensive or identical with it. It will be obvious, therefore, that presbyters might be called, as they are, in the Greek *episcopi*, without being bishops, just as apostles might be, and are, in the Greek, called *diaconi*, without being deacons; in both cases the larger and more general signification of the Greek word including what the more strict and confined English term does not.[1]   And so it is with the derivatives of both; bishopric means only the office of a bishop, as deaconship means only the office of a deacon; but the Greek *episcope* and *diaconia* not only mean the same, but have also other and very different meanings. After this explanation it will be idle to object that the actual nomenclature of the Church does not (as we admit) corre-

---

[1] *Diaconus* and its derivatives occur no less than ninety-eight times in the Greek New Testament; and yet they do not refer to the name and office of a deacon more than six times *at the very most* (viz. Acts vi. 3; Phil. i. 1; 1 Tim. iii. 8, 10, 12, 13), even as we understand the office; and perhaps not even once as Presbyterians understand it. The Westminster divines were willing to allege in support of their lay diaconate, only 1 Tim. iii. 8, where the office appears to be plainly a clerical one, and Acts vi., where the name does not occur. See Lightfoot's Journal, pp. 83–93, and the remark of Dr. Yonge, ibid., p. 97.

Episcopus and its derivatives oc-cur only eleven times, and it may be doubted (see below, Lecture ii.), whether they are used at all in the strict sense which we now attach to the words bishop, bishopric, epis-copate, &c., although our trans-lators, certainly with no advantage to the cause of episcopacy, but rather the reverse, have employed them, as the nearest equivalents in the greater part of those instances: viz. in Acts i. 20; Phil. i. 1; 1 Tim. iii. 1, 2; Titus i. 7; 1 Peter ii. 25. The other instances are Luke xix. 14 ('visitation'); Acts xx. 28 ('over-seers'); 1 Peter ii. 12 ('visitation') v. 2 ('taking the oversight'); Heb. xii. 15 ('looking diligently').

spond with the Scriptural nomenclature. And yet, if the objection should be made, we can at least reply that the same objection lies equally against the presbyterian nomenclature. For instance, we know what a presbyterian *minister* is, and what a presbyterian *deacon* is. Well : minister is simply a translation of the Scriptural word *Diaconus* ; but a 'deacon' and a 'minister' in the presbyterian vocabulary are never the same. Again : we know what a presbyterian 'elder' is ; he is mainly a layman. But elder is simply a translation of the Scriptural word *Presbyterus* ; and it is more than probable—it is certain (if you will believe, not me, but a high presbyterian authority[1]) that the Christian presbyters of the New Testament were never laymen, but always clergymen.

Before I quit this matter for the present, you will, I hope, have understood perfectly that the names bishop, presbyter or elder, and deacon, as we are familiar with them in their English form, are all strictly technical and official, having, not only a limited meaning, but a fixed relation to each other, and that they do not now admit of being used otherwise ; but that it was not so with any one of the original words, episcopus, presbyterus, and diaconus, from which they are etymologically derived. All these in the Greek, when St. Paul used them, were capable of a wide, and varied, and indefinite signification, with little or no marked distinction from each other, and all of them, but especially

Our present nomenclature of the ministry explained.

[1] See 'The Theory of the Ruling Eldership,' by Principal P. C. Campbell of Aberdeen.

E

the last, are so used in the New Testament, as they had been previously used in the Septuagint and in other Greek authors. And this is by no means an uncommon case in regard to the altered use and relationship of many similar words, as will be shown hereafter.[1] Remembering, then, that as *diaconus* and *diaconia* were used of every kind of ministration, high or low, sacred or secular, so *episcopus* and *episcope* were used of various kinds and degrees of superintendence or authority—much as we ourselves now employ the words overseer or superintendent, which have etymologically the same signification—remembering this, we shall find no real difficulty in the fact that those names are applied to presbyters in the New Testament ; we shall readily understand how the Ephesian presbyters, in the Acts xx. 28, may be spoken of by St. Paul as having been made *episcopi* —' overseers in [2] the flock to feed the Church of God ;' how in this Epistle to Timothy, iii. 1, 2, the words, 'If a man desire the office of a bishop,' literally, ' desire the superintendence ' (τῆς ἐπισκοπῆς); and, again, ' a bishop,' literally, ' *the* superintendent ' (τὸν ἐπίσκοπον), then, must be blameless '—how these words *may* refer to the pastoral charge of a congregation, and to the presbyter who is to occupy such a charge.[3] Above all, we shall bear in mind that the ques

---

[1] See below, Lecture ii., especially the quotation from Bentley.

[2] Not ' over,' as our translation renders it.

[3] See the passage from St. Clement of Alexandria, quoted below, Lect. ii., where, though he recognises bishops as the first order of the threefold ministry, yet he speaks of presbyters as ' pastors who guide, or rule, the Churches.'

tion with which we are dealing is one, not of names, but of things; not what Timothy may have been called, or what the presbyters under him were called, but what they were in relation to him and he to them. They were 'overseers' in relation to their respective flocks (and the Scripture more than once[1] expressly confines their 'oversight' to their flocks), but he was to be *their* overseer. They were clergy ordained; he was to be an ordainer of clergy.

But besides this apparent difficulty, which has been raised out of the indistinctness of the clerical nomenclature, as used at first in the New Testament and in some of the most ancient of the early Fathers, we are met here by a further objection, which also turns upon a question of words and names, rather than upon any substantial argument or matter of fact. In order to get rid of the conclusive argument which the appointment of Timothy affords to the Scriptural and apostolical authority of a threefold or episcopal ministry, it has been attempted to show that the office which St. Paul assigned to him was the office, not of a bishop, but simply of an evangelist,[2] and that the office of evangelists was altogether extraordinary, and not to be continued in the Church. This subterfuge is suggested because, in his Second Epistle to this same Timothy, St. Paul has used the words, 'Do the work of an evangelist' (εὐαγγελιστοῦ, iv. 5). But what are the words which immediately follow these? They are 'Make full proof of thy ministry,' literally, 'thy deaconship'

2. Objection from the name of evangelist being applied to Timothy

---

[1] Acts xx. 28; 1 Pet. v. 2.   [2] 'Irenicum,' p. 340.

(τὴν διακονίαν), as in the First Epistle he had called him, 'a good minister,' literally, 'a good deacon (διάκονος) of Jesus Christ' (1 Tim. iv. 6); so that, if in order to exclude Timothy from the episcopate, we are to insist upon his being an evangelist and nothing more, we might with almost equal justice insist upon his being no more than a deacon; whom the presbyterian system will not allow even to preach the Gospel—the very thing which an evangelist (as the name implies) had especially to do. Such are the inconsistencies to which we are reduced when we have recourse to mere verbal subtleties for the evasion of evidence which we are unwilling to accept! The truth is, we know little or nothing about evangelists as distinct officers of the Church. The word occurs only in two other passages of the New Testament, viz. Acts xxi. 8, when Philip, the deacon, whom we know to have preached and baptized (as our own deacons do), is spoken of as 'Philip the evangelist;' and Eph. iv. 11, 'He gave some apostles, some prophets, and some evangelists, and some pastors and teachers,' &c. We seem, however, to be safe in supposing that they were officers specially employed to preach the Gospel in new regions.[1] But Ephesus, where Timothy was to abide, was not now a new region. Apollos had done the work of an evangelist there[2] even before St. Paul himself first visited it. And, again, what right have we to conclude that an evangelist or missionary preacher would be entitled to ordain, as Timothy

---

[1] See Eusebius, H. E., iii. 37.

[2] Acts xviii. 24, 28. A.D. 54. See Hooker, book v. c. xxviii.

is instructed to do in this Epistle? No. A bishop may Timothy proved to have been bishop of Ephesus. well be told to do the work of an evangelist, especially among the heathen part of the population of his diocese, as our colonial and missionary bishops are wont to do ; but we see no reason why an evangelist should be told, virtually, as Timothy is, to do the work of a bishop (especially in a Church like Ephesus, where there were presbyters already) if presbyters are the proper persons to do that work. The truth is, that this expression, so far from proving what it has been alleged to prove, proves rather the direct contrary. It proves that Timothy was not an evangelist. For consider : If we were to tell a presbyter to do the work of a presbyter —or any other official to do the work of his office—would not this be paying him a poor compliment? would it not be almost tantamount to an affront? In like manner, to tell an evangelist to do the work of an evangelist would be flat and unmeaning, not to say impertinent. Whereas to tell one who was not an evangelist merely, to do the work of an evangelist beyond his own ordinary duty is natural and consistent with the character and relations of the parties, and with the circumstances of the case. We cannot, therefore, doubt that Timothy was placed at Ephesus, not as an evangelist merely, but in the office which all Christian antiquity has assigned to him, viz. as a bishop. I could produce to you no less than twenty distinct testimonies from ancient writers or documents to this effect,[1] while not a single wit-

---

[1] A considerable portion of these testimonies is to be found in Bingham, vol. i. p. 63 sq. It is true, as Whitby has pointed out, that there

ness is producible to the contrary, or to throw doubt upon the rest; but I shall be content to quote only one passage, because the evidence which it affords is of such a kind that it is scarcely possible to conceive any more satisfactory or more complete.[1] I allude to a statement which is contained in the 'Acts of the Fourth General Council,' held at Chalcedon, A.D. 451. At that Council, in the course of a debate respecting the filling up of the Ephesian bishopric, which had been declared vacant, it was mentioned by Leontius, bishop of Magnesia, that, 'From Timothy to the time then present, there had been twenty-seven bishops of that see, all of whom had been ordained in Ephesus itself;'[2] and though the accuracy of the statement as to all the ordinations having taken place in Ephesus was disputed by some, who put in a counter-claim in favour of Constantinople as the patriarchal see, yet no one questioned the fact of the succession, as Leontius stated it. Among those twenty-seven are doubtless to be reckoned, as successors of Timothy, not only (as I have before remarked) the angel of the same Church, to whom St. John writes in the Book of Revelation, but Onesimus, whom St. Ignatius,

Statement of
Leontius at
Council of
Chalcedon.

---

is none of them earlier than the latter part of the third century; but, he adds, 'this defect is abundantly supplied by the concurrent suffrage of the 4th and 5th centuries.'—*Pref. to Notes on Ep. to Titus*, p. 316. Dr. Crawford on Presbyterianism, p. 47, note, has quoted the former

remark, but omits the latter.

[1] I do not hesitate to affirm this, notwithstanding the cavils against the evidence which may be seen in 'Irenicum,' p. 302 sq.

[2] Concil. Labbé, vol. iv. p. 700. See Usher, vol. vii. p. 47.

in his Epistle to the **Ephesians,** mentions as their **then** bishop.[1]

But you will perhaps desire to ask me, 'If Timothy was a bishop, why **does** not St. Paul call **him** by some name which would sufficiently designate him as such, and so remove all cause of doubt? And, in return, I would wish to ask you two questions. First, Why are **not** 'the seven' (Acts xxi. 8) of whose appointment we are informed in the sixth chapter of the Acts, and whom we all assume [2] to have been deacons—why are they not called by that name, or by any other official designation either there or elsewhere in the New Testament? Again, Why were **not the** disciples of Christ **called** Christians till they were so called (as we read in Acts xi. 26) at Antioch, **some ten years after the** beginning of the Christian Church? It will not **be denied** that many thousands had lived—and not **a few had** died—who were really Christians during that interval, and yet they had never received the name. Is it **not** reasonable to suppose that what had happened in the case of so large a number of the earliest members of the Church and happened in the case of the lowest order of the ministry, **might have** happened also for a time in the case of the **highest order of** the same ministry, and in regard to **one of the first** appointments to that order?

I venture, then, to say, with perfect confidence, that we

No difficulty in the fact that Timothy is not called prelate in the New Testament.

[1] See c. ii., a passage preserved in the Syriac version.

[2] It is one of the two texts upon which the Westminster divines found the obligation and perpetuity of the deaconship. See below, Lect. ii.

have found the true constitution of the Christian ministry—
with a bishop, presbyters, and deacons (in fact, though not
yet fully in name) resting upon Scriptural and apostolic authority in the Church of Ephesus—probably the first of the
Gentile Churches which was fully built up, as it was certainly
the Church in which St. Paul had laboured more continuously than in any other.   And the same ministerial organisation which we have thus found in regard to Ephesus, we

Titus proved
to have been
bishop of
Crete. may also find in regard to Crete. This appears evident
from St. Paul's Epistle to Titus, written about the same
time. What Timothy, as an individual chief pastor, was
instructed to do at Ephesus, that Titus, as an individual
chief pastor, was instructed to do in Crete, viz. to ordain
presbyters (i. 5) by his own single authority, only taking
care that they possessed the necessary qualifications (i. 6–9).
And that he did this, in the character of bishop of Crete,
and not as a theoretical evangelist, still less as a fancied
moderator of a presbytery, is the concurrent, unanimous
testimony of Christian antiquity,[1] as it was in the case of
Timothy.[2] On the other hand, there is not a syllable in

---

[1] See Usher, vol. vii. p. 64. San-
croft's first Sermon, Life, vol. ii. p.
303 sq. and 335; who both consider
him to have been metropolitan, or
archbishop.

[2] Professor Lightfoot does not
concur in this conclusion. He regards Timothy and Titus only as
St. Paul's delegates. 'It is (he says)
the conception of a later age, which

represents Timothy as bishop of
Ephesus, and Titus as bishop of
Crete. St. Paul's own language
implies that the position which they
held was temporary.   In both
cases their term of office is drawing
to a close when the apostle writes.
See 1 Tim. i. 3, iii. 14; 2 Tim. iv. 9,
21; Tit. i. 5, iii. 12, p. 197.' To me
it does not seem necessary to draw

either of those Epistles to indicate that the government, which till now had been monarchical in St. Paul's own person over both Churches, was henceforward to become oligarchical or republican ; which surely was to have been expected if the presbyterian system, and not the episcopal, was to follow after his own decease.

It may be asked, Why did St. Paul write an Epistle to Titus, as well as to Timothy, on Church regimen ? Would not the Epistles to Timothy have served for Titus also ? I give the answer in the words of one of the most learned of our recent commentators on the New Testament.

Examples of Ephesus and Crete both necessary.

' The principal inference—and it is an important one—to be derived from the fact in question, seems to be this : that by writing to the two chief pastors of two places, so different in population and habits as the polished capital of Asia, Ephesus, and the almost savage island of Crete, and by *prescribing the same form of Church regimen to both*, the Holy Spirit has taught the world by St. Paul that this form of Church government, which is no other than that of Diocesan Episcopacy, is designed by the great Head of the Church for all countries and ages of the world.' [1]

---

this conclusion from any of those passages. But the question is—were not the appointments of Timothy and Titus *such* that the episcopal successions of Ephesus and Crete might be fairly said to have been founded in them respectively? The Professor does not notice the statement made by Leontius at the Council of Chalcedon. See above, p. 54.

[1] Bishop of Lincoln, ' Introduction to the Epistles to Timothy and to Titus,' p. 421. On the other side, comp. Stillingfleet's 'Iren.,' p. 185 sq., where the *obligation* of

Besides the history of St. John upon the question before us, I have now examined the history first of St. Peter and then of St. Paul—one, the special apostle of the Jews dispersed throughout the world, the other, the special apostle of the Gentiles. It remains to examine from the same point of view the history of St. James, surnamed the Less, to distinguish him from the apostle of the same name, the son of Zebedee, and brother of John. And this examination will carry us still further upwards to the fountain head, in regard both to time and place; the time being the first thirty years of the Church's life, immediately after our Lord's resurrection; the place being Jerusalem itself, the parent and pattern of all the Churches.[1] **We need not** enquire whether there were deacons at Jerusalem; for this we gather from Acts vi. 1–16, although the name of deacon does not there occur. Neither need we ask whether there were presbyters at Jerusalem, for this also we know from Acts xi. 30,[2] and else-

---

continuity is denied, because St. Paul (so far as we see in Scripture) makes no provision for a successorship to either Timothy or Titus. Such an objection implies a low estimate of the spiritual guidance vouchsafed to the primitive Church.

[1] See Mosheim, 'De Reb. Christ.,' p. 134, and Bishop of Lincoln on Isaiah liv. 1, 'Zion, the mother of us all'—where St. Jerome and the Synodal Epistle of the Council of Constantinople are quoted to prove that Jerusalem (and not Rome, as the Council of Trent asserts) is 'the Mother of all the Churches.'

[2] Mosheim, 'De Reb. Christ.,' p. 124, infers from the use of νεώτεροι in Acts v. 6, (whom he considers to have been deacons before the appointment of 'the seven') that πρεσ·βύτεροι were already instituted in the Church at Jerusalem. See also 'Hist. Eccles.,' p. 46, where he interprets 1 Pet. v. 5 in the same way. On the other hand, St. Chrysostom, Hom. xiv. on Acts, has

where; although, it so happens, there is no record of their institution. Our only enquiry, therefore, is in regard to the first order of the ministry, the order of Bishops. And again it will be seen that the plainest intimation of Holy Scripture concerning matters of fact are sustained by the fullest and most authentic testimonies of Christian antiquity.

During the great forty days after His resurrection Christ appeared on ten different occasions. It was a time of the deepest interest and importance. Everything that He then did and said had a more than ordinary significance. In reference to the whole of that time, St. Luke tells us that He 'spake to them of the things pertaining to the kingdom of God' (Acts i. 3),[1]—that is, to the Christian Church. On one of those ten occasions, we learn from St. Paul—what none of the Evangelists had mentioned—that 'He was seen of James,' singly (1 Cor. xv. 7). Who was this James, and why was he singled out for this great distinction? Why, again, do we find him introduced repeatedly in the history of the

As seen in various passages of the New Testament.

raised a doubt whether 'the seven' were really deacons.

[1] Yet Mosheim, H. E., p. 44, says that neither Christ Himself nor His Apostles gave any express direction (disertò aliquid præceperunt) respecting the external form and government of the Church; whence he infers that such matters are in the main left to the prudence of ecclesiastical and civil rulers. At the same time, he admits that the arrangements made by the apostles were *inspired*, and consequently that the form of government which they established at Jerusalem, and which from them was universally received in all Churches, must be regarded as divine. He will not, however, grant that it must therefore be immutable and perpetual. His own position unhappily forbade him so to do.

Acts, and in the writings of St. Paul, in such a way as to imply some marked pre-eminence even among the apostles—a pre-eminence for which we had not been prepared, and which is nowhere expressly notified or accounted for in the sacred text? For example—why was it that St. Peter (A.D. 44), when he had been miraculously released from prison by an angel, sent, especially, to let James know, as we read in Acts xii. 17? Why was it that on three (if not four) several occasions,[1] which embrace together a period of at least twenty years (A.D. 37–58), James was found by St. Paul in residence at Jerusalem, and visited by that great apostle and missionary of the Gentiles, as one whom it concerned even him to see and to confer with ; and that, on the last of those occasions, when he and his fellow travellers 'went in unto James, all the presbyters were present ;' (like the clergy with their bishop) as if to receive them in solemn synod?[2] Why was it that, at the first council of the Christian Church, held at Jerusalem (A.D. 50), where not only presbyters, but the apostles were present—why, I ask, was it that James (who, if one of the Twelve at all, which is uncertain,[3] was certainly of no special eminence as *such*) spoke after all the rest, claimed to be 'hearkened to,' and finally declared in

---

[1] First visit, A.D. 37, Gal. i. 18, 19 ; Acts xxii. 17–21 ; 2 Cor. xii. 1–9. Second visit, A.D. 50, 51, Acts xv. 2 ; Gal. ii. 1–10. Third visit, A.D. 58, Acts xxi. 18.

[2] See Acts xxi. 18. Mosheim, 'De Reb. Christ.,' p. 134, who (though he questions the actual episcopate of St. James at Jerusalem) considers it clear, from this text, that he exercised a kind of prelacy. Comp. below, p. 66.

[3] See Professor Lightfoot, p. 195.

set form his own 'sentence,' as the determination of the assembly? See Acts xv. Why, again, was it that at Antioch (A.D. 51) certain persons of Jerusalem, who represented themselves as having 'come from James,' had sufficient influence to induce both St. Peter and St. Barnabas to alter their course of conduct upon a difficult question of the first importance? See Gal. ii. 12. Why is it that St. Jude, at the beginning of his Epistle, denominates himself, and is denominated by St. Luke, both in his Gospel and in the Acts, as 'brother of James?' Finally, why is it that in the New Testament the Epistle of James is placed before those of St. Peter, St. John, and St. Jude, and is addressed 'to the twelve tribes scattered abroad?'—and why does the writer of that Epistle give directions to those that are sick to 'send for the presbyters of the Church?' and on the other hand, to the presbyters themselves, when so sent for, to 'pray over them?' (v. 14).

All these are questions which closely concern the interpretation of the sacred text, and they require an answer from intelligent students of the New Testament. 'To the law and to the testimony!' was the cry of old; and for our parts, we have never shrunk from that appeal: only we have been anxious not to put novel and strange interpretations upon the Word of God. We reply, therefore, to these questions as Christian antiquity has taught us to reply. We account for all those passages of the New Testament concerning St. James—and it is worthy of notice that those are the only passages which do relate to him; so that all the inspired testimony which

How those passages are to be interpreted.

we have points to one and the same conclusion—we account for them, I say, in the only way in which they ever have been, or can be, satisfactorily accounted for ; viz. by the fact that James, during all that time, was bishop of Jerusalem, and as such, the earliest bishop of the Christian Church.[1] I now proceed to bring forward the evidence upon which that fact is established.

Evidence of the Fathers respecting St. James as bishop of Jerusalem.

1. Hegesippus, a converted Jew, born about the time of St. John's death, bears witness thus :—'James, the Lord's brother, who was surnamed the Just, received the government of the Church of Jerusalem *with the apostles.'* Euseb. ii. 23. Jerome, ' de Vir. Illustr.,' c. xi.

2. Clement of Alexandria, who flourished before Hegesippus' death, i.e. before the close of the second century, testifies the same more fully thus :—'Neither Peter, nor James (the son of Zebedee), nor John—though they had been distinguished by our Lord's especial favour—claimed

---

[1] Professor Lightfoot concurs substantially in this conclusion. He writes : ' It seems vain to deny, with Röthe, that the position of James in the Mother Church furnished the precedent and the pattern of the later episcopate,' p. 204. See also pp. 195, 206. But he also draws attention to the fact, that in Acts xi. 30, where the presbyters are mentioned, St. James is not named ; and from this (compared with xv. 4, 23; xvi. 4), he infers that ' though holding a position superior to the rest, he was still considered a member of the presbytery; that he was in fact the head or president of the college,' p. 126. Compare what is said below, p. 66 sq.

Eusebius has μετὰ with the genitive, but in St. Jerome we read ' post apostolos,' as if he had found μετὰ with the accusative. The text being so far doubtful, we cannot be quite certain as to the precise meaning of the phrase. Possibly it may mean 'in accord with,' i.e. having their concurrence and approval.

to himself the honour to be made bishop of Jerusalem after His ascension, but they chose James the Just to fill that office.'—Institut. lib. vi. ap. Euseb. ii. 1.

3. The author of the 'Clementine Recognitions,' which cannot be placed later than the beginning of the third century, and most probably belong to the second, not only speaks of James as bishop of Jerusalem, but assigns his appointment to our Lord Himself. 'The Church of Jerusalem,' he writes, 'was governed by most upright regulations (justissimis dispensationibus) by James, who was ordained bishop in it by the Lord.' Book i. c. xliii. Patr. Apostol. Cotel., i. p. 503. See also the 'Apostolical Constitutions,' lib. vii. c. xlvi. Ibid. p. 385.

4. Eusebius, who was born about 270 A.D., and became bishop of Cæsarea in Palestine, describing the course pursued by the apostles immediately after the ascension of Christ, testifies as follows :—' First, Matthias was chosen by lot to be an apostle in the place of the traitor Judas. There were also appointed, by prayer and laying on of hands of the apostles, approved men, seven in number, . . . to the office of deacons, for the public service. Then, too, it was that James, called the brother of our Lord, whom our forefathers, on account of the excellence of his virtue, surnamed the Just, was called to occupy the see (or *throne*) of the Church at Jerusalem—so our records inform us—as the first bishop.'—H. Ecc., ii. 1. And the same Eusebius, in his Chronicle, under the very year of our Lord's death, A.D. 33, testifies again, 'James, the brother of our Lord, is ordained,

by the apostles, the first bishop of the Church, at Jerusalem.'
But to return to his work upon Church history.　In several
other parts of that work he not only repeats his testimony to
the same effect, and records the martyrdom of James, A.D. 62,
and the election of Symeon as his successor in the see, but
after Symeon, carries on the catalogue of all the bishops in
succession down to his own time.　See ii. 23; iii. 5, 7, 11;
iv. 5; v. 11; vii. 19.

5. Cyril, who was himself bishop of Jerusalem about ten
years after the death of Eusebius, A.D. 349, in one of his
catechetical lectures, speaks of James as 'formerly bishop of
this Church;' and, again, in another lecture, as 'the first
bishop of the diocese.'　Lect. iv. 28; v. 21.

6. Epiphanius, who was bishop of Salamis, or Constantia,
the metropolis of Cyprus, while Cyril was still alive, A.D.
366–402, mentions James as 'the brother of our Lord,
and first bishop of Jerusalem,' adding that 'by him and by
the apostles before named, successors of bishops and presbyters were appointed in the House of God.'　Hær. lxxix.
c. iii.　Elsewhere he calls him 'the first who occupied the
chair of the episcopate.'　Hær. lxxviii. c. vii.; see also Hær.
xxix. c. iii.

7. Jerome, who was contemporary with Epiphanius, and
who resided near Jerusalem during the latter part of his life,
testifies that 'James, who is called the Lord's brother, and
surnamed the Just, was ordained bishop of Jerusalem by the
apostles immediately after the Passion of our Lord.'　He
also states that 'he presided over the Church of Jerusalem

for thirty years, i.e. to the seventh year of the Emperor Nero ; when, having been thrown down from the roof of the Temple, he thus suffered martyrdom, and was buried near the spot.' De Vir. Illust., c. ii.   See also Commentary on Isaiah, vol. iv. p. 175 (where he is called 'a thirteenth apostle'), and Commentary on Galatians, vol. vii. p. 330 sq.

8. Augustine, who was bishop of Hippo in Africa from A.D. 395–430, testifies that 'James was bishop of the Church at Jerusalem,' and 'the first bishop.'—Vol. ii. p. 118.   Ibid. p. 674.

9. Chrysostom, who became bishop of Constantinople in A.D. 398, testifies that 'James was the Lord's brother, and bishop of Jerusalem ;' that 'the Lord Himself is reported to have ordained him, and made him the first bishop ;' that 'because he was bishop in the Church of Jerusalem, therefore he spoke last at the council,' of which we read in Acts xv. ; and that 'when Paul went up to Jerusalem, about questions of doctrine, he immediately visited James : for he was a person so much esteemed that he was the first who was appointed to the episcopate.'—Vol. ix. pp. 386, 414, 279 ; vol. viii. p. 90.

Here then are nine different witnesses—and it would be easy to produce more [1]—men of credit, men of intelligence —following one another in succession, down from the time of the apostles to the end of the fourth century—speaking

Summary of the evidence concerning St. James.

---

[1] E.g. the Ancient Syriac documents, which belong to the Ante-Nicene period, p. 46. Comp. Lightfoot, p. 209.

F

to us from all parts of Christendom, and all testifying the same thing : that James was bishop of Jerusalem—the first bishop—appointed (as some say) by the apostles, or (as others report) by our Lord Himself ; and thus they enable us to account for those passages of the New Testament to which I before referred, and which, as I then remarked, have received, and can receive, no satisfactory explanation except in accordance with the statements of these witnesses. Those passages were all of the nature of undesigned coincidences, and if we take them collectively, and then corroborate the conclusion to which they lead by the clear and unanimous declarations of witnesses, so many and so trustworthy, we obtain an amount of circumstantial proof which must, I am persuaded, carry complete conviction to every fair and impartial mind.[1]

His relation as bishop to the (other) apostles.

It is readily admitted that the twelve apostles, so long as they remained together at Jerusalem, acted in a corporate capacity, after the manner of an episcopal synod ; and in that capacity exercised collectively a general and supreme control ;[2] so as to leave little or no room for the exercise of

---

[1] Mosheim, ' De Reb. Christ.,' p. 135 sq. considers that Jerusalem set the example of episcopacy, and was ' under a bishop,' a considerable time (satis diu) before the end of the first century. He also admits that James undoubtedly exercised a certain *prelacy* at Jerusalem, especially after the departure thence of the *other* apostles (for he assumes that James *was* one of the twelve); but he does not allow him to have been formally the first bishop. His reasoning, however, upon this latter point appears to have little or no weight ; and in denying James' episcopate while he grants him to have been ' antistes,' he makes a distinction without a difference. See below, p. 75 sq., notes, and above, p. 33, note. He takes no notice of 1 Cor. xv. 7.

[2] See Acts ii. 14, 27, 42; iv. 35, 37; v. 13; viii. 14. That the apostles continued to form an order

an individual and **distinct episcopate,** such as was afterwards exercised over the **Gentile** Churches which he founded, **by** St. Paul. And that **collective** administration was adopted, we may suppose, **in order to give additional** weight to the arrangements **which** they made in **common for** the organisation of the Church in that city, **and which,** being thus **agreed** upon, they would afterwards **introduce into all** the **other** Churches which they respectively **set on foot.**[1] If they **remained, as** they **appear to have done, at** Jerusalem, during the events recorded in the first eight chapters of the Acts, up to the conversion of St. Paul in the ninth chapter, this would include a **period of only four years** ;[2] not too long for the purpose contemplated, nor, **perhaps, for the** preparation required **before they set off upon their several missions**

distinct from that of presbyters, is proved by the double use of the article, which our translation unhappily has not preserved, in Acts xv. 6, and elsewhere in that chapter; '*the* apostles and *the* elders (presbyters).' It is true the *copula sine articulo* occurs in verse 2 of that chapter, but not without a various reading. Compare below, Lect. ii.

[1] See Mosheim, 'De Reb. Christ.,' p. 77, note, and p. 112. He assigns the observance of the Lord's Day as the Christian Sabbath, the origin of parochial churches (p. 116), 'and the institution of both the presbyterate and diaconate' (p. 124) to the common counsels of the apostles at Jerusalem. See also pp. 132, 134.

[2] According to Apollonius, a writer of the second century, the apostles remained together at Jerusalem twelve years. See Clem. Alex. 'Strom.,' iv. 5, sub fin., and Euseb. H. E., v. 18. But this calculation (though followed more or less by Greswell, ii. p. 58) seems excessive, and not altogether in accordance with the sacred text. That *eventually* 'they went forth and preached *everywhere*,' we learn from Mark xvi. 20.

throughout the world.[1]   But surely there is nothing in these circumstances which militates in the least degree against the conclusion at which we have arrived in regard to the episcopal appointment of James.   It is still quite probable that that appointment might have been indicated by our Lord Himself, (as is stated by the author of the Clementine Recognitions, and by St. Chrysostom,) and yet that three or four years must be allowed to elapse, in that critical period of the Church's infancy, before the plan would be fully ripe for execution ;[2] and when ripe, it is equally probable that it would (according to the statements of Clement of Alexandria, of Eusebius, and Jerome) be carried formally into effect by the apostles ; who, in the meantime, would seem to have retained the chief administration of the Church in their own hand.[3]   All this, I say, is quite probable ; and quite consistent with supposing that James may have held during those few first years a position of temporary subordination to the twelve, similar to that of some ancient bishops, resident in monasteries, who, within the monastery, were subordinate to the abbot.   Be this, however, as it may,—the first Scriptural evidence to which I have referred in support of James' episcopate, and permanent residence, as bishop, at Jerusalem (excepting only his private interview with our

---

[1] See Euseb. H. E., iii. c. i.; and Greswell, 'Dissert.,' where other testimonies from the Fathers are quoted at length.   Vol. i. pp. 146-150.

[2] Compare the gradual process by which the twelve themselves were raised by our Lord to the full exercise of the apostolic office.   See above, p. 20.

[3] See Greswell, vol. ii. p. 59.

Lord before His ascension), does not occur in the history till three years after St. Paul's conversion, or, in other words, till seven years after the great day of Pentecost.[1] Before that time to have placed him singly in a position of public pre-eminence might only have tended to mark him out for instant death : but from that time forward, or shortly after, when 'the Churches had rest throughout all Judæa, and Galilee and Samaria, and were edified,'[2] it would seem, as I have shown, absolutely certain that all Christian Church authority at Jerusalem, even when the most eminent of the apostles were present there,[3] was made to culminate in St. James ; just as it is certain that, after James' martyrdom (in A.D. 62), all Church authority culminated in his successor, Symeon, the second bishop, and so in those who followed after. Doubtless we might have felt more thoroughly satisfied upon the point, if we had found the first institution of the episcopate expressly recorded in the sacred text ; but such is not the way in which (as I shall show hereafter) it has pleased God to deal with us in regard to other matters of the same or scarcely less importance; it is not the way in which He has actually dealt with us in the case of the presbyterate,[4] the first institution of presbyters being nowhere

The time at which he would be likely to appear as bishop.

---

[1] See Gal. i. 19 ; Acts ix. 27.

[2] Acts ix. 31.   About A.D. 38. Euodias is placed by Eusebius as first bishop of Antioch in A.D. 43. See Clinton F. R., appendix, p. 548. And even according to Mosheim, James was the first of Christian 'antistites.' See above, p. 66, note.

[3] As at the council of which we read in Acts xv. Greswell supposes that Peter and James were the only apostles, at that time, present in Jerusalem. Vol. i. p. 145.

[4] And perhaps in the case also of

recorded in the New Testament;[1] and if this omission is to be urged as weakening the proof in favour of episcopacy, it must also be urged as weakening the proof (if, indeed, there be any Scriptural proof,) in favour of presbytery. At the

But still in an unobtrusive position.

same time, it must be borne in mind, as tending to account for the incidental and unobtrusive manner in which the position of James is indicated rather than expressed in the sacred narrative, that the authority of the Jewish high priest was still, throughout the whole time of James' episcopate, partially recognised by the Christian community;[2] and that, both on this account, and in order not to provoke his jealousy in particular, and the furious hostility of the Jews in general, there was manifest occasion for secrecy and concealment.[3] We read in the Acts (xxi. 20), that so late as A.D. 58—only four years before James' martyrdom—there were 'many thousands' of converted Jews, who, nevertheless, were 'all zealous for the law,' i.e. the Mosaic system of ritual and government,[4] and who therefore, we may suppose, would be unfriendly to any measure tending to give unnecessary prominence to the Christian hierarchy.

Summing up of the evidence as derived from the New Tes-

I now return to the point of time from which we set out upon the foregoing Scriptural and historical investigation, viz. the end of the first century. But before we pursue the

the diaconate. See above, p. 66, note, for the opinion of Mosheim.

[1] They are first mentioned in Acts xi. 30.

[2] See Acts xxiii. 5.

[3] See the author's Synodal Ad-

dress for 1864. p. 30, and above, p. 24.

[4] See also concerning St. Paul himself, Acts xviii. 18, 21, 22 ; xx. 16 ; xxi. 26.

enquiry further let us pause, in order to review the evidence
which so far has been laid before us.

We have been looking back from that original starting-place, over a period of seventy-seven years, up to the very first beginning of the Church's life, and what have we seen ? Inverting now the order in which that survey has been taken, and tracing it downwards in its natural course, we have seen, first, James in Jerusalem acting as bishop, speak-
ing as bishop, in residence as bishop with his presbyters around him, and, moreover, as bishop, writing to the members of his scattered flock an epistle, in which he reminds both them and their presbyters of their relative position and duty towards each other ; and what we have thus seen done at Jerusalem, we have every reason to conclude was designed to set the example to all other Churches.   Further, we have seen St. Paul, in regard to the various Gentile Churches which he founded, at first and during the greater part of his ministry, writing and acting as bishop, in his own person, with supe-riority over presbyters, and, towards the close of his career, devolving his episcopal powers, including ordination, upon Timothy at Ephesus, and upon Titus in Crete.   We have seen St. Peter acting as bishop, more especially in relation to a portion of the converted Jews, dispersed throughout the world ; and writing an epistle, in which, while he con-descends to call himself their fellow-presbyter, he neverthe-less reminds his presbyters of their duty as St. James had done, and exhorts them, as St. Paul had done, to superintend and feed their respective flocks (v. 1, 2).   We have seen

St. John, in relation like St. Paul to a portion of the Gentile Churches,[1] though writing once and again with condescension similar to that of St. Peter (ii. Ep. 1, iii. Ep. 1), yet acting as an arch- or metropolitical bishop, at the direction of Christ Himself, by the letters which he addressed to the angels or bishops of the Seven Churches; not upbraiding them because they were bishops, but impressing upon them the duties which as bishops they were required to perform. All this we have seen in Scripture itself; and, moreover, we have seen it all abundantly confirmed by the earliest testimonies of trustworthy, though uninspired, Christian authors; testimonies which, in regard to any matter of mere secular history, would be accepted without controversy. Those authors—and Scripture with them (as we have seen) to a great extent—combine to represent to us, within this primi-

List of the earliest prelatical ministries. tive and apostolic age, the Church of Jerusalem as constituted with a prelatical ministry, the Church of Antioch as constituted with a prelatical ministry, the Church of Ephesus as constituted with a prelatical ministry, the Church of Rome as constituted with a prelatical ministry, the Church of Alexandria as constitued with a prelatical ministry, the Church of Crete as constituted with a prelatical ministry, the Churches of Smyrna, Pergamos, Thyatira, Sardis, Philadelphia, and Laodicea, all severally constituted with a prelatical ministry. And ancient records, more or less

---

[1] It would seem from Gal. ii. 9, that St. John, as well as St. James and St. Peter, went, at first, chiefly, if not exclusively, to 'the circumcision.'

authentic, would enable us to extend this catalogue [1] of pre-latical ministries to other places, still within the same time, that is, be it remembered, the first seventy-seven years of the Church's life. If ever 'authoritative example' is to be allowed to supply the place of positive precept—as we all allow it to do in the case, for instance, of the canon of Scripture, and of the Christian Sabbath—surely we may make the same allowance in the present question. For, to state once more the conclusion of this portion of our argument in a comprehensive form, we have seen that the facts which have been brought before us all conspire to represent and establish one and the same principle, viz. ' the apostolic rule merging into the episcopal.' [2] We have seen that the candid admission of Dr. Tulloch—if we will examine the

---

[1] See Bishop Taylor, 'Episcopacy Asserted,' c. xviii. Works, vol. vii. p. 72. Pearson, 'Vind. Ignat.,' pp. 539–545. Lightfoot, pp. 207, 211 sq., 214.

[2] See Sadler's 'Church Doctrine —Bible Truth,' p. 272. Professor Lightfoot would probably demur to the statement of the text. He regards the episcopate as having been developed out of the presby-terate. 'If,' he writes, 'bishop was at first used as a synonym for presbyter, and afterwards came to designate the higher officer under whom the presbyters served, the episcopate properly so called would seem to have been developed from the subordinate office. In other words, the episcopate was formed not out of the apostolic order by localisation, but out of the presby-terial by elevation; and the title which originally was common to all came at length to be appropriated to the chief among them.'—P. 194. I do not see why both views may not stand, as applicable in different places, and under different circum-stances. Compare Lect. ii. sub init. bishops regarded as successors of the apostles; and Hooker an Bentley, quoted below, in the same Lecture.

matter fairly and thoroughly—requires to be extended so as to reach not only 'the later age of St. John,' but the later age of St. Peter, the later age of St. Paul, the later age of St. James ; in all of which we have found ' episcopacy as an order distinct from presbyters. This is simply a matter of history, which no candid enquirer can deny.'

Uniformity of the results so far obtained. That the apostles, in the first foundation of Churches, did to a certain extent adapt the arrangements which they made according to the necessities of each particular case, this we do not deny ; [1] but the uniformity of result in which (as we have seen) those arrangements issued, has left us no room to doubt that, however separated, they were working together upon one and the same foreordained plan. And what we have already seen will become, as we proceed in our historical investigation, still more manifest. We shall be less and less inclined to agree with those who have supposed [2] that different apostles, proceeding upon different principles, adopted different forms of organisation in the constitution of the ministry ; because we shall find it impossible to conceive how *such* differences, if they had existed, should have disappeared and coalesced into the uniform system which everywhere prevailed in the second century, without the presence of any influence whatever to account for such

---

[1] See above, **p. 23, and note.**

[2] See ' Irenicum,' pp. 322, **331,** 341 ; where a view, not to be rejected if kept within due bounds, is **exag**gerated to serve the author's theory.

St. Ignatius expressly **asserts that** the same episcopal ministry was established *everywhere* by the apostles. See below, Lecture ii.

amalgamation. In saying this, we are quite content that the obligation derived from apostolic practice should be referred not merely to that practice itself (which, we grant, has not been held sufficient to bind the Church in matters of lesser moment),[1] but to 'the law and reason which was the ground of it.' And that law and reason we consider to be the necessity of union and order ; which, as we before [2] observed, are not to be obtained without uniformity of constitutional organisation throughout the body.

Now, in opposition to all this evidence, inspired and uninspired, what is the ground which was formerly taken up by the opponents of prelacy ? The more learned and more moderate disputants (such as Mosheim, in the last century,[3] a German Lutheran, and therefore a presbyterian from inherited necessity), have indeed admitted the primitive and apostolic [4] institution of an 'antistes,' or superior, who was

What is to be said on the other side.

View of the more learned disputants, such as Mosheim.

---

[1] See 'Irenicum,' pp. 341–345.

[2] See above, p. 18 sq., and again, below, Lect. iii., and comp. 'Irenicum,' pp. 347, 371.

[3] He died in 1755.

[4] See Mosheim 'De Reb. Christ.,' p. 132. 'Viventibus et probantibus apostolis.' In 'Hist. Ecc.,' p. 47, he adds to what is stated in the text : 'Videtur Ecclesia Hierosolymitana, numerosa in primis, apostolis delapsis et ad exteras gentes profectis, *antistitem* sibi primum elegisse, cujus exemplum reliquæ familiæ

(branches of the Church) paulatim secutæ sunt.' Comp. 'De Reb. Christ.,' p. 134. He had before remarked : 'Ecclesiæ Hierosolymitanæ exemplum, *ex præcepto apostolorum*, reliqui omnes cœtus in diaconis constituendis imitabantur.' Why are we to suppose a precept of the apostles 'for the appointment of deacons,' and not also for the appointment of 'antistites,' both in Jerusalem and in all the other Churches, when the proper time arrived for such appointments?

called first 'angelus,' and afterwards 'episcopus,'[1] and who, they grant, was permanently 'set over' his brother presbyters so soon as their number was sufficient to render his appointment proper and desirable—in short, a nascent prelate, such as was to be expected in a nascent Church. By these admissions they have allowed all that is pleaded for by moderate Episcopalians (who desire to see neither dioceses too large, nor diocesans too lordly); only they have failed to recognise an actual three-fold ministry in the earlier apostolic period, because, as they remark,[2] in the Acts of the Apostles and in St. Paul's epistles, they see mention made of presbyters and deacons, but none of an individual as exercising rule and authority in any Church. They forgot that James at Jerusalem (by their own confession[3]) and St. Paul himself, and Timothy and Titus after him, are all examples of such individuals, so far as was possible and suitable in the circumstances of that

[1] Mosheim, 'De Reb. Christ.,' p. 133; 'Hist. Ecc.,' p. 47.

[2] See Mosheim, 'De Reb. Christ.,' ibid.

[3] Mosheim speaks of James as the 'antistes' of the Church at Jerusalem, 'Hist. Eccl.,' pp. 32, 47. What is the difference between *ant*istes and *præ*latus, or *præ*positus? this last word being used by him as well as the first. He also says of James, 'cœtui Hierosolymitano *præ*fuit.'—'De Reb. Christ.,' p. 134. In like manner Dr. P. C. Campbell, admitting as undeniable 'the all but universal prevalence of episcopacy very soon after the death of the apostles,' yet considers that 'this episcopacy was not *prelatical* but *presidential.'—On Lay Eldership,* p. 75. Would it not be difficult to distinguish between the two? Johnson's Dictionary defines a *president* 'one placed with authority over others.' Dr. Campbell adds, 'and even if sanctioned, yet not *prescribed*, by the apostles'—a distinction which it would be still more difficult to establish. See above, p. 75, note 4.

infant age ; and they also forgot that bishops when they address their clergy—as St. Paul addressed, for instance, the Ephesian presbyters at Miletus—do not commonly speak of their own duties, but of the duties of those who are subject to their superintendence. Other less learned and less scrupulous opponents, such as our own Scotch and English Anti-Prelatists in the 17th century, (who could not but feel conscious that they had placed themselves in a position which was aggressive in the extreme against all episcopal jurisdiction,) determined, in the first place, to listen to no evidence, however trustworthy, external to Scripture (even though the evidence might only profess to give the sense of Scripture, as the first Christians understood it) ; and then took care that Scripture should be interpreted only in such a way as to give no support to the authority against which they had rebelled. Take, for instance, the case which has had most influence upon posterity, and which will enable me to substantiate more easily what has now been said—I mean the case of the Westminster Assembly. That Assembly consisted of about one hundred and twenty English 'divines' and thirty laymen, assisted by four 'divines' and two laymen, as commissioners from Scotland.[1] It was appointed by an ordinance of the Long Parliament, which

Conduct of the Westminster Assembly.

[1] Hetherington's 'History of the Westminster Assembly,' p. 112, where the names may be seen, 151 in all. The English lay members consisted of ten lords and twenty commoners. There were twenty-one members added afterwards, in consequence of non-attendance or death of others, p. 114. Several Episcopalians attended at first, but none after the signing of the Solemn League and Covenant, p. 135.

set forth, that ' Whereas it has been declared by the Lords
and **Commons** assembled in Parliament that **the** present
Church government by archbishops, bishops, &c. &c., is
evil, **and** justly offensive **and** burdensome to the kingdom,
&c. &c., therefore they **are** resolved that the same shall
be *taken away,* and that such a government shall be settled
in the Church as may be *most* *agreeable to God's holy* word.'
This ordinance passed on June **12, 1643.**[1]   In obedience to
it, but in disobedience **to the royal proclamation** of June 22,
which **forbade their** meeting, the Assembly met; and on
September 25 all **the** members who were present, together
with the members (228 **in** number) of the House **of Com-**
mons, subscribed, in the Church of St. Margaret, Westminster,
the Solemn League and Covenant, by which they **pledged**
themselves to endeavour ' the extirpation of prelacy.'[2]   This
they did before they had made any attempt whatever to
discover the kind of form of Church government which would
be ' most agreeable to **God's word** '—a duty which they did
not commence till the 23rd of the following month.[3]   Thus,
as they had met to carry out, so far as episcopacy was con-
cerned, a foregone conclusion on the part of the Parliament,
so they themselves **were self-excluded from a full and fair**
examination **of the Scripture upon the** matter, and simply

---

[1] Hetherington, p. 97.

[2] Ibid. pp. 111, 127, 130.   Lightfoot, pp. 10, 15.   Baillie understood
' all kinds of episcopacy.'   Letters,
vol. ii. pp. **228, 252 sq.**   Bishop Leigh

ton, however, after the Restoration,
argued otherwise.   Works, iv. p. 386
sq.

[3] Lightfoot's Journal, p. 26.

prejudged and condemned episcopacy without a hearing.[1]
Under such circumstances nothing was left for them but to
endeavour, by whatever means, to make good that which they
had taken up—taken up, must it not be said? most unad-
visedly, most presumptuously. And how did they contrive to
do this? In the first place, they pronounced the apostles
to have been officers only *pro tempore*, and entirely extraordinary; and then they drew a line, hard and fast, between
them and any other church officers whom they, the Assembly,
might afterwards allow to be ordinary and permanent. They
alleged as a ground for this distinction, in regard to the
apostles, that there is 'no promise in Scripture for their
continuance;'[2] whereas we think we see such a promise
very clearly in the concluding words of St. Matthew's Gospel.
'Lo! I am with *you* alway, even unto the end of the world;'[3]

The resolutions adopted by the Assembly contrary to Scripture.

---

[1] The utterly exclusive and self-sufficient animus of the Assembly is evident from what Baillie, one of the Scotch commissioners, wrote under date April 19, 1644, respecting John Davie, who had been chosen as one of the superadded members of the Assembly: 'If he should come to us with the least tincture of *episcopacy*, or *liturgic learning*, he would not be welcome to any I know.'—Vol. ii. p. 166. In writing some months afterwards to the same correspondent, he admits 'the impossibility ever to have gotten England reformed by human means, as

things here stood, *without their brethren's help* (i.e. from Scotland). The *learnedst* and most considerable part of them were *fully episcopal*.'—Ibid. p. 250. Comp. Lecture ii.

[2] See Lightfoot, p. 27. Thus they necessarily granted the entire absence of connection (which some Presbyterians have been anxious to maintain) between the apostolic order and that of presbyters. See above, p. 66, note 2.

[3] 'These words belong to the apostles as to a *perpetual* corporation.'—Bishop of Salisbury's *Five Discourses*, p. 45. See also below.

if not also in Ephesians iv. 11–13 : 'He gave some (to be) apostles . . . for the perfecting of the saints, for the work of the ministry . . . till *we all come* to the measure of the stature of the fulness of Christ.' [1]   And, moreover, we might ask, is there any promise in Scripture more distinct, or, strictly speaking, any promise at all for the perpetuation of presbyters, or of deacons? However, by this proceeding (which constituted τὸ πρῶτον ψεῦδος—their fundamental mistake), they at once excluded every argument adverse to ministerial parity which might be drawn from the examples of apostolical prelacy, such as you have heard.   It mattered nothing to them that the ancient Fathers not only call the apostles 'bishops,' [2] which they were according to the greater exigencies of the Church, as it was at the first; but they have

And to the testimony of the Fathers.

p. 85, note. Dr. Crawford, p. 109, (where he remarks that 'Christ at His ascension made no promise that the apostolic office should be *perpetuated*, but simply that *all faithful* ministers of the Gospel, when *baptizing*, &c., might in all ages rely on His countenance and assistance,') appears to have forgotten Tertullian ' De Bapt.,' c. xvii., where we read, ' Dandi quidem Baptismum habet jus summus sacerdos, qui est episcopus ; dehinc Presbyteri et Diaconi ; *non tamen sine episcopi auctoritate.*'

[1] I am aware that this observation involves the consequence that the other officers there named were also to be continued ; viz. prophets, evangelists, pastors, and teachers ; and such I believe to be the true interpretation of the passage. The main *functions* of them all are still given to the Church ' for the perfecting of the saints,' &c. Bishops perform more or less the main functions of all *five* ; presbyters the main functions of the four last ; deacons the main functions of three —of the prophet, as reading and expounding Scripture ; of the evangelist, if licensed to preach the Gospel ; of the teacher, as catechising the young.

[2] See Bilson, p. 295.

also called bishops ' apostles,'[1] which (it may be said) they
are, according to the lesser exigencies of the Church as it
now is. At a later period of their discussions, however, Perplexities
of West-
minster
Assembly.
the presbyterian part of the Assembly, when they came to
endeavour to construct from Scripture their own precon-
ceived system, were not a little perplexed by the manifest
rank which the apostles, before their dispersion, occupied at
Jerusalem. It was wished to establish the proposition, that
'the several congregations in Jerusalem were (from the first)
under one presbyterial government,' and in order to reconcile this with the recorded facts, it was argued that the
apostles, though gifted with authority proper to their office
as such, were also presbyters, and that it was as presbyters,
not as apostles, they acted in the government of the Church![2]
The discussion was a long and tedious one (from the 1st to Opposition
on part of
the Inde-
pendents
the 14th of March, 1644), in consequence of the opposition
of the Independents ; but during all that time no one, on

---

[1] See Bingham, i. p. 66 sq.,
quoting Theodoret and Pseud. Ambrose. See also Jerome, Comment.
in Philem. 1, where he gives to
Timothy (and apparently also to
Sosthenes and Silvanus) the title
of apostles, vol. vii. p. 606 ; and on
Gal. i. 19 he says that 'in course of
time others were ordained *apostles*
by those whom the Lord had chosen.'
—Ibid. p. 330.

[2] The entry in Lightfoot's Journal
is curious, as indicating the difficulty
in which they found themselves :
March 6, 1644, *afternoon*.—'Then
fell we upon our proposition about
a presbyterian government in Jerusalem before the dispersion (of the
apostles) ; and there was *a good long
silence* before anyone spake to it,
and it was called to the question.
At last Mr. Seaman spake to it.'
—Page 199. For the full discussion
see pp. 186–214.

either side, appears to have drawn attention either to the fact [1] that in Acts xv. 6 the double use of the article proves '*the* apostles' to have formed an order distinct from that of '*the* presbyters,' or 'elders;' or to the historical testimony in favour of the prelacy of James,[2] and to the argument in support of it to be deduced from that same chapter.

How the cases of Timothy and Titus were dealt with.

But to return to 'the fundamental mistake' made, as I have said, by the Westminster divines in denying continuity to the apostolic body, as such. The position of secondary apostles, such as Barnabas, they evidently found an embarrassing one ;[3] and as they could not so easily reconcile it with the designs which they had in view, therefore, passing them by, their next step was to extend their category of church officers, temporary and extraordinary, so as to include *evangelists* also. By this means they seemed to themselves to get rid of the case of Timothy, upon the plea (to which I have before referred) that he is instructed by St. Paul to 'do the work of an evangelist;' the fact that he is called by various ancient writers bishop of Ephesus, and never an evangelist merely, not having been considered (so far as appears) worthy of notice. And when Timothy had been thus disposed of as an officer extraordinary, and not to be continued, in

---

[1] See above, p. 66, note. This omission is the more remarkable because, on a former occasion, one of the members (Dr. Temple) showed that he was aware of the difference implied in the use of the copula *with* or *without* the article in Greek syntax. See Lightfoot, p. 54.

[2] The only references to James in Lightfoot's Journal are at pp. 209, 211.

[3] Lightfoot, p. 28.

defiance of the episcopal succession which history records
at Ephesus from **Timothy downwards** ; when this had been
effected, it was an obvious expedient to dispose of Titus
also in the same way ; though he is *not* told to do the work
of an evangelist, nor is the title of evangelist ever applied to
him, either in the Scripture or elsewhere among the ancients ;
and though he is called expressly bishop of Crete by Eusebius
(following, as he says, previous records), by St. Jerome, by
St. Chrysostom, by Pseud. Ambrose, by Theodoret.[1] So far,
then, from the Assembly's point of view—utterly narrow and
unauthorised as it was—all at the first appeared smooth and
successful. It was not long, however, before they themselves
began to discover, as arising out of these conclusions, sundry
inconveniences which threatened to prove fatal to the whole
procedure. On the one hand, the denial of a successorship
to the apostles in the episcopal order, seemed to leave little
logical ground for a continual succession in their own order,
such as the Presbyterians were anxious to maintain against
the Independents. On the other hand, the removal not
only of the apostles, but of Timothy and Titus into the rank
of officers extraordinary and not to be continued, had left
little or no Scriptural authority for the perpetuity of any
ordination other than that which the Independents argued
for, viz. ordination conveyed simply by the ruling members
themselves of each separate congregation.[2] I have already

No Scriptural authority left for Ordination.

---

[1] See the passages quoted in
Bingham, vol. i. p. 64.
[2] Hetherington, pp. 172, 175.

The main discussion was upon 1
Tim. iv. 14, whether ' the presbytery '
in that text is to be confined to

shown in part, and shall hereafter show much more fully, that these conclusions of the Assembly, in denying bishops to be proper successors of the apostles, and in denying Timothy and Titus **to have been** among the first of such successors, were entirely at **variance, upon** the matter of fact, with the conclusions **of the primitive** Christians; who must have known the **truth, and** who had no prejudice (as the **Westminster divines** certainly had) **to warp their** judgment. The primitive **Christians did not, indeed,** doubt that the **twelve apostles and St.** Paul held in many respects **a** peculiar **and** unique position; and so far they would **have agreed** —as we **agree**[1]—**with the** Westminster divines; **but this** persuasion did not lead them to infer that the apostolic order, in all its ordinary functions of ruling, ordaining, **confirming, preaching, and ministering the worship** and sacraments of the Church, was to be discontinued at the apostles' **death. On the contrary, they held that the** apostles them-

---

' preaching presbyters,' as the Presbyterians argued, or to ' ruling elders,' as the Independents wished. It does not seem to have occurred to either party, that the preposition ' with ' (not ' by ') implies the effectual action of a higher authority. See below, p. 89.

[1] Champions of episcopacy have sometimes erred in **breaking down** this barrier. I agree with Dr. Crawford, that 'no one can read St. Paul's Epistles to Timothy without perceiv-

ing how wide and marked an interval there was between their respective positions.'—*Presbytery or Prelacy*, p. 37, note. In part, this **would be** owing to difference of age, and still more, to the fact that one was the convert and disciple of the other. At p. 43, Dr. Crawford overlooks the circumstance that *we* consder the germ not only of episcopal, but of metropolitical authority, to be Scriptural, and derived from the apostles.

selves made provision [1] for the continuation of their own order, in regard to all those functions, and that in so doing they acted in accordance with Christ's implied directions, when He gave the promise to which I just now referred.[2]

But supposing that both these cases—the case of the apostles, and the case of Timothy and Titus—were capable of being disposed of as the Westminster divines determined ;—supposing this, there would still remain—first, the difficulties that arise out of the case of James at Jerusalem ; who is seen in *Scripture* to have occupied a position, apparently permanent and distinct from his apostleship (if he was an apostle)—a position which was at once peculiar and pre-eminent ; and who is seen in *history* to have had after his death a regular continuation of successors in the same position. Next, there would remain the difficulties that arise out of the 'angels' of the Seven Churches. And, lastly, there would remain the difficulties that arise out of the cases of the episcopal successions at Rome, at Antioch, at Alexandria, which the most ancient Church history records as having existed during the apostolic age. Yes ; when

No notice taken of St. James.

Nor of the 'angels' in Revelation.

---

[1] See St. Clement of Rome, c. xlii. (quoted in appendix to the author's Syn. Address, 1864, p. 108 sq.), who was himself one of those so appointed by the apostles. The passage, however (though so understood by Röthe), admits of a different interpretation. Comp. Lightfoot, pp. 201, 203.

[2] See above, p. 79. Matth. xxviii. 20. The words in Acts i. 2 —'He through the Holy Ghost had given commandment *to the apostles* whom He had chosen'—seem to determine the application of the text of St. Matthew to the apostles, and to them only.

you have got rid of the apostles (as prelates wholly extraordinary and only temporary), you have still to get rid of

Nor of the
great epis-
copal suc-
cessions at
Rome, An-
tioch, &c.

the prelatical successions, founded by apostles, in all the
most conspicuous centres of European, Asiatic, and African
civilisation—and in some instances continued and traceable
down even to the present time ; you have still to get rid
of these ; and these you never can get rid of so long as
authentic history shall continue to be read and received as
such. What then, I ask, was the Westminster Assembly to
do with these last-named difficulties ? So far as can now be
discovered from the reports of their discussions as given by
three of their own body, Lightfoot, Baillie, and Gillespie, they
took no notice of them at all ! Subsequent champions of the
presbyterian cause, when challenged to account for them, have
followed, for the most part, the same course ;[1] and whenever
they have departed from it, what is the utmost they have been
able to advance ? Some have been content with the modern
fiction of a non-prelatical moderator ; the skirts of whose
official robe (scantily as he himself is clad) are to be extended
so as to cover all the ordinary precedents of primitive prelacy,
and this, although moderatorship, as regards either name
or thing, has no existence in Scripture or any ancient
author. Others have had recourse to the ancient dream
of St. Jerome, respecting quarrelsome presbyters, who, in
spite of apostolic rule and to the disparagement of apostolic forethought, soon required a *boná fide* prelate to keep

---

[1] The case of James is not alluded
to in the Free Church Catechism of
1847, nor in 'Presbyterianism Defended,' by Dr. Crawford.

them in good order; or, again, it may be that he him-self was too proud, too arrogant and ambitious, in those days of persecution and martyrdom, to remain in his proper rank!—Dreams which, I trust, I shall be able to dispel effectually in my next lecture. Only let me add here, in reference to those primitive successions of bishops at Rome, and Antioch, and Alexandria, and to the silence which has been maintained regarding them; however such silence may have been allowed to pass unnoticed in the days of the Westminster Assembly (when there was no certain Chronicle of facts, such as that of Fynes Clinton, easily accessible to the general reader), in the present age, when we are properly required to take into account the discoveries of science in the interpretation of the word of God, there can be no sufficient reason why we should not be obliged to pay at least equal regard to the testimonies of history. The Westminster Assembly has pronounced that 'it pleased God to create, or make of nothing, the world and all things therein in the space of six days;' which we know from science to be untrue. The same Westminster Assembly has pro-nounced that it pleased Christ and His apostles to institute the ministry of His Church in a republican parity, which we know from history, sacred and profane, to be equally untrue.

And now, of all the incidents in this discussion, so far as we have pursued it hitherto, that which must strike a com-petent enquirer as most remarkable, is this: that a system which was founded upon certain fact should have been over-thrown to make room for one resting only upon uncertain

Conclusions of Assembly not founded on Scripture.

speculation; and that a system which had been objected to as resting insufficiently upon Scriptural proof, should have been supplanted by one which (if the truth is to be spoken) positively rests upon no Scriptural proof at all. Let me show what I mean by this latter **statement.** Of course, when we establish the existence of the threefold ministry, we establish, *ipso facto,* the existence of **clerical presbyters** ; and there is one passage of the New Testament, and only one, viz. 1 Tim. iv. 14, in which presbyters are spoken of, apparently, as gathered into a presbytery.[1]   But even from that passage, and still more from every other in which presbyters are mentioned, we may see plainly they were not supreme; they were not self-sufficient ; they had some one over them, some one from whom, as a superior, they received directions. The presbyters at Jerusalem received directions from St. James ; the presbyters of the Jewish dispersion received directions from St. Peter; the presbyters in Crete received directions *first* from St. Paul, *then* from Titus ; the presbyters at Ephesus received directions *first* from St. Paul, *then* from Timothy, *then* from the angel whom St. John addresses. The presbyters of the other six Churches of the Apocalypse received directions, some of them probably, if not all, from St. Paul *first*, then from St. John, and then from their respective angels or bishops. And in that single passage of St. Paul to Timothy in which the presbytery is mentioned, the language which is used, and which has reference to ordination, implies that there had been an authority engaged in that

[1] See 'Irenicum,' pp. 335. 353 sq.

sacred function, associated indeed with the presbyters (as is still the practice in our own ordinations), but superior to them; for the ordination is spoken of as administered 'with' the laying on of their hands, but not 'by' it, as is the case in the ordination which St. Paul himself administered, perhaps on the same occasion, to the same Timothy : ' Stir up the gift of God which is in thee *by* the putting on of my hands,' 2 Tim. i. 6.

But more than this. It is certain that we have express provision made in the New Testament (for instance, by St. Paul) for carrying on the ministry and government of the Church by the authority of individuals, such as Timothy and Titus ; and it is equally certain that we have no provision made for the carrying on the ministry and government of the Church by the authority of a board of coequal officers without a superintendent. St. Paul directed the Ephesian presbyters, who met him at Miletus, to take heed to themselves and to the flock ; but he did not authorise them to ordain other presbyters, or to exercise discipline over each other; as he did afterwards authorise Timothy in Ephesus and Titus in Crete, both to ordain clergy, and to superintend them in the discharge of their duty. It is well observed by a modern writer, that ' The Three Pastoral Epistles of St. Paul are the only Epistles [1] in which there are any directions whatsoever respecting the government of the Churches. In no other Epistle is there one word respecting the choice, qualifications, or ordination of ministers ; and these three

On the contrary, inconsistent with Scripture.

---

[1] Excepting those of St. John to the Seven Churches.

Epistles are written to individual companions of the apostle, not to Churches. . . . Nor is there any intimation whatever that the authority conferred on those individuals was temporary or abnormal, to be speedily succeeded by some more popular or democratic form.'[1]　I repeat, therefore, that the edifice which has been raised in this country over the ruins of the threefold ministry, through the pretence that that ministry was insufficiently grounded upon Scriptural proofs, so far from being able to produce more satisfactory evidence in its own behalf, either Scriptural or historical, will be found by strict investigation to be literally based upon no evidence at all.　This will be demonstrated still more thoroughly as we proceed.　It will then be seen that the interpretation which has been put upon the texts and facts of Scripture, upon the one side, is in perfect harmony with history and tradition, whereas on the other side it is at variance with them both.

Recent testimonies of eminent Presbyterians.

In the meantime, before I conclude the present lecture, allow me to offer one remark—or rather to produce one all-sufficient witness—in order to show that in what I have just now said, respecting the baseless and visionary character of the system by which the three-fold ministry has been displaced, I have not spoken rashly, or in the spirit of a partisan, but really and truly in the character which I profess, of a lover of truth and peace.　In an early part of this lecture I drew your attention to the fact, that a learned Principal of one of our universities has recently declared,

[1] Sadler's 'Church Doctrine—Bible Truth,' p. 383 sq.

that ' The existence of episcopacy, as an order distinct from presbyters, ever since the days of the apostles, is simply matter of history, which no candid enquirer can deny.' I have now to point out, that a learned Principal in another of our universities has recently admitted, with no less candour and love of truth, that when champions of presbyterianism [1] have made their system of lay eldership to rest upon the authority of St. Paul, in 1 Tim. v. 17, they have done what a sound interpretation of the sacred text will not justify.[2]

More than this : in the able treatise which is devoted to a discussion of that point, the author plainly declares that the distinction between preaching and ruling presbyters, which such champions have professed to draw directly from Scripture, is not Scriptural ; is, in short, nothing better than a baseless theory; and that the name of *lay elder*, and the term of *ordination* in connection with his appointment, are indefensible and ought to be abandoned,[3] as tending to engender and keep alive incorrect and unscriptural notions respecting the Christian ministry. Such notions, I need scarcely say, have never been accepted by the Anglican, or

---

[1] Such as the authors of the ' Second Book of Discipline ' and Dr. Miller of Princeton. See Principal Campbell's ' Lay Eldership,' pp. 8, 38.

[2] See ibid. pp. 2, 20, 32, and comp. 'Irenicum,' p. 336 sqq.

[3] See ibid. pp. 69 sq., 109. He considers, however, that the institution of lay assessors or councillors, (not presbyters or elders in the New Testament sense) is sufficiently based upon 1 Cor. xii. 28 and Rom. xii. 8 ; such assessors being the questmen, sidesmen (synodsmen), or *testes synodales*, and church wardens of the English Church. He rests the admission of laymen into synods upon Acts xv. 23. See pp. 5, 8, 12, 15.

Eastern, or Roman Churches, and, though sanctioned by
Calvin in his writings (but not in his practice[1]), have been
disallowed by many of the ablest of the foreign Reformed
divines.   If only we could have, upon both sides, more of
the fair and candid spirit, combined with the needful learning and intelligence, which have been shown by the two
eminent presbyterian divines to whom I have referred,[2] I am
persuaded that the barriers which now separate Episcopalians and Presbyterians would be speedily removed[3] (through
the blessing of God upon our earnest endeavours for that
end); and a reunion might be effected by building, not upon
the treacherous shifting sand of man's imagination,[4] but
upon the solid and immovable rock of divine truth.   And is
there not a cause for such reapproachment on either side?

[1] See ibid. p. 2. Calvin's own consistory at Geneva was not in accordance with his theory, p. 17.

[2] I am sorry that I cannot extend this remark to *all* that has been written by the former of those divines, especially in some recent numbers of the 'Contemporary Review.' Not only Hooker, but Chillingworth and Stillingfleet, if they were alive, would, I am sure, complain of the treatment they have there received.

[3] It is feelingly remarked by Principal Campbell: 'Surely the visible Church is not always to remain in its present divided condition,' p. 66; and his treatise on the so-called 'Lay Eldership' is evidently written with the charitable design of removing one stumbling-block out of the way of reunion. At p. 67, in speaking of 'the Protestant Episcopal Church of the United States' of America, he throws out the valuable and important hint, that 'its admirable constitution combines the advantages of presbytery and episcopacy.'

[4] 'We have been in a pitiful labyrinth these twelve days about ruling elders; we yet stick into it.' Thus wrote Baillie (a Scotch Commissioner to the Westminster Assembly), from London, under date December 7, 1643; vol. ii. p. 115.

On the one hand, who does not feel the havoc which was
made of the Christian ministry, as the apostles instituted it,
when men forsook the ground of authoritative example, of
Christian precedent, in order to indulge their own temper,
to give effect to their own devices? Instead of the well-
regulated gradation—which our *à priori* reasoning had led us
to anticipate—from the deacon to the presbyter, and from
the presbyter to the bishop ; instead of this, no gradation
was left at all; no bishop at the head, no clerical deacon[1] at
the foot, and the presbyter, who alone remained, yet lost his
name ; while the office was at once bisected and aggran-
dised, so as to give to each of the two sections more than its
due. But though all this must be matter for regret—and
for amendment—however we may estimate the conduct
which provoked it, yet, on the other hand, justice requires
us to pay the deserved meed of praise to those who, notwithstanding their own mistakes upon other points, in one
most essential respect hit the blot and supplied the defect of
the true system, as it had come to be administered in later
times. Ecclesiastical councils, emancipated from all undue
interference on the part of the civil power, were again made
what they had been from the first at Jerusalem ; and the lay
brethren were again, not only allowed, but invited and required to recover and to hold their own (and if more than
their own, this was owing to the violence of a just recoil from

---

[1] Principal Campbell quotes Dr.
Claudius Buchanan's 'Christian Researches' as tending to prove that
deacons are an order of the clergy,
and ought to come *before* lay representatives, p. 12 sq.

past exclusion) in the administration of all Church affairs.[1] Let these last words be a proof that if we are bold, according to the light and ability which God has given, to challenge and reprove the shortcomings of others, with the view to their amendment and for the common good, we are no less willing and desirous that our own defects should be challenged and reproved, with the same view to correction, for the benefit of the Church which is our common mother, and of the country which we all love.

[1] It should always be borne in mind that the distinguishing characteristic of the Reformed Church of Scotland, as compared with the Reformed Church of England, is *Church government by kirk sessions, presbyteries, synods, and general assemblies*; and that this government is not inconsistent with the threefold ministry, but rather requires the threefold ministry to harmonize and complete it. See the author's Synodal Address for 1870, and the presbyterian testimonies there quoted, p. 26.

LECTURE II.

My former lecture contained a Scriptural and historical *Enquiry re-commenced* survey of the apostolic age, tracing it upwards from the *from the end of first cen-* death of St. John in the year 100, to the first infancy of the *tury.* Church, after our Lord's ascension, at Jerusalem. I now return to my original standing-point, the conclusion of the first century ; and again starting from thence and proceeding downwards in the natural course, I propose to carry on the same investigation into the period which immediately suc- ceeded, that is, into the earliest of the post-Scriptural and post-apostolic times. And if we shall still discover traces everywhere of the same result, which *à priori* reasoning had led us to expect, and which we have seen exhibited in Scrip- ture and in the practice of the apostles, we may, I think, conclude with perfect safety, that we have found the truth of which we were in search.

1. In the first place, then, when writers towards the end of the second century, such as Irenæus, bishop of Lyons, and Tertullian, presbyter of Carthage—a European and an African—in disputing with heretics, confront them with the challenge to show, in behalf of their doctrine or discipline,

what the Church had to show in behalf of hers—viz. a regular descent of the bishops of the several dioceses in direct succession from the apostles—when we see this, and when we find that the challenge was never met; is it possible to conceive an evidence in favour of a prelatical ministry, as primitive and apostolical, more satisfactory—more decisive? Let me offer to you, then, some specimens of this evidence.

Testimony
of Irenæus. And first, from Irenæus ; of whom we know that, having been previously a presbyter of Lyons, he succeeded Pothinus as bishop in A.D. 177 (see Clinton, sub ann.). We also know that in his youth he had been a disciple of Polycarp, bishop of Smyrna, the disciple of St. John. This venerable author has left us a large and elaborate work against heresies. In that work, book iii. chap. iii., he thus writes :—

' In every Church it is in the power of all, who may wish to see the truth, to contemplate clearly the tradition of the apostles manifested throughout the world; and *we* are in a position to reckon up those who were by the apostles instituted bishops in the Church and [to demonstrate] the succession of these men to our own times. . . . They (the apostles) were desirous that those persons should be perfect and unblamable in all things, especially as they were leaving them to become their successors, *suum ipsorum locum magisterii* tradentes, i.e. *delivering up to them their own place of government.*'

But it may be asked, 'Are we sure that Irenæus, when he wrote thus, did not mean simple ' presbyters,' and not 'bishops,' in the sense in which we now understand this latter term, that is, of persons holding singly a permanent official rank above presbyters? This is a question which may be fairly put, more especially as in the preceding chapter of this third book,[1] and elsewhere, viz. lib. iv. c. xxvi.,[2] the same writer speaks of those whom he there calls 'presbyters,' in the same way.[3] But the answer is clear and certain,[4] both from what he had said in the first book, and from what he goes on to say immediately after the passage you have heard. In the first book, c. xxiv., he had spoken of

[1] See Harvey's note on that passage. 'While the apostles lived, and exercised control over the Churches which they established, the subordinate spiritual ruler (ὁ προεστὼς) of each Church was not distinguished in point of ecclesiastical title from the *presbytery.'*—Vol. ii. p. 7.

[2] The words of this passage are : 'It is necessary to obey those *presbyters* who are in the Church ; those who possess, as I have shown, succession from the apostles ; who, along with the succession of the *episcopate*, have received the same gift of Truth according to the goodwill of the Father.'

[3] 'When we refer them (the heretics) to that tradition which originates from the apostles, and which is preserved by means of the succession of *presbyters* in the Churches, they object to tradition, saying that they themselves are wiser, not merely than the presbyters, but even than the apostles.' On this use of the name 'presbyters' see Bishop Pearson, 'Vind. Ignat.,' p. 546, who shows that, though bishops were still sometimes (though very rarely) so called, yet an individual bishop was never called ' presbyter,' nor an individual presbyter ever called ' episcopus,' by Irenæus, or any other writer after the apostolic age. Ibid., p. 549. (See also Clinton, 'F. R.' sub ann. A.D. 177.) In pp. 538–543 he exposes the error of Blondel and Salmasius (also of Stillingfleet, p. 311 sq.) in regard to the passage of Eusebius, 'H. E.,' v. 4.

[4] I have no scruple in saying this, notwithstanding the captious remark in ' Irenicum,' p. 306 sq.

H

Hyginus (bishop of Rome) as 'holding the ninth [1] place of the episcopal succession from the apostles downwards' (ἐπισκοπικῆς διαδοχῆς ἀπὸ τῶν Ἀποστόλων). In the third book, after the passage just now produced, he continues thus :

Episcopal successions according to Irenæus—

' Inasmuch as it would be tedious in a work such as this, to reckon up *the (episcopal) succession* of *all* the Churches' —well—this being so, what does he propose to do ? He proposes to give—and he does give—the names of the

At Rome.

bishops of Rome,[2] one by one, from the first foundation of that Church by St. Peter and St. Paul [3] (St. Peter as representative of the Jews, and St. Paul of the Gentiles) down to his own time,—that is, to Eleutherius, the twelfth in succession, and then bishop. Now no one, I think, at the present day,[4] will venture to assert that all, or any of these

---

[1] The correctness of this calculation, which is questionable, does not affect the relevancy of the passage to the purpose for which it is quoted. St. Cyprian makes the same statement, Ep.lxxiv. ad Pomp., c. ii.

[2] On the early episcopal succession at Rome as recorded by Irenæus and others, see Bishop Pearson, Minor Works, ii. pp. 266-572, and Lightfoot, pp. 218-222, and p. 166 sq., note. In the time of Pius, the 8th or 9th of the succession (A.D. 127-142), we find the word cathedra, 'chair' or 'see' used as a recognised phrase, indicating a more or less prolonged ex-

istence of the episcopal office. See Lightfoot, p. 220.

[3] 'Those two apostles, the joint-founders of the Church of Rome, left it, however, in charge of Linus when they proceeded, St. Paul to the West, and St. Peter into Pontus.' —Harvey's *Irenæus*, vol. ii. p. 10.

[4] See Bishop Pearson, 'Vind. Ignat.,' in answer to Salmasius, p. 550 ; but Professor Lightfoot, p. 219, considers that the prelatical position of the bishop at Rome was *at first* less marked than at Antioch 'or Smyrna, and than it soon afterwards became at Rome itself. He calls Clement 'the presbyter-bishop.' —Page 222.

were not bishops in the prelatical sense, that is, having presbyters under them *in a lower degree* : although, at the same time,
it is to be borne in mind, as tending still further to clear up
the point, that the generic name 'presbyteri' might be and
was still sometimes used in a laxer acceptation,[1] to designate,
or include, bishops ; just as the name 'priest' is often used
in the Old Testament to designate, and in the plural to include, the high priest. We know from an extant letter of
Cornelius, the twentieth Roman bishop, A.D. 250, that he
had forty-six presbyters under him.[2] And the same unquestionable distinction between the bishop and his presbyters holds good when Irenæus in the same place
goes on to mention next the episcopal succession in the
Church of Smyrna, of which he states that Polycarp was
appointed bishop by the apostles ; for in the extant epistle
of Polycarp he and his presbyters are distinctly specified.[3]
And once more : the same distinction holds good, where
Irenæus mentions, lastly, the episcopal succession in the
Church of Ephesus ; of which he tells us that it was founded
by St. Paul, and that St. John 'tarried' with it so late as the
time of Trajan ; virtually producing, therefore, those two
apostles as instituting and sanctioning the episcopate of that
Church, in which, as we know from Scripture, and as I
pointed out fully in my former lecture,[4] there was a body of

At Smyrna
and Ephesus.

---

[1] See Sclater, p. 217 sq. ; also
above, p. 97, note 3, and below, p. 116.

[2] See Euseb., vi. 43.

[3] See title of the epistle, and
capp. v. and vi.

[4] See above, p. 45.

presbyters even in the time of St. Paul; a body which
Timothy was instructed to enlarge, by ordaining others.

There is one other passage of Irenæus which I cannot
refrain from quoting, because, while it bears further testimony
to the fact of the episcopal succession having been derived
from the apostles, it contains 'a wholesome doctrine' which
is only too much needed in our own times. In the thirty-
third chapter of the fourth book he writes as follows :—

Warning of
Irenæus
against
divisions.

'The truly spiritual Christian' (he is alluding to the text of
St. Paul, 1 Cor. ii. 15, *He that is spiritual judgeth all things*)
—'The truly spiritual Christian will judge those who cause
divisions; men who are destitute of the love of God, and
who look to their own private advantage rather than to the
unity of the Church ; who, for any trifling occasion that may
arise, cut and dissever, and, so far as they can, destroy the
great and glorious body of Christ ; men who talk of peace while
they are waging war, who strain at a gnat but swallow a
camel. For *it is not possible that they should effect any improvement sufficient to compensate for the injury which they
cause by their schism.*' Then, after condemning all such
persons, he goes on to say : 'True knowledge consists in
these things—in the doctrine of the apostles ; in the primitive system of the Church throughout the world ; in the
character, or marks, of the body of Christ, according to
*the succession of the bishops, to whom they (the apostles) en-
trusted the several local or particular Churches which now exist,*
and which preserve the traditional rule of faith (i.e. the
Creed) in its perfect form, neither detracting from it, nor

adding to it; in the reading of Holy Scripture, unadulterated by apocryphal admixtures, and in sound and careful exposition founded upon safe and reverent interpretation of the sacred text ; and (lastly, he adds), in the gift of charity, which is more precious than knowledge, more glorious than prophecy, and more excellent than all other gifts.'

Such is the guidance which Irenæus gives us for the discovery of the truth, writing before the end of the second century.[1] For my own part I know not where peaceable and humble-minded Christians could find directions more Scriptural, more trustworthy, more suitable to heal our present divisions, and to restore to us the concord which we so sadly need.

I quite admit that the passages which I have quoted, as they occur in Irenæus, are introduced for no other purpose than to confute the teachers of heretical doctrine ; there being at that time no question in regard to Church government, or the right constitution of the Christian ministry ; but it cannot be denied that they also afford, upon this latter point, incidental evidence which is highly valuable in itself, and goes directly to confirm the conclusions to which we are led by a long and orderly array of other proof.

The evidence of Tertullian follows about twenty or twenty-five years after that of Irenæus, at the very beginning of the third century, or, in other words, only one hundred years after St. John's death. In his treatise ' De Præscriptione Hæreti-

Testimony of Tertullian.

---

[1] Professor Lightfoot remarks, p. 218, ' When Irenæus wrote, episcopacy was certainly a venerable institution.'

corum,' that is, 'on the Church's rule for discerning and
arguing with heretics,' he thus writes :—

'If there be any heresies which dare to represent themselves as of the apostolic age (in order that they may appear
to have sprung from the apostles, because they existed in
their time), we can say : Well, then, let them show the
original records (*origines*) of their Churches ; let them *unfold
the catalogue of their bishops*, so coming down in succession
from the beginning, that their first bishop shall have had as
his ordainer and predecessor some one of the apostles, or of
such apostolic men as continued steadfast in the apostles'
fellowship.   For in this manner do the apostolical Churches
transmit their registers (*fastos*); as the Church of Smyrna bears
record that Polycarp was placed there by St. John ; as the
Church of Rome avouches that Clement was ordained by
St. Peter ; and so, too, of the other Churches.[1]   They in like
manner exhibit those who, as having been appointed to the
episcopate by the apostles, have handed down the apostolic
doctrine' (c. xxxii. vol. ii. p. 44 sq.).   We shall see presently,
that there can be no doubt respecting the meaning of the

---

[1] There is another passage to the same effect in the 'De Præscriptione,' c. xxxvi., which Professor Lightfoot quotes, p. 213, but of which he questions the strict historical accuracy, so far as concerns the use of the term 'apostolic see' in regard to Philippi, Thessalonica, and Corinth. But concerning Philippi, see below, p. 162 ; concerning Thessalonica, see the tradition mentioned by Origen on Rom. xvi. 23, and referred to by Lightfoot, p. 213 ; concerning Corinth, see below, p. 161 ; and Lightfoot himself, p. 214.

word 'episcopate,' as used by Tertullian. He intended by it simply the first order of the threefold ministry.

The same line of argument was afterwards employed by Optatus, bishop of Milevi, in Numidia, and by St. Augustin, bishop of Hippo, in confuting the Donatists, who had separated from the Church. The former, after tracing the episcopal succession of the Church of Rome from St. Peter downwards to Siricius (the thirty-eighth), who was then bishop (A.D. 385), gives to his opponents this challenge : ' Do you now produce the origin of your episcopate (*cathedræ*), inasmuch as you claim to yourselves to be the Church.' [1] In like manner Fulgentius, bishop of Ruspa, in Africa, at the beginning of the sixth century, who wrote against the Arian heresy, commends the orthodox faith, 'which,' as he writes, 'through a series of successors in the see (*cathedra*) of Peter the apostle at Rome or at Antioch, in the see of Mark the evangelist at Alexandria, in the see of John the evangelist at Ephesus, in the see of James at Jerusalem, is preached by the bishops of those cities even to the present time.' [2]

Of Optatus, St. Augustin, and Fulgentius.

Now it is morally impossible that any men in their senses could have given challenges such as these to the host of heretics throughout the world, unless the facts had been really such as the challengers assumed ; that is, unless *bonâ*

Force of this evidence.

---

[1] ' De Schism. Donat.,' ii. c. iii. p. 950. See Bishop Pearson's Minor Works for the passages of St. Augustin, vol. ii. p. 309; and comp.

' Irenicum,' p. 305.

[2] ' De Trin.,' c. i. p. 498. See Bishop Pearson, ibid.

fide episcopal, and not merely presbyterian, succession had been actually traceable to the apostles in the Churches thus referred to. Remember, I say nothing of the value of the argument for the purpose to which they applied it, viz. *as a test of the true doctrine*; still less do I insist upon the episcopal succession as the sole and indispensable channel for conveying the grace of sacraments, and other ordinances of the Gospel. Those are points with which I am not now concerned. I simply assert the impossibility of an appeal under such circumstances to facts which had no real existence, to evidence which was not plainly and notoriously true, and also free from all ambiguity in regard to the real character and position of those whose names and succession in an office of pre-eminence were thus produced, or alluded to as notorious and capable of production. And I wish you to observe further, in connection with this line of proof, that it was the common language of Christian antiquity to speak of bishops as successors of the apostles. For instance, it is Jerome himself who says, 'Apud nos apostolorum locum episcopi tenent.'[1] *With us bishops hold the place of the apostles.* And as it will be impossible to deny that the apostles in the New Testament had a pre-eminence of jurisdiction over all other ministers, so it will follow that they who succeeded them—and succeeded them, as Firmilian, bishop of Cappadocian Cæsarea in Asia, writing A.D. 250, and Cyprian, bishop of Carthage in Africa, writing A.D.

Bishops commonly called 'successors of the apostles.'

[1] Epist. ad Marcellum, vol. i. p. 476.

254, both express it, 'vicariâ ordinatione,' i.e. by an ordination that put them in the apostles' room—must have had a similar pre-eminence ; otherwise it would be a delusion to call them successors.

We have seen that Irenæus felt himself precluded, by the character of his work, from exhibiting more than two or three examples in which the succession of bishops might be traced up to the apostles, viz. Rome, Ephesus, and Smyrna. Happily, however, in the History of Eusebius, which succeeds immediately to the Acts of the Apostles, any deficiency in that respect, which we might otherwise have had occasion to regret, is amply supplied. Eusebius, who was made bishop of Cæsarea, in Palestine, about the beginning of the fourth century (A.D. 306), and who wrote his History, as he tells us, on purpose 'to record the (episcopal) successions from the apostles, together with the events which had occurred in the Church, and the persons who had presided in the principal dioceses down to his own time,'—Eusebius, I say, has given us the names of the bishops, one by one, not only in the see of Rome, but also in the three other patriarchal sees of Jerusalem, of Antioch, and Alexandria.

Testimony of Eusebius to episcopal successions.

I must again repeat, let no one imagine that there can be any room for doubt in regard to the true clerical character and rank of those who composed those several successions. They were from the first what no one denies they were afterwards, prelates or bishops, in the modern sense of this latter

Meaning of that term.

---

[1] See 'Patrologia,' vol. iii. p. 1168, vol. iv. p. 403; 'Irenicum,' p. 308.

name, and bishops only; though necessarily at first with
fewer subordinate clergy, and with a jurisdiction more
limited, and less accurately defined. In the history of
Athens we are duly informed respecting the magistrates
called archons; that for many years their office continued to
be for life, that then it became a decennial, and ultimately
an annual one. But we have no information, no hint whatever, in the history of the Church, of an inverse change, or
of any change at all, having taken place in the *office* of
bishops. We must therefore conclude that no such change
occurred, unless we will suppose that the original authors to
whom I have referred, when they spoke of those episcopal
successions, were consciously intending to delude their
readers; and that subsequent historical and chronological
writers—writers, some of them at least perfectly impartial,
such as Gibbon, or such as Fynes Clinton—who have
accepted their testimony to the catalogues in question,
allowed themselves to be deluded upon a matter of such
importance.

Instances of
presbyters
advanced to
episcopate.

It will serve to put the point upon which I am now insist-
ing in a still stronger light if I can show that there are upon
record, during the same period, instances of individuals
who had been presbyters, and who were afterwards promoted
and ordained to the episcopate as to a higher rank. And
instances of this can be shown. For example, we know
that Irenæus had been a presbyter of the Church at Lyons
before he succeeded Pothinus as its bishop (Euseb. v. c. iv.).
Again, we learn from Origen, as quoted by Eusebius (lib. vi.

c. xix.), that Heraclus, who succeeded Demetrius as bishop of Alexandria, had previously been a presbyter of that Church. So, too, Dionysius had been a presbyter of Rome, and Cyprian had been a presbyter of Carthage (see his Life by Pontius, his deacon, c. iii.), before they became bishops. (Euseb. vii. c. vii.; Jerome, 'de Vir. Illustr.,' c. lxix.).

It must be confessed that in the earliest times there is some difficulty in proving a distinct ordination of those who were raised from the second to the first order in the ministry; and opponents of prelacy have not been slow to take advantage of this difficulty, as enabling them to maintain that the distinction between the two orders is not essential, and that, having been introduced merely as a human arrangement, it may be dispensed with or maintained according to circumstances, and simply upon grounds of greater or less expediency. The only Scriptural evidence which bears directly upon the point is derived from the analogy, before referred to, between the Jewish and the See Lecture 2. Christian ministry; and this, it cannot be denied, is of great weight. It is certain that the high priest received a separate and distinct consecration from that of the ordinary priests,—a consecration which consisted in being vested with a special dress, in receiving a special unction, and in offering a special sacrifice.[1] Of evidence which is post-Scriptural to the same effect I know of none more conclu-

---

[1] See Exod. xxviii.-xxx.; Levit. viii. xvi. Selden, 'De Successione in Pontificatum,' lib. ii. capp. vii.-ix. vol. ii. pp. 182-197; Jerome, Epist. lxiv. ad Fabiolam, vol. i. pp. 615-617.

sive [1] than that which is afforded by the earliest canons of the Church ; such as the so-called 'apostolical canons,' and the canons of the first Œcumenical Council [2]—to both of which I shall have occasion to refer presently. Meanwhile, in the dearth of records to throw full light upon those early times, we can only suppose that the Church fell into the way of trine ordination as it fell into the way of infant baptism and of the observance of the Lord's Day ; and that, as no express notice has come down to us of the institution of either of those usages, which, nevertheless, we retain without scruple, so neither need we scruple to retain this usage, which comes to us recommended by at least equal claims of reason and propriety, as well as of prescriptive right.

But to proceed with the question of successorship to the apostles.

The earliest known ministry a threefold one.

2. A second method of proving the point upon which we are engaged—viz. the prelatical character of the earliest episcopate—is to be found in the fact that the ministry to which the apostolical succession appertained was invariably a threefold one, composed of the three orders, bishops,

---

[1] Bishop Beveridge, in his note upon the Second Apostolical Canon, p. 14, remarks upon the impossibility of the trine ordination having been *recognised* so universally as we find it was by the earliest Councils, unless it had been instituted by the apostles.

[2] The fourth canon of that Council is as follows : 'It is most fitting that a bishop should be instituted by all the bishops of the province ; but if this be not practicable . . . . three at all events must meet together, and when they have received the consent of those who are absent, signified by letter, then let them *perform the ordination.*'

priests, and deacons ; a ministry in which, as a rule,[1] the
same individual who rose to the highest, must have passed
through the lower orders ; a ministry, in short, the same as
that which we found laid down in Scripture in the directions
which St. Paul addressed to Timothy as first bishop of the
Church in Ephesus, for his own guidance, and for the guidance of those who were to come after him. Let me now
request your attention to the evidence of this fact, as we
meet with it in writers who come next to the penmen of the
New Testament.

The earliest uninspired Christian document is the Epistle
of Clement [2] to the Church at Corinth. It was written from
Rome very soon—probably not more than two years—after
St. Paul's martyrdom in A.D. 68 ; and, if so, thirty years
before the death of St. John. The evidence, therefore,
which it affords, belongs properly to the period embraced in
my former lecture—the period of the first century—the
Scriptural and apostolic age. It is very important to bear
this in mind.[3] It serves to account for the still unsettled

Testimony of
St. Clement.

---

[1] But this was not always observed. Deacons were sometimes
made bishops, as St. Athanasius of
Alexandria ; and even laymen, as
Ambrose of Milan, and Nectarius
of Constantinople, and Demetrius
of Alexandria. See Bingham, book
ii. c. x. 5, 7, vol. i. pp. 143, 145 ;
Neale, 'Hist. of Alex. Church,' vol.
i. p. 12.

[2] It is probable but not certain

that the Clement who is mentioned
by St. Paul, Phil. iv. 3, was the
same as the author of the Corinthian
Epistle, and bishop of Rome. See
Lightfoot, p. 166 sq.

[3] Professor Lightfoot does not
concur in this early date. He considers the Epistle of Clement to
have been 'probably written in the
last decade of the first century,' p.
216; in ' the later years of Domitian,

state of the Corinthian Church—much as we have seen it in
St. Paul's own Epistles written twelve years before.   Whether
St. Clement was already become bishop of Rome when he
wrote it we cannot certainly tell.   If he was—and according
to Tertullian, who represents him as having been ordained
bishop by St. Peter,[1] he must have been—he doubtless
wrote the Epistle in that capacity : at all events, it appears
from the first chapter, that he had been formally consulted
by the Corinthian Church (as Polycarp, bishop of Smyrna,
afterwards was by the Church of Philippi[2]) in its difficulties.
In this most primitive document, then, we appear to find a
sufficiently distinct recognition of the three orders of the
Christian ministry (as the intended normal constitution of
that ministry) in the comparison with the Jewish high priest,
priests, and Levites—all distinctly named, as holding peculiar
and distinct offices in the elder Church (c. xl.[3]), a comparison repeated afterwards more than once by St. Jerome.[4]
Again : when Clement writes (c. xlii.) that 'the apostles,

---

about A.D. 96.'—Page 166.

[1] ' De Præscrip. Hæret.,' c. xxxii.

[2] See his Epistle, c. iii.

[3] Following a conjecture of
Neander, Dean Milman, 'Hist. of
Christ.,' vol. iii. p. 259, writes, 'this
passage is rejected as an interpolation by all judicious and impartial scholars'—a statement which,
being certainly incorrect, appears to
me singularly partial and injudi-
cious. The passage is accepted in
' Irenicum,' p. 326, and admitted to

contain 'a parallel of the Church
officers in the Gospel to those under
the Law.' I am glad to find myself
supported by Professor Lightfoot,
p. 248, in demurring to Dean Milman's 'arbitrary criticism.'

[4] See below in this Lecture.
Athanasius calls Hilary the deacon
a Levite. 'Hist. Arian.,' c. xli. vol.
i. p. 368. Jerome gives the same
name to the Roman deacons. See
below, p. 175, note 2.

preaching through countries and cities, appointed the first
fruits of their labours—after they had proved them (ἐοκι-
μάσαντες) by the Spirit—to be overseers and ministers
(ἐπισκόπους καὶ Διακόνους) of those who should afterwards
believe;' we see just such a germ of the future complete
threefold ministry as is found, for instance, in St. Paul's
Epistle to the Philippians, where the apostle himself is still
the prelate of the Church.[1]

From the Roman bishop, and probable fellow-labourer of
St. Paul, St. Clement, we come next to the bishop or metropolitan [2] of Antioch, St. Ignatius, the disciple of St. John.
I do not think that any person of competent learning, who
has thoroughly studied the controversy respecting the Ignatian Epistles will venture to dispute the genuineness of the
seven now generally accepted in their shorter form,[3] and
still less of the three—to Polycarp, to the Ephesians, and to

Testimony
of St.
Ignatius.

---

[1] See Lightfoot, p. 96.

[2] In his Epistle to the Romans he
calls himself 'bishop of Syria,' of
which Antioch was the metropolis.
See Hammond, ' Dissert.,' ii. c. vii.
sect. 14.

[3] The opinion of Dean Milman,
who belonged to the sceptical or
hypercritical school (see note 3, in
last page), is thus expressed : ' My
own opinion is decidedly in favour
of the genuineness of these Epistles
—the shorter ones, I mean—which are
vindicated by Pearson. . . . . The
object of the writer does not seem to

be to raise the sacerdotal power, but
rather to enforce Christian unity.'
Ibid. vol. iii. p. 256. Compare
Hammond, ' Dissert.,' ii. c. xxii.
83 ; Professor Lightfoot, however,
accepts only the Curetonian Syriac ;
but though he regards 'the short
Greek recension as probably corrupt or spurious,' he concludes
'from internal evidence that it can
hardly have been later than the
middle of the second century ; ' and
' its witness, therefore,' he adds, ' is
highly valuable.' See pp. 210 sq.,
232, 240.

the Romans—so far as they are preserved in the Syriac version, first published in 1845. The saintly bishop of Antioch
was, as I have said, a disciple of St. John, and suffered
martyrdom not many years after St. John's death, viz. A.D.
115.[1] Doubtless the temptation is great to dispute the authority of writings which, coming from such a source, must
ever be felt, not only to give a strong testimony, but to
convey a severe censure against those who have reduced the
true ministry of the Church to a republican parity, and I
may add, against those also who have exaggerated it into an
autocratic supremacy.[2] But love of the truth will not yield
to that temptation ; and even so long as there is uncertainty,
so long as there is *any ground* of probability that these
Epistles may be genuine—much more when the balance of
proof must be seen greatly to incline to that conclusion—no
fair and candid reasoner will desire that the evidence which
they afford should be left out of view. And what, then, is
that evidence?[3] Of those seven Epistles, which purport to
be written by St. Ignatius as a condemned martyr on his
way towards Rome, and which, whether written by himself
or not, we know[4] to have been in existence in the second
century, there is not one which does not make distinct men-

---

[1] According to Clinton, 'F. R.,'
p. 101. Others say A.D. 107, and
others A.D. 117.

[2] See Bishop Pearson's 'Vind.
Ignat.,' p. 350.

[3] Stillingfleet's remarks upon it

maybe seen in 'Irenicum,' p. 308 sq.

[4] From the testimony of Polycarp (Ep. ad Phil., c. xiii.); of
Irenæus (lib. v. c. xxviii.); of Origen
(Prol. in Cant. Canticor.). See
also Euseb. iii. 34.

tion of the threefold ministry, of a bishop, presbyters, and deacons—excepting only the Epistle to the Church of Rome —the Church in reference to which such mention, under the circumstances, would be most likely to be suppressed, and, as matter of evidence, is least required. In three of the Epistles we find the name of the bishop of the Church to which the Epistle is addressed—viz. Onesimus, bishop of Ephesus [1] (with a deacon named Borrus) ; Damas, bishop of Magnesia (two of whose presbyters, Bassus and Apollonius, and a deacon, Lotio, are also mentioned by name) ; and Polybius, bishop of Tralles, —particulars not consistent with the notion of forgery.[2] I propose to give but two specimens [3] of the Ignatian evidence out of upwards of thirty distinct testimonies which might be produced. And I shall take the first specimen from one of the three Syriac Epitomes. In the epitomised version of the Epistle to Polycarp, who is denominated in the inscription 'bishop of Smyrna,' we read as follows : ' Be studious of unity, than which nothing is more precious. . . . . Cleave to your bishop, that God also may (cleave) to you. I give my life for those who are subject to the bishop, to presbyters, to deacons. With them may my portion be in the presence of

---

[1] Mentioned also in the Syriac Epitome.

[2] See Lightfoot, p. 211.

[3] For a general view of the other testimonies to be found in the Ignatian Epistles, and of the conclusions to which they lead, see Hammond, 'Diss. Sec.,' capp. xxv. xxvi. Also Appendix to the author's Synodal Address for 1864, pp. 114-120.

I

God !'[1] (capp. i. vi.). You will remember that this is quoted, not for the sake of the sentiment, but simply of the testimony—testimony to the fact of the existence of the three orders in that primitive age (the first quarter of the second century), when there was no controversy respecting the form of the ministry to tempt to the fabrication of such representations. The other specimen which I have to give will show not only the same institution of an episcopal ministry, and the same motive for maintaining it—viz. regard for unity—but also that in the opinion of Ignatius it rested upon the sanction of Christ Himself, and that it was already universally received. Thus, then, he writes in his Epistle to the Ephesians, ch. iii. : ' Since love suffers me not to be silent, I have taken upon me, first of all, to exhort you that ye abide in unity according to the will of God. For as Jesus Christ, our inseparable Life, was [the fulfilment of] His Father's will, so the bishops, settled everywhere to the utmost bounds [of the earth], are by the will of Jesus Christ.'

Testimony of ' Martyrdom of Ignatius.'

Similar proof in support of the threefold ministry is to be derived from the narrative of the martyrdom of St. Ignatius, which, if not actually written by the companions of his journey, as it purports to be, is unquestionably a document of primitive times. In that narrative we read : ' The cities and Churches of Asia had welcomed the holy man through their bishops, and presbyters, and deacons ' (ch. iii.).

---

[1] On the conclusive character of this evidence in favour of the three-fold ministry, see Cureton's ' Corpus Ignatianum,' Pref p. xvi. See also Lightfoot, pp. 96, 233 sqq.

From Ignatius—the Asiatic bishop—passing over the apo- Hermas
stolic Hermas (brother of Pius, bishop of Rome), who seems,
however, to mention the three orders, under the names of
' bishops, doctors or teachers, and deacons,' in his third Vi-
sion, ch. v.[1]—we come next to Clement of Alexandria, and
Tertullian, both African presbyters at the close of the *second*
—that is, as I must frequently remind you, the *first* post-
apostolic—century. In the former, Clement, we find at Testimony
of Clement
of Alex-
andria.
least one passage in which the three orders are distinctly
named, viz. in his book of ' Miscellanies,' where, speaking of
the degrees of celestial glory, and comparing them with the
dignities of the Church below, he writes : ' In my opinion
the gradations (προκοπαὶ) here in the Church, of bishops,
presbyters, and deacons, are imitations of the angelic glory,
and of that Economy which, the Scriptures say, awaits those
who, following the footsteps of the apostles, have lived in
the perfection of righteousness, according to the gospel '
(Strom. vi. c. xiii. vol. ii. p. 793). In another passage, however, of the same work (vii. 1), he mentions only two orders,
viz. the presbyterate and diaconate, the former 'for improvement,' the latter 'ministerial.' In like manner, in his ' Instructor ' (i. 6), he does not scruple to speak of himself and
his fellow-presbyters as ' Pastors who had rule over (προηγου-
μένοι) the Churches.' And again, in his ' Quis Dives,' &c.,
(c. xlii.), in the well-known anecdote respecting St. John, the

---

[1] On the testimony of Hermas
see Lightfoot, p. 216 sq. He considers 'the notices in the Shepherd
too vague to lead to any result.'

names presbyter **and** episcopus appear [1] to be used indifferently of the same person.   But it will be obvious, that while each of these latter three passages is capable of being interpreted so as to comprehend a threefold division of orders or degrees of ministry,[2] it is not possible to interpret the first passage so as to reduce the three orders to only two.   In short, the fair inference to be drawn from Clement's testimony, taken as a whole, is the same which has already been drawn from that of Irenæus, viz. that the generic name presbyter was still sometimes used in a laxer sense, so as to include the episcopus or overseer of the presbyters.   In Tertullian there are three passages at least which bear testimony to the ministry as threefold, viz. in 'De Baptismo,' c. xvii. vol. i. p. 1218; in 'De Fugâ in Persecutione,' c. xi. vol. ii. p. 113; and in 'De Monogamiâ,' c. xi. vol. ii. p. 493.

Testimony of Tertullian.

---

[1] I say 'appear,' because Bishop Pearson regards 'presbyter' in that passage as descriptive of age, not of clerical office. 'Vind. Ignat.,' vol. ii. p. 551.

[2] In reference to the first of those three passages, which represents the duty of the presbyterate to be 'to improve,' while that of the diaconate is 'to serve,' the Church, Dr. Lightfoot remarks: 'The functions of the bishop and presbyter are thus regarded as substantially the same in kind, *though different in degree*; while the functions of the diaconate are separate from both.' In re-

ference to the last, he observes: 'Clement, like Irenæus, regards the bishop as a presbyter, *though the converse would not be true*,' p. 227. The passage in the 'Instructor,' iii. 12, upon which Bishop Pearson, 'Vind. Ignat.,' p. 567, has laid so much stress as testifying to the threefold gradation of the ministry, and claiming for it the authority of Scripture, Dr. Lightfoot dismisses as incompetent for that purpose, because it assumes that the names episcopus and presbyter are *not* used synonymously in the New Testament, p. 224, note.

In the first of these passages, not only the distinct existence of the three orders, but the gradation of their power,
and the principle upon which it rests, are plainly marked, as
may be seen from the words which I proceed to quote :
' The chief priest, i.e. the bishop, has the right of giving
baptism ; after him the presbyters and the deacons ; not,
however, without the bishop's authority, out of regard to the
Church's honour, on the preservation of which depends the
preservation of peace.' Again I must remind you that I am
not defending sentiments but ascertaining facts, and with
this object I must beg you to observe that in each of the
four testimonies of the Alexandrian Clement and of Tertullian to which I have now referred, as specifying the three
orders, the mention of them is introduced, not as a matter
of doubt or disputation—for there had been no dispute
upon the point, nor did any arise till two centuries later—
but simply as matter of illustration, or as a statement of acknowledged fact.[1]

Slightly later than Clement and Tertullian, but still in the
early part of the third century, flourished Origen, another
presbyter, and successor of Clement as a teacher in the
school of Alexandria. His testimony, frequently[2] repeated
in various parts of his voluminous writings, is precisely the
same as that of the other two. In his Commentary on St.

Testimony of Origen.

---

[1] Professor Lightfoot observes,
p. 213, 'Episcopacy was the only
form of government known or *remembered* in the Church when Ter-

tullian wrote ;' i.e. within a century
after the death of St. John.

[2] See Bingham, i. p. 55 ; Pearson,
'Vind. Ignat.,' p. 272 sq.

Matthew alone there are four several passages in which the three orders are distinctly enumerated just as we enumerate them at the present day (see vol. iii. pp. 501, 646, 690, 752). In one of those passages we read of persons who prided themselves upon the fact that their fathers or forefathers had been bishops, or priests, or deacons—in which case they must have been contemporary with the apostles or nearly so ;[1] in another it is plainly intimated that the three orders are derived from Scripture.[2]

One more testimony remains to be cited, which sets the coping stone upon this line of proof. I allude to the collection called 'Apostolical Canons,' of which though the date is uncertain, Mosheim, a Presbyterian, admits that they exhibit the discipline received among the Eastern Christians in the second and third centuries ;[3] and Bishop Beveridge, who had examined the subject thoroughly, came substantially to the same conclusion.[4] There seems, therefore, to be no sufficient reason why we should not regard and speak of them in the same way as the Westminster Shorter Catechism speaks of the so-called 'Apostles' Creed,' only substituting the word *discipline* for the word *faith*: 'This collection of canons, though not composed by the apostles,

[1] Vol. iii. p. 690; see Pearson, ibid. p. 276.

[2] Vol. iii. p. 646; see Pearson, ibid. pp. 273, 281.

[3] See 'Hist. Eccl.,' c. ii. 19, p. 50.

[4] He considered that the collection was formed towards the end of the second or at the beginning of the third century. See in his 'Synodicon' the note on canon ii. p. 15. explaining the cause of the absence of express evidence respecting ordinations in the early Church. See also Bishop Pearson, 'Vind. Ignat.,' p. 546.

is a brief sum of the Christian discipline, agreeable to the word of God, and anciently received in the Churches of Christ.' The first of those canons is in these words : 'Let a bishop be ordained by two or three bishops, a priest by one bishop, and so likewise a deacon.'[1] And this canon is still observed by all the Churches of the Anglican communion, by all the Churches of the East, and by all the Churches subject to the Church of Rome ; except that they now insist upon the presence of at least three bishops for the consecration of a bishop, according to the fourth canon of the Council of Nicæa, before referred to.[2]

The testimonies now produced do not descend later than 200 years after our Lord's ascension. No one who is acquainted with early ecclesiastical history, with the writings of the Fathers or the decrees of Councils, will need to be told that from that period[3] similar testimonies to the true constitution of the ministry become, in consequence of the greater mass of evidence, infinitely more abundant. For instance, we learn from Eusebius (vi. 43) that a very large synod, which chronologists place in A.D. 251, assembled at Rome to take into consideration the false teaching of

Testimony from later times still more abundant.

---

[1] See Bruns., 'Canones Apost. et Concil.,' p. 1 ; and Bingham, book ii. ch. xi. 4, vol. i. p. 153 sq.

[2] See above, p. 108. The canons of that Council distinctly recognise the three orders again and again. See canons 3, 15, 16, 18. It is also to be observed, that the 13th canon speaks of the 'Old Canonical Law,'

with reference, probably, to the 44th of the so-called 'Apostolical Canons.'

[3] Concerning the evidence of the Clementine Homilies, which belong, most probably, to the second century, and of the 'Ancient Syriac Documents,' edited by Cureton and Wright, see Lightfoot, p. 209.

Novatus, 'at which sixty bishops, and a much greater number of presbyters and deacons were present.' Such was
the Church's experience in Europe. We have similar testimony, to the same effect, about the same time in regard to
Africa and Asia; in the seventh Council held under Cyprian
at Carthage,[1] on the baptism of heretics, in A.D. 258, at
which were assembled upwards of eighty bishops, with presbyters and deacons (Patrol, vol. iii. p. 1052); and in the
Council held at Antioch, against Paul of Samosata, in A.D.
264 (Euseb. vii. 30). Or if we descend into the following
century, to the reign of Constantine, it is calculated, according to Gibbon, that there were then as many as 1800 bishoprics altogether in the East and West ; and we know that
some 318 bishops,[2] besides presbyters and deacons, actually
came from all parts of the then civilised world—from Spain
and Gaul, from Italy and Greece, from Macedonia, from
Libya, Egypt and Arabia, from Palestine, and the various
provinces of the East—in order to attend that first great
General Council to which I just now alluded, which was held
at Nicæa in A.D. 325. Even from our own distant island we
read of a bishop of London, a bishop of York, and a bishop,
priest, and deacon from the diocese of Lincoln, among those
who were present at the Council assembled at Arles, in the

Including
evidence
from our
own island.

---

[1] In one of his letters, epist. lix.,
he alludes to a Council, held before
his time, at which ninety bishops
were present. See Lightfoot, p. 222,
note.

[2] Their names, and the names of
the sees which they represented,
may be seen in Labbe's 'Concilia,'
ii. pp. 50-54.

south of France, somewhat earlier, viz. in A.D. 314.[1] In short, the prevalence of that threefold ministry was so universal, so unexceptional, wherever Christianity itself had spread, that the existence of a Church without a bishop, priests, and deacons, would have been thought no less incongruous, no less impossible, than the existence of a Church without the possession of the Scriptures, or without the observance of the Lord's Day. And this uniformity of the ministry is the more remarkable, because in rites and ceremonies (the discussion of which has been sometimes improperly mixed up[2] with the question of the ministry and of Church government) great differences in different places were unquestionably allowed without any injury to the cause of peace and unity.[3] Nor was this all. The heretical bodies also which had separated from the Church—such as the Arians, the Novatians, the Donatists, the Luciferians, the Nestorians, sects which prevailed over different and widely distant parts of Christendom—all retained the same

Heretical separatists kept the same form of ministry.

---

[1] See Labbe's 'Concilia,' vol. i. p. 1430. The names of the three bishops were Restitutus, Eborius, and Adelphius. 'There is reason to believe that there were, even at that period, two other bishops in Britain, one of whom was in Wales, and *the other in Scotland.* In like manner Britain sent three bishops to the Council of Ariminum in A.D. 359.'—Cosmo Innes' *Scotland in the Middle Ages,* p. 46. When Augustin landed in England, A.D. 596, there were seven British bishops and one archbishop (of St. David's). See 'Theoph. Anglic.,' part ii. c. i.

[2] For instance, in the 'First Book of Discipline,' c. xx., 'Not that we think that one *policy* and one *order of ceremonies* can be appointed for all ages, times, and places.'

[3] See Firmilian, quoted in 'Irenicum,' p. 323, and Augustin, ibid. p. 60, also p. 382.

form of ministry; which it cannot be supposed that they would have done if they had considered that the Church was in error in this respect, or if there had been any tradition or belief that a different system had been instituted or sanctioned by the apostles.

Pretended exceptions of the Goths, &c.
In making these last remarks I have not forgotten that an exception to this universal uniformity has been thought by some to have been discovered among our own forefathers; that much has been said about a Culdean church without bishops; and, moreover, that the Goths have been assigned to us as companions of our singularity in this respect.[1] In such a case, where the multitude of unquestionable examples over all parts of the Christian world was so very great, it might be sufficient to say that as there are *lusus Naturæ* in every department of creation, so in this case the exception only proves the rule. But the truth is, that notwithstanding the learned researches and peremptory conclusions which have been put forth upon the point, there is good and sufficient reason for believing that the supposed exception never really existed.[2]

No just comparison between the universal prevalence of episcopacy and the western prevalence of popery.
It has also been attempted to cast a slur upon this entire argument by confounding the universal acceptance of an episcopal ministry with the upgrowth and wide extension of popery; and this representation has been largely and successfully made use of in former times, for the purpose of creating a prejudice against prelacy and in favour of a system

[1] See 'Irenicum,' p. 374 sq.
[2] See Bishop W. Lloyd's 'Historical Account,' chaps. v.–vii.

of ministerial parity. **Nor** is **this to** be wondered at, when it is considered that in **order** to detect the fallacy there **is** required some knowledge of early ecclesiastical history, of which the mass of **our** population, and, I **fear it must be** added, **not a few even** of our better educated classes, are sadly ignorant. Of the upgrowth of popery, **and of the causes** which led **to** it, I shall have occasion to speak pre- **sently ;** and then it will be seen that, so far from any natural or necessary connection existing between the two, there has been nothing more fatal to the legitimate autho- rity of bishops than the **power of the popes.** In the mean- time let it be **borne in** mind that the universal prevalence of a prelatically constituted ministry throughout the entire East of Christendom has been, if possible, still **more re-** markable than its **prevalence in the West ; and** that through- out the **East** (where, be it also remembered, was the first cradle of the Church) the usurpations of **popery have been** disallowed all along from the beginning—and **still are—no** less resolutely than since the Reformation they have been re- jected **by ourselves.** There is, in fact, nothing with which travellers in **the East,** who attend to matters of this kind, are **more struck at the** present day than the entire absence among all Christian communities, orthodox or heretical, **of any** semblance of **presbyterianism, or** of the existence of any other form **of ministry than that which** we call prelatical. The late **well-known missionary Dr. Joseph Wolff, after** stating that he himself **once held wild and irregular views in** Church matters, **has left upon record the following testimony :**

Testimony of Eastern travellers.

'The very fact that all the Eastern Churches, without one single exception, have bishops, priests, and deacons, and the very fact that a presbyterian Church is not known, is to me a sufficient proof that episcopacy is of divine origin, and that the doctrine of apostolic succession is a Scriptural doctrine.'[1] In an earlier part of the present century the interesting researches of Dr. Claudius Buchanan conveyed similar testimony respecting the Syrian Christians on the coast of Malabar, who appeared incredulous when, as a ·Scotchman, he told them of a Church, without deacons in holy orders, and without a bishop to superintend the presbyters; while at the same time it appeared that the same body of Christians had placed themselves in an attitude of the staunchest Protestantism against the Church of Rome, whose unscrupulous aggressions they had had only too much reason to resent.[2]

3. Hitherto it has been my aim in the present Lecture to prove, *first*, that bishops, i.e. individuals holding a permanent position above presbyters, and, strictly speaking, bishops only, were regarded as successors of the apostles by the primitive Christians who lived in the earliest post-apostolic age ; and secondly, that during the same age the ministry in which the said individuals occupied the foremost rank was universally a threefold one, consisting of a bishop, presbyters, and deacons. I now proceed, in the third place,

[1] See 'The Primitive Church in its Episcopacy,' p. 67; also Dr. Wolff's 'Travels to Bokhara,' vol. i. p. 189.

[2] See Dr. Buchanan's 'Christian Researches in Asia,' pp. 120-123.

and still in continuation of the same branch of evidence, to establish the fact **that no attempt** was made to question the Scriptural authority **of the same** episcopal or three-fold ministry **till the fourth** century; **and that no sooner was** the attempt **made than it was** put down **and condemned by** the universal conscience and witness of the **Church.**[1]

The first attempt to question the threefold ministry made by Aerius in the fourth century.

Three authors, all of whom lived within the last quarter of the fourth, and the first quarter of the fifth century, viz. Epiphanius, bishop of Salamis, the metropolis of Cyprus in the east of the Levant; Philastrius, bishop of Brescia, in Northern Italy; and St. Augustin, bishop of Hippo in Western Numidia; each of these—an Asiatic, a European, and an African—composed a treatise against heresies or false doctrines; and each has included Aerius in his list of heretics.[2] This man, who was a presbyter of Sebaste in Lesser Armenia, and had previously been ambitious of a bishopric, but without success, and who was still living when Epiphanius wrote,—this Aerius, unable to digest his morti-fication and disappointment, took upon himself to broach the opinion (besides being an Arian, and holding other unsound

---

[1] Young Stillingfleet argues, that Aerius was condemned because he denied the lawfulness of episcopacy and for his separation; otherwise Jerome must have been condemned too. See 'Irenicum,' pp. 276, 404. It is true that Jerome's error was simply theoretical. He did not deny the right of bishops to their pre-eminence (quite the contrary), and what he has denied, more or less, in two passages—the Scriptural and apostolic origin of the right—he has asserted in many more. See below, in this Lecture.

[2] Epiphanius, 'Hær.,' lxxv. vol. i. pp. 904–912; Philastrius, ' De Hæresibus Liber,' c. cxxii. p. 70; St. Augustin, 'De Hær.,' c. liii. vol. viii. p. 55.

doctrines) that there ought to be no difference between a bishop and a presbyter. The arguments which he used were all drawn from Scripture, and appear to have been precisely similar to those which it was found convenient to have recourse to, in order to justify a foregone conclusion, in the later stage of the Continental Reformation, and with which in this country we have become familiar, since the days of Andrew Melville, and still more of Alexander Henderson. For instance, he referred to Philippians i. 1, and to 1 Timothy i. 14, without troubling himself (so far as appears) to compare this latter text with 2 Timothy i. 6.[1] But the true interpretation of Scripture upon such a point, however speciously attacked, was not to be so easily overthrown in that early age ; being attested, as it then was, by a uniform tradition, and by the experience of universal Christendom. Consequently the teaching of Aerius (notwithstanding the support it might have derived from the wild statement which St. Jerome put forth not long after, and to which I shall presently refer at length)—this teaching, I say, this discovery of Aerius, appears to have become extinct with his own death ; and no more is heard of it until it was revived by the supposed 'necessity' of untoward circumstances which embarrassed, for the most part, the legitimate progress and development of the Reformation in the sixteenth century.

Meanwhile, we have now to turn our attention to a cor-

[1] See Epiphanius, ibid., and Bishop Pearson, 'Vind. Ignat.,' pp. 326, 565 sq., 571.

ruption of the truth the very opposite of that which was broached by Aerius.

I remarked in my former lecture, that an indication of the probable design of a uniform ministry, and of our being able to discover it, is to be found in the fact that elements of identity underlie the diversities of system which actually exist, and that the diversities themselves can all be traced historically to one and the same common origin.

We have now arrived at that stage of our enquiry when the grounds of that remark are to be made good. And this will form the fourth and last stage of investigation under that second main head of our general argument with which we are now engaged.

4. It has been shown, then, I think conclusively, that the apostles formed a distinct body, having prelatical authority, each in his own person ; that they severally made provision for a successorship to themselves in all the ordinary functions of their prelatical office ; and that their successors from the first were, and have been ever since, known by the name of bishops, having presbyters and deacons under them, as necessary to complete the clerical ministry.

We have also seen, that in the fourth century an attempt was made by Aerius to call in question the Scriptural authority of that successorship, and to prove that the apostles in fact had no successors, and that no higher order than that of presbyters ought to be maintained in the Church. It has been seen, moreover, that the time was not yet ripe for any such attempt. More than a thousand years were to pass before it could be renewed; and then it would be made, and would partially succeed as a reaction from an attempt which, as I have said, was of the very opposite kind, and which also appeared for the first time in the fourth century.

Upgrowth of popery. I allude to the pretensions in behalf of the see of Rome, when there began to be advanced—though in a way scarcely perceptible, and certainly with no intention of producing the extreme results which eventually flowed from them—pretensions whereby, over and above the successorship of bishops to the apostles, which Aerius denied, there was asserted a special successorship to one apostle, viz. St. Peter, which was to give to one bishop—the bishop of Rome—an official rank and authority superior to and distinct from the rank and authority of all the rest ; and thus the threefold ministry, which Aerius would have reduced to two orders, was virtually increased to four. Happily, not only the teaching of Scripture,[1] but the testimony of the Church's history for the first 300 years and upwards[2] is no less conclusive against the exorbitant claims of the single bishop of Rome, than it is against the opposite claims of the disappointed presbyter of Sebaste. I cannot say, more conclusive ; on the contrary, I must confess, that full as much apparent testimony is to be derived from both these sources—from Scripture, and from antiquity—in favour of the papal excess, as is to be derived from them in favour of the presbyterian defect; for such is the nature of these two extremes in comparison with the

---

[1] See a tract entitled 'The Episcopate,' by the Rev. H. Dodds.

[2] See the author's Address, Perth Lecture, 1854, pp. 17-22.

printed in the Report of the Norwich Church Congress, 1865 ; and true system of the Church's ministry. We have no difficulty in tracing the steps which gradually led up to the gigantic structure of the papal supremacy. The use of St. Peter's name, not without some semblance of a primacy among the apostles being assigned to him in Scripture; the unquestionable primacy of Rome itself as *princeps urbium* in the civilised world; the learning, sanctity, and fidelity of some of its first bishops; the value of a centre to look to and to rally round during the early childhood of the Church, in days of persecution or in days of heresy, and when—the Church being still confined within one empire, and speaking, for the most part, one language—the recognition of such a centre involved none of those practical inconveniences which render it both undesirable and impracticable at the present day: and again, at a later period, when the irruption of barbarians from all sides had broken up the order of Christian society throughout Europe, the obvious advantage of guidance and of authority, the best and most powerful that could be had, in dealing with the new elements, so as to bring them, as far as might be, under a control which, in proportion as it was uniformly systematised, would be more widely felt:—these, and such as these, were the causes which led men to acquiesce in, or promote—too often through the use of force or fraud[1]—a development of the

Causes which led to papal supremacy

---

[1] 'History deposed unhesitatingly that Rome rose to the eminence she occupied in the thirteenth century, when at her zenith . . . *most un-righteously*, as concerns the Church —the whole Church I mean—by *fraud and force*; by the weapon of the weak and the weapon of the

K

threefold ministry, which practically destroyed its divine symmetry, and introduced a power utterly inconsistent with the teaching of Scripture, and with the testimony and example of the Church during the apostolic and post-apostolic age. And how was this power to be maintained? It was to be maintained partly by denying, partly by undermining, the legitimate authority of the highest order of the threefold ministry—that is, of the bishops, as each and all equally [1] successors of the apostles; and then by obtruding the pope alone into their place. And this was done.[2] Contrary to the prevailing sentiment of the primitive Church, first, the schoolmen, in the pope's interest, invented a distinction whereby, though they allowed bishops to be superior to presbyters in power and jurisdiction, they made them to be

---

strong alternately put into her hand, and employed by her as legitimate for the spread of her power, to the dismemberment and destruction of the Church at large; the most striking specimens of each kind being the *Pseudo-Decretals,* including of course the Pseudo-donation, and *the Crusades.'*—Ffoulkes' *Letter to Archbishop Manning.*

[1] See St. Jerome, 'Epist. ad Evang.,' i. : 'Ubicunque fuerit Episcopus, sive Romæ, sive Eugubii, sive Constantinopoli, sive Rhegii, sive Alexandriæ, sive Tanis, ejusdem meriti, ejusdem est et sacerdotii.'— Vol. i. p. 1194.

[2] See the author's 'Discourse on Scottish Reform.,' 2nd ed., pp. 16 sq., 93–97. It is strange that a Church historian like Gieseler, vol. i. p. 89, should not have understood the real drift of 'admissions' made by the Roman canonists and schoolmen to the effect that bishops and presbyters are of one order. See also Stillingfleet's 'Iren.,' pp. 273, 300, and Professor Lightfoot, p. 228: 'The substantial identity of order (of bishops and presbyters) was maintained *even* by popes and councils.' Yes, by popes, and by councils so far as they were overruled by popes. But see the next note.

both of one and the same order.[1] In this they were followed by the Jesuits ;[2] and to the present day, though the Church of Rome reckons altogether seven orders in the ministry— four of them being inferior, and only semi-clerical—the epis- copal order is not included,[3] but is regarded as merged in that of presbyters, while the pope sits alone, *extraordinary*, and supreme above them all !

This is what is meant by papal supremacy. This is what the Eastern patriarchs, in the encyclical letter which they addressed to the present pope in complaint of his aggression upon their jurisdiction twenty years ago, called —and justly called—' the great heresy of modern times, as Arianism was the great heresy in the earlier ages ' (p. 9). Acting upon the new notion of the schoolmen, and calcu- lating that whatever tended to depress the episcopate would elevate themselves, the popes did not scruple to give dispen- sations whereby presbyters were authorised, on occasions,

Supremacy of the pope denounced by Eastern patriarchs.

---

[1] See Bishop Pearson's Minor Works, i. p. 275; Bingham, i. pp. 52, 270, and ix. p. 245. At the same time, it is not to be forgotten that the Council of Trent, mainly through the influence of the Spanish bishops (see Father Paul's History, pp. 552 sqq., 686), pronounced anathema against any 'who shall say that there is not in the Catholic Church a hierarchy, instituted by divine ap- pointment, which consists of bishops, priests, and deacons.' See below, p. 138.

[2] Some of our earlier divines, e.g.

Hooker, Field, Mason, Mede, Usher, have followed the scholastic distinc- tion, speaking of only *two orders*, but *three degrees.* Compare Bishop Pearson, 'Vind. Ignat.,' p. 279. But Bishop Andrewes, ' Opusc. Posth.,' p. 183, has shown that the pretended distinction of order and degree is not founded on Scripture or the Fathers. And so also Bingham, ut supra.

[3] The seven Roman orders are : presbyter, deacon, subdeacon ;— acolyte, exorcist, reader, doorkeeper.

Policy of the pope to impair the authority of bishops. to perform episcopal acts. And worse than this : not only did they encourage throughout Christendom the institution of rich and powerful monastic bodies, which they set free from episcopal jurisdiction by making their establishments extra-diocesan ; but they took upon themselves to appoint legates or vicars, by whom their own supreme authority was to be represented and enforced in other countries beyond Italy ; an abuse which our great dramatic poet has exposed in the accusation against Cardinal Wolsey, which he puts into the mouth of the Earl of Surrey :—

> You wrought to be a legate, by which power
> You maimed the jurisdiction of all bishops.
>
> *King Henry VIII.* Act iii. Sc. 2.

In this manner, when episcopacy had been depreciated to serve the interests of the papacy,[1] and when its rights and position as a distinct order in the ministry had become obscured and confounded with those of the presbyterate, the way was prepared for the downward course which fol-

---

[1] See Pearson's M. W., i. p. 274 (and Churton's Pref., p. lviii.) : ' Nothing is more certain than that all diminution of the rights of episcopacy had its source in the papal usurpation.' See also ibid. pp. 286, 434. Bishop Taylor, vi. p. 809 : ' I shall say one thing more, which is indeed a great truth, that the diminution of episcopacy was first introduced by popery ; and the popes of Rome, by communicating to abbots and other mere priests special graces to exercise some essential offices of episcopacy, have made this sacred order cheap, and *apt to be invaded.*' Archbishop Bramhall, i. p. 252 : ' Though the popes do not abolish the order of bishops, or episcopacy, in the abstract, yet they limit the power of bishops in the concrete at their pleasure, by exemptions and reservations.'

lowed naturally upon the overthrow of the papal usurpation ; a downward course which, in this and other Protestant countries, has been going on from the time of the Reformation to the present day. And, much as there is to condemn in the avowed doctrine and in many of the practices of the Church of Rome, I cannot but consider that a less amount of injury to the cause of Christianity, and to the propagation of the Gospel throughout the world, has arisen from these than from the usurped dominion of the same Church ; which, through the opposition which it roused, has given occasion, more or less directly, to those divisions by which our modern Christendom is disturbed and rent.

Injurious effect of this policy upon the Scotch and foreign Reformers.

The various steps of the downward course just now referred to, are to be traced no less easily than the steps of the ascent which I before described. When the people, exasperated into lawlessness by a long period of great and grievous provocation, shook off the power of the pope, and assumed it to themselves, it was not unnatural for them to suppose that as the pope had often allowed presbyters to act as bishops, and had reduced bishops into little more than presbyters, through their subjection to himself, they (the people) might do the same ; they also, with at least equal propriety, might treat their own national bishops as presbyters, and their presbyters as bishops. And this they did : they turned the acts of the papacy against itself.[1] Hence it

Gradual departure from the true system of the ministry.

---

[1] On 'The Defects of the Reformation as due originally to Excesses of Popery' see the author's 'Disc. on Scottish Reform.,' p. 16, and Append. ch. v.

is that, according to the just remark of Charles Leslie,
'Whosoever would write the true history of presbyterianism

must begin at Rome, and not at Geneva.'[1]   First came the
system of Knox (1560) with the shadow of episcopacy in
the persons of superintendents, but without the laying on of
hands,—a system professedly **founded** upon the principle
which, however familiar to us now, **had** been till then un-
heard of, that the ministry of the Church admits of variation.[2]
Next came the system of Andrew Melville (1580), with laying
on of hands restored,[3] but with no superintendents to lay
them on, and with the assertion of simple equality in the
power and authority of all pastors, or preaching **presbyters**,
and with the novel introduction of lay elders (otherwise called
ruling presbyters) **as a** permanent 'spiritual function,' to
share with the pastors the government of the Church ; the
diaconate being also permanently converted into a lay
office :[4] **a system** founded upon the **opposite** principle of
setting a limit **permissible** to variety in the constitution of
the ministry, at least so far as to exclude[5] even the shadow

---

[1] Leslie's Works, vol. vii. p.
127.

[2] 'We do not think that any
policy can be appointed for all
ages, times, and places.'—*Scotch
Confession of Faith,* 1560, c. xx.

[3] Melville himself, like Calvin,
never, I believe, received even presbyterian ordination.

[4] In the *first* 'Book of Discipline'
provision had been made (c. x.)
for election of laymen as elders and
deacons ; but neither office was to be
permanent.   Both officers were to
be elected *annually.*

[5] Grub, 'Eccles. Hist.,' ii. 225,
goes further. He considers that
the system laid down in the *second*
'Book of Discipline,' is there held
to be 'of perpetual authority, . . .
and therefore *unalterable under any
circumstances whatever.'*   But he

of episcopacy before allowed. Next followed the Glasgow
Assembly of 1638, which formally renounced and condemned episcopacy, 'as having no warrant nor fundament
in the Word of God ;' and shortly after, the Westminster
Assembly (1643–47), which, having first taken a solemn
pledge in the house of God to do their utmost to extirpate
prelacy, proceeded to examine the Word of God, and there
found what for fifteen centuries had never been found there—
viz. that a ministerial platform of coequal clerical pastors, of
semi-lay, ruling presbyters, and lay deacons, is alone of Divine
appointment, and, as such, of perpetual obligation ; to which
they added, as at least 'lawful and agreeable to the Word
of God,' graduated government by congregational assemblies
(otherwise called kirk sessions), classical assemblies, or presbyteries, synodical assemblies, and general assemblies ; a
system which bore upon its front its own condemnation,
because, while it claimed, for the most part, to be of universal obligation, it professed to be framed 'in a method of
their own ;'—for human originality in the things of God is
equivalent to untruth,[1] according to the favourite but much-
abused maxim[2] of the Puritans themselves, which on this
occasion they appear to have forgotten. Then came, in Origin of In-
open antagonism to the last system, the system of Indepen-

dependency.

---

adds, 'It cannot, however, be said
that the *divine right* of the presbyterian system was even now distinctly set forth.' On the exclusion of episcopacy see ibid. pp.
212, 219.

[1] See 'Acts of General Assembly,'
p. 114.

[2] See 'Confession of Faith,' 1560,
c. xviii., and comp. author's 'Disc. on
Scottish Reform.,' Appendix, c. iii.

dency, by which each congregation was to form in itself a complete Church. Such were the retrogressive, downward steps of the great reaction from the upward development and ascendency of popery; till at last Quakerism was reached, without any ministry at all, and with women permitted, if not preferred, to preach! And now we have had, within the last quarter of a century, symptoms of a counter-reaction. Not only has the Free Church endeavoured to restore the diaconate, which (though pronounced to be of perpetual obligation) had become practically obsolete, to its original **Irvingism.** place in the presbyterian system; but the sect of the Irvingites, not content to accept the threefold ministry in its Catholic form, have added, by an invention of their own, a fourth order, whom, in repudiation of the feeling of reverence which influenced the primitive Christians,[1] they do not scruple to call 'apostles.'

Consistent position of the Church of England. In striking contrast with all this change and inconsistency —with all that excess on the part of Popery, and with all this defect on the part of an heterogeneous and discordant Protestantism—stands out the simple position of the Church of England; which—when it had shaken off the papal usurpation, under which it had groaned, more or less (though not without continual protests), for three centuries—it accepted and announced, not, however, as something new and original, but as old and traditional; which it announced, I say, at the commencement of the Reformation,[2] and from

---

[1] See Theodoret in Ep. i. ad Timoth., c. iii. vol. iii. p. 652.

[2] It must be admitted, however, that in the minds of many of the

which, up to the present time, it has never deviated so much as a hair's breadth—a proof at once of consistency and truth! The announcement was made in these words, which form the first sentence of the preface of our Ordination Services :—

'It is evident unto all men diligently reading the Holy Scripture and antient authors, that from the apostles' time there have been these orders of ministers in Christ's Church —bishops, priests, and deacons.'

Controversy may beat against these words, like waves against a rock, but it will never move them. And anyone who has studied the aberrations of the human mind in the spirit of a sound philosophy will recognise, I think, a further confirmation of the historical argument which has now been traced, in the fact that the Church, which has certainly produced the greatest and most learned of the Reformed divines, has also given the most consistent witness to the truth ; standing now, as it has ever stood, equally removed from both those extremes, whereby the true proportions of the organisation of the Christian ministry have been exceeded or curtailed.

But the evidence is to be extended further yet. I have produced the uniform testimony of the Churches of the An-

---

Anglican reformers, as individuals, and especially of Archbishop Cranmer, there was much confusion and unsoundness upon the point, arising out of the same causes which had produced similar results in the views of Knox and his associates. See 'Irenicum,' pp. 392 sq. 404.

glican communion—English, Irish, Scotch, American, Colo-

Its agreement with the Churches of Russia and of the East.
nial. The testimony of all the Eastern Churches and of the Church of Russia (which, be it remembered, are as much opposed to popery as Western Protestants are) is to the same effect, as may be seen from the following words of the larger Catechism of the Russian Church: 'The necessary degrees of order in the Church are three, viz. those of bishops, priests, and deacons.'[1] But, strong and valuable as both those testimonies are (representing, as they do, the uniform conclusion of the two most numerous communities of Christians in the world, next to the Roman Catholics), I am not sure that the confessions which have come from the two extremes themselves are not even still more conclusive. On the one hand, it was decreed in the Council of Trent, mainly through the influence of the Spanish and French bishops, and greatly against the will of the Ultramontane party,[2] as follows :—

'If anyone shall say that there is not in the Catholic Church a hierarchy, instituted by divine appointment, which consists of bishops, priests, and deacons, let him be *anathema*' (Session xxiii. c. vi.).

Opinion of Calvin.
And to this, on the other hand, we have the corresponding[3] anathema of Calvin himself. His words are these :—

---

[1] Page 96. See also the 'Confession of Dositheus,' Patriarch of Jerusalem, stating the faith of the Oriental Church in 1672; Kimmel's 'Monumenta,' vol. i. p. 437 sq.

[2] See above, p. 131, note, and the History of Father Paul there referred to.

[3] But Calvin's 'anathema' was prior to that of Trent.

'If they (the Romanists) would *show* us an hierarchy in which the pre-eminence of bishops should be placed upon such a footing as that they would not refuse to be subject unto Christ and to depend upon Him as their only head '— in allusion to the false headship of the bishop of Rome, as episcopus episcoporum—'and in which they would so cultivate a mutual brotherhood, as to acknowledge no other bond of union than the truth of God ; then, indeed, if there be any who could not reverence such an hierarchy, and pay it entire obedience, they would be worthy, I confess, *of every possible anathema* (nullo non anathemate).' [1]

Such, in principle, is the hierarchy which we now *show*, and which the Church of England *shows*. But the divines of the Westminster Assembly swore to extirpate what the learning and the judgment of Calvin would not suffer him to condemn, nay, even obliged him to anathematise those who should condemn and disallow it.

In like manner, it was Luther himself, who, in the last work which he wrote, and published in 1545, only a year before his death, gave this testimony :— Of Luther.

'Let the bishops cease to persecute and blaspheme the Gospel ; let them provide for the Churches true teachers ; let them put away forms of worship which are impious and idolatrous, and restore such as are pure and true : and then the duty which *we owe to them* shall be fully paid ; then will

---

[1] 'De Necessitate Reform. Eccles.,' Op., viii. 60. See also his letter to the king of Poland, December 1554, 'Epist. et Resp.,' pp. 187-191.

we acknowledge them as our fathers indeed ; then will we gladly submit ourselves to their authority, which *we see to be thoroughly fortified by the word of God* (Verbo Dei communitam).'[1]

The members of the **Glasgow** Assembly of 1638 could *not see* this : the divines of the Westminster Assembly could *not see* it ; they saw the reverse : but the Father of Protestantism could see it, and all the more clearly the nearer he approached to his latter end.

I have now gone through what I considered to be necessary in order to exhibit—in as clear and, at the same time, in as succinct a manner as I could—the argument upon the question before us, so far as it is to be drawn from a strict investigation, first of the Scriptural, and then of the historical evidence. But there is one thing which is still wanting in order to complete this portion of the subject, viz. to notice the principal objections which have been raised, more or less, against such a representation of the said evidence as that which has been now given ; and the consideration of these will occupy the remainder of the present lecture.

1. First, then, the objection with which we are most familiar arises out of the form in which that portion of the historical proof which we derive from Scripture is communicated to us. It is felt that this might have been made far

Objections to be now considered.

1. Objection. That Holy Scripture would have been more explicit if one form of ministry had been obligatory.

---

[1] Luth. **Op.,** viii. 591 sq.; Seckendorf, ii. 553; Calvin, ' Inst.' lib. iv. c. iv. 1, 4, (quoted in ' Irenicum,' p. 405 sq.; and by Usher, vii. p. 69,) speaks to the same effect. See further testimonies below, in Lect. iii.

more direct and definite than we see it is, and hence it is inferred that no obligation can lie upon us to accept as matter of duty what is only to be proved with difficulty, if proved at all.[1] The case is put in the ordinary popular way by Sir Walter Scott in the ' Legend of Montrose,' where the author is describing in his own person the two opposing parties—' the Prelatists and Presbyterians of the more violent kind '—in the days of Charles I. : ' It was in vain remarked to these zealots that had the Author of our holy religion considered any peculiar form of Church government as essential to salvation it would have been revealed with the same precision as under the Old Testament dispensation ' (chap. i. p. 9). In these words, if we take them to represent the objection referred to as made in the present day, there is the ordinary twofold fallacy. First, there is what logicians call ' ignoratio elenchi,' or misstatement of the question. Even in the time of the Covenant, I doubt whether the most violent zealot would have said — and certainly none of us say at the present day—that a particular form of Church ' is essential to salvation.' But what some of us do say—and maintain—is this : that a particular form of Church government is (upon other grounds, and not least for the sake of unity) expedient, if not necessary, for the good order, and welfare, and extension of the Church—

Fallacy of this objection.

---

[1] Comp. Ezek. xx. 49, from whence it would seem that a similar objection was raised against the warnings of the old prophets : ' If he had really a message from God *which was designed to guide us,* would it be delivered in such dark and ambiguous terms?'

all which being matters of concern to Christ Himself, must be also matters of concern to all good Christians.   And then the argument itself—that if one particular form of Church government had been essential in the Christian Church it would have been revealed with the same precision as in the Jewish—this argument, I say, is equally fallacious.   For what right had we to entertain any such expectation, when we know that in the parallel case of the observance of the Lord's Day no precise revelation is to be found upon the point?   No ; rather it would be fair and reasonable to argue that a threefold ministry having been already revealed and made obligatory under the Law—just as a weekly Sabbath had been revealed and made obligatory—there was no further occasion for an express command, and that the absence of such renewed command only leaves us to infer equally in both cases that, *mutatis mutandis*, the original order is still to be observed.[1]

Other points of duty on which Holy Scripture is not more explicit.

But it may be well to state our answer to this popular objection a little more fully.   The truth, then, is, that so far from being entitled to look for a precise, explicit revelation, *totidem verbis*, upon a point like this—the right constitution of the Christian ministry—the evidence which we have regarding it is exactly of the same kind (viz. circumstantial rather than direct) which it has pleased God to give us in regard to other practical matters of scarcely, if at all, less importance.[2]   I have already mentioned the case of

[1] See the author's Synodal Address for 1866, p. 18, note.

[2] See Hammond's Works, vol. i. p. 398 sq.; vol. iv. p. 742.

the observance of the Christian Sabbath. There is also the case of infant baptism. But that which is the strongest perhaps of all, and certainly the most important, is the case of the canon of the **New** Testament.[1] Surely nothing can be more essential than that we should be left in no uncertainty upon a matter on which the whole system of Christianity entirely depends. And yet no one can pretend that the canon of Scripture, and especially of the New Testament Scripture, has been revealed to us in any way whatever. No one can point to any authoritative declaration emanating from an apostle, or council of apostles, to give it the sanction which the objection we are considering assumes to be necessary. No one can say that it has been ascertained otherwise than by traditional usage and historical research,—usage and research which are doubtless sufficiently conclusive ; but certainly not more conclusive than the usage and research precisely similar which enable us to ascertain the true ministry of the Church ; while, in regard to this latter, we may also gather evidence clear and sufficient (not in my opinion only but in the opinion of great divines, such as Hooker [2]) to the same effect from Revelation itself. Moreover, it must be admitted that upon grounds far less sufficient, far less conclusive, we receive without question the most important facts and deductions of secular history. Nor can I omit to remark, as a further justification of the

Canon of Scripture.

---

[1] See above, **Lect. i. p. 5.**

[2] 'Ecc. Pol.,' book **v. c. lxxviii.** § 9. 'It *clearly* appeareth by Holy

Scripture,' &c. &c. I might have added, in the opinion of Luther also. See above, p. 140.

dealing of God's providence with us in these respects, that
there is a manifest advantage in circumstantial evidence
over that which is direct in such a case ; because it leaves far
less room for suspicion of forgery, which might be raised by
interested persons against a single text, containing a direct
and express command.

If, notwithstanding all that has now been said, it be still
objected that there are few persons competent or inclined to
conduct with the requisite care an investigation such as circumstantial evidence confessedly demands, and such as we
admit to be necessary in the present case ; then we reply
(as was indicated in my former lecture), that there was a
time, during the first ages of the Church, when no such investigation was called for ; because, when one and the same
threefold ministry was everywhere in existence, no question
could be raised concerning it ; or, if raised, it would, as in
the instance of Aerius, be immediately set at rest by the
unanimous voice of the universal Church.   And if occasion
has since been given for the question, and no unanimous
voice is now heard to settle it ; then we further reply, that
this state of things is due to misgovernment on one side,
and to insubordination on the other ; and while it is plain
that the goodness of God cannot fairly be made responsible
for the consequences of human faults, it is equally obvious
that the faults themselves are punished most appropriately
by the increased doubts and difficulties which such mis-
conduct has tended to create.

But after all (to sift this objection still more thoroughly),

See First
Lecture, p. 6.

what was there that we could reasonably expect from Scripture in regard either to the record of fact, or delivery of
precept, which we have not received? If men ask us to
show them a full-blown diocesan system—with a threefold
ministry—in every place where the Gospel was first preached,
during Scriptural times, they ask what implies a misconception of the circumstances of the case ; and the Scripture
itself has taught us to protest against any such demand.
There is abundant evidence that the Church was everywhere to be built up by degrees, and only out of materials
thoroughly and cautiously prepared.[1] In no place, so far
as we read, did the apostles ordain presbyters upon a first
visit ; though it is probable this may have been done at
Ephesus, where St. Paul's first visit extended to the unusual
period of three years. In default of men regularly trained
and willing to devote themselves to the clerical profession,
as now they do, from early manhood, there was at first large
employment of extraordinary and miraculously gifted ministrations of which we have now no experience. St. Paul
himself was not formally ordained as apostle of the Gentiles
(Acts xiii. 1, A.D. 45) till ten years after his miraculous conversion and primary call on the way to Damascus (Acts ix.
A.D. 34). At Ephesus, after the Church had existed there
about twelve years, Timothy was warned not to ordain 'a
novice' (1 Tim. iii. 6). Again, the apostles, when persecuted in one city, would have to break off their missionary

A mistake
to suppose
the teaching
of Scripture
insufficient.

---

[1] See above, Lect. i. p. 22. Also   1864, p. 26 sq., and for 1866, p.
the author's Synodal Address for   25.

L

work, and (as their divine Master had enjoined) flee to another. In the matter of precept, we could scarcely look for more, under such circumstances, than general injunctions to maintain unity and uniformity, to practice subordination, and to show all due respect and obedience to constituted authorities—and of such injunctions there is no lack. Nor, in regard to historical fact, can we reasonably complain that we have been left without the needful guidance, so long as we can find, during Scriptural times, what we have discovered in the Church of Jerusalem, in the Church of Ephesus, in the six other Churches of Lýdian Asia, in the Church of Crete—out of Scripture itself; and out of uninspired but trustworthy authorities, in the Church of Rome, in the Church of Antioch, in the Church of Alexandria, not to mention others[1]—still during Scriptural times : so long as we can find *thus early* such and so many instances of an episcopal or threefold ministry ; and *can find no instance whatever, either in or out of Scripture, of the Papal system on the one hand, or the Presbyterian system on the other*, during the same primitive period ; so long as this is so, to ask for more evidence, is surely of a piece with the conduct of the unbelieving Jews, who, though Christ had wrought so many miracles before their eyes, still professed themselves dissatisfied, still continued to ask for some further sign.

2. Objec-
tion. 2. A second objection, which may be disposed of in a few words, has been raised upon the remark that the most

---

[1] See above, Lect. i. p. 72 sq.

important arrangements in the organisation of the Church— Apparently accidental character of primary organisation. for instance, the appointment of 'the seven' whom we suppose to be the first deacons (Acts vi.)—appear to have arisen out of circumstances purely incidental, and not from forethought or design. Hence it has been argued[1] that such arrangements must be still subject to the control of circumstances, so as to be variable at our own discretion, and can have no legitimate claim to be received as of perpetual obligation. But there seems to be no good reason why God should not employ the incidents in the history of the Church as He employs all other incidents, in order to accomplish His own purposes in His own good time. This was the ground that was taken by more than one of the Westminster divines in discussing the very point referred to as an example, viz. the Institution of the Diaconate. Its perpetuity was insisted on, and the very same objection in regard to it was overruled by Mr. Vines, because, as he argued, 'that which is occasional in the rise, yet may be perpetual in the use;' and again by Mr. Rutherford, who pleaded that, 'though the occasion was the murmuring, &c., yet the motivum was the good of the Church to the end of the world; as the occasion of St. John's Gospel was [the heresies of] Ebion and Cerinthus, but the motivum was the good of the Church for ever.'[2] Moreover we cannot be

---

[1] See Dr. Caird's Essay in 'Good Words,' July 1863.

[2] See Lightfoot's Journal, pp. 87, 89. Mr. Rutherford also referred to 'the Epistle to Philemon, and the case of Zelophehad,' as additional examples to the same effect. St. Luke's Gospel is another case in point.

quite certain that the appointment of the seven did really form the first institution of the diaconate. Mosheim and others are decidedly of opinion that it did not,[1] and that deacons had been previously instituted and employed in the Church; although we find no mention of the fact in the Acts, as we also find no mention there of the institution of presbyters at Jerusalem. Again, St. Chrysostom (*in loc.*) has raised a doubt whether the seven were deacons at all in the clerical sense; or rather, he considers it very manifest that they were neither deacons nor presbyters, but were appointed only for the particular purpose specified in the history. So that of this objection it may be said :—

Nil agit exemplum litem quod lite resolvit.

And, after all, it is to be borne in mind that the institution of the third order of the ministry, though it may be illustrated by the appointment of 'the seven,' yet it does not rest upon that appointment for its binding force, so much as upon the injunctions which St. Paul gives in his first Epistle to Timothy; one of those three which are called the pastoral or hierarchical epistles, because they deal expressly and authoritatively with matters of this description.

3. Objection.

3. I now proceed to notice a third objection which has been repeatedly urged against the threefold ministry, from the fact that the names which we give to the first and second

[1] See above, Lect. i. p. 58, note 2. The heading of the chapter in our authorised translation may be thought to leave the matter uncertain.

orders appear to be used in the New Testament, not as we use them, with a plainly marked distinction between the two, but indiscriminately,[1] and with reference (perhaps exclusively) to the second order alone. Common fairness required that, before this objection was pressed as it has been, account should have been taken of the similar or rather much greater diversity, which also exists between the New Testament use of the name of the third order of the ministry, and its employment not only by us, but by Presbyterians themselves, and by every other denomination of Christians. If we find, as we do find, in the New Testament, such a laxity of use of the original word διακονία (deaconship), that it is applied even to the apostleship, and that apostles are called by the name of deacons, and yet we conclude nothing from thence either against the apostleship, or against the diaconate, as distinct offices in the ministry; if this be so—as unquestionably it is—then, *à fortiori*, if we find a similar laxity of use of the original word, ἐπισκοπή (episcopate or bishopric), so that it is applied to the presbyterate, and that presbyters are called *episcopi* (bishops or overseers), we are bound in like manner, if we would be fair

---

[1] See 'Irenicum,' p. 287 sq., and Professor Lightfoot, pp. 93–97. It is due, however, to Bishop Pearson, as the greatest scholar among Anglican divines, to state that he never yielded the point of the indiscriminate or synonymous use of the names *presbyter* and *episcopus* in the New Testament; and he has shown that the confusion, if it exists, was not noticed by the Fathers till after the third century. See 'Vind. Ignat.,' pp. 556, 571 sq. He also proves that after the time of the apostles, that is, from the beginning of the second century, the name of *episcopus* was never given to a simple presbyter. (Ibid., p. 547 sq.)

Those
names not
capable of
proper
translation.

and consistent, to conclude nothing from thence against
either the presbyterate or the episcopate as distinct orders.
The truth is that each of those three names has been rendered untranslateable by change of circumstances; having
been originally all used laxly and even interchangeably, and
now (in their anglicised form of bishops, presbyters, and
deacons) being all used strictly and definitively; or, rather, in
order to translate them properly, inasmuch as we can derive
no theory from their employment in the New Testament, we
must take our theory with us (which has been derived not
from names but facts), and apply it in the best way we can—
translating at one time strictly and definitely, according to
the modern use, at another time laxly and indiscriminately,
according to the ancient use. It may be doubted whether our
translators have been always successful in this difficult task.[1]
They have sometimes perhaps been lax where it would have
been better to have been strict, as in Acts xx. 17, and in
Titus i. 5, where they have translated 'presbyters' by 'elders;'
but more frequently they have been strict where it would
have been better perhaps to have been lax; as where they
have spoken of the ' bishoprick ' of the fallen apostle Judas
(Acts i. 20); where they have translated the same word 'the
office of a bishop' in 1 Tim. iii. 1; where they have translated ἐπίσκοπος 'bishop' in Titus i. 7; and where, in the
first verse of the Epistle to the Philippians, we read 'with
the[2] bishops and deacons,' when ' overseers and ministers,'

[1] They are right in Acts xx. 28,
' overseers;' and in 1 Pet. v. 2,   ' oversight.'
[2] There is no definite article in

in the then immature and unsettled state of the Church of Philippi, might probably have been safer and nearer to the facts.[1]

Here, then, we are dealing, strictly speaking, with a question not so much of Church order, as of criticism and scholarship. And upon such a question it is satisfactory that we are able to produce the authority of perhaps the most eminent scholar and the most gifted critic whom the world has yet known—I mean Richard Bentley. In his controversy with the freethinker, Collins, who had attacked our translation of the New Testament, and, among other passages, had objected that, in Acts xx. 28, the word (ἐπισκόπους), which is rendered 'overseers,' ought to have been translated *bishops*, Bentley had occasion to take up this matter. Already, in discussing the right translation of the word 'ecclesia,' which originally meant, not a Church, but a political assembly, he had been led to remark, that 'political words in different languages are seldom totally equivalent: and those foreign words that are not interpreted but adopted, and retained, as *apostle, bishop, priest, deacon*'—each of which is merely a Greek word turned into English—'have always a narrower sense where they are

the Greek; but a preposition going before renders its insertion in the translation at least excusable.

[1] Bentley seems to intimate the same, when he remarks, 'if our awkward freethinker had changed the tables and expostulated, not why here (Acts xx. 28) *overseers*, but *why not everywhere else*, he could not have been so easily answered.' 'Works,' vol. iii. p. 380, See below, p. 161 sq.

transplanted than in their first soil.'[1]   He then proceeds
thus, in reference to the text which I just now mentioned :—

Acts xx. 28.   'Here, instead of *overseers*, he (Collins) would have it
rendered *bishops*, that it might appear that *bishops* and *presbyters* in Scripture phrase are synonymous words.   And
what if they should be so, *iidem presbyteri qui episcopi* ; the
first the name of their age and order, the latter of their office
and duty?   Does he think to fright your bishops with this?'
—For Bentley is writing not in his own name, but as a
foreigner, a German, in a letter to an Englishman.—' Does
this affect the cause of episcopacy?   How then came
Theodoret a bishop, Theophylact an archbishop, and

---

[1] Thus (1) διάκονος (with its derivatives, διακονία the noun of office,
and διακονέω the verb), of our three
clerical names the widest in signification, and found most frequently,
besides being used to denote the
position of a domestic servant and
of a civil magistrate, is applied ec-
clesiastically not only to deacons
properly so called, but to presbyters,
bishops, apostles, and even to our
Lord Himself.

(2.) πρεσβύτερος (with its derivative πρεσβυτέριον), besides being used
to denote an elder, or senior in
point of age, is applied ecclesiasti-
cally to Jewish elders and to Christian presbyters, perhaps also to
bishops, certainly by apostles in
speaking of themselves.

(3.) ἐπίσκοπος, (with its derivative

ἐπισκοπή, the noun of office, and ἐπι-
σκοπέω the verb), though found much
more rarely, besides being used in
more general senses not ministerial,
is applied probably to the presbyterate, perhaps to the episcopate,
certainly to the apostleship and to
the office of our Lord Himself.

(4.) Even the word Ἀπόστολος,
which became official sooner than
any of those, continued to be used
in a non-official sense as equivalent
to messenger, if the translation in
Phil. iv. 18, 2 Cor. viii. 23, is correct.

See the author's Synodal Address for 1864, Appendix, c. ii.,
'On the Nomenclature of the Orders
of the Threefold Ministry, as used
in the New Testament and in the
earliest of the Fathers.'

Chrysostom a patriarch, not to be aware of it, when they expressly *affirm* what our writer would have *appear*? They, with all Christian antiquity, never thought themselves and their order to succeed the Scripture ἐπίσκοποι, but the Scripture ἀπόστολοι; they were διάδοχοι τῶν Ἀποστόλων, *the successors of the apostles.*[1] The sum of the matter is this :— though new institutions are formed, new words are not coined for them, but old ones borrowed and applied. Ἐπίσκοπος, whose general idea is *overseer*, was a word in use long before Christianity; a word of universal relation to economical, civil, military, naval, judicial, and religious matters. This word was assumed to denote the governing and presiding persons of the Church,[2] as διάκονος (another word of vulgar and diffused use) to denote the ministerial. The *presbyters*, therefore, while the apostles lived, were ἐπίσκοποι, *overseers*. But the apostles, in foresight of their approaching martyrdom, having selected and appointed their successors in the several cities and communities, as St. Paul did Timothy at Ephesus and Titus in Crete four years before his death, what names were these successors to be called by? Not ἀπόστολοι, *apostles*; their modesty, as it seems, made them refuse it; they would keep that name

How the name *episcopus* came to be restrained to bishops.

---

[1] See above, p. 104.

[2] The two nearest English equivalents of the Greek ἐπίσκοπος are *overseer* and *superintendent*; and it is remarkable how far removed they both of them are from any meaning connected with episcopacy. An *overseer* of an English parish is not the bishop, nor even the incumbent, but a lay official; and a *superintendent* may now signify the manager of almost any kind of work, *except ecclesiastical.*

proper and sacred to the first *extraordinary* messengers of Christ, though they really succeeded them in their office, in due part and measure, as the *ordinary* governors of the Churches.' I may add that the name would cease to be equally appropriate when they were no longer to be *sent out* to institute new societies of Christians, but rather were to stay at home and *superintend*, each in his own diocese, those already instituted. ' It was agreed, therefore,' he proceeds, ' over all Christendom at once, in the very next generation after the apostles, to assign and appropriate to them the word ἐπίσκοπος or *bishop*. From that time to this, that appellation, which before included a *presbyter*, has been restrained to a superior order. And here's nothing in all this but what has happened in all languages and communities in the world. See the *Notitia* of the Roman and Greek Empires, and you'll scarce find one name of any state employment, that in course of time did not vary from its primitive signification. So that should our Lutheran presbyters '—Bentley, as I have said, is writing in the character of a German—'contend they are Scripture bishops '—as so many of my opponents in the public journals have done— 'what would they get by it? No more than lies in the syllables. The time has been when a commander even of a single regiment was called *imperator* : and must every such nowadays set up to be *emperors?* The one pretence is altogether as just as the other.' [1]

[1] 'Remarks upon a late Discourse of Freethinking, by Phileleutherus Lipsiensis.' Bentley's 'Works,' vol. iii. pp. 378-380.

These are the observations of one who, in the province of criticism, has had no superior. The assertion, however, which he makes respecting the change of name from apostle to bishop, as the received designation of the highest order of the ministry in the very next generation after the apostles, is pronounced by a living Presbyterian divine to be 'against all probability. We cannot suppose,' he writes, 'that a whole class of Church rulers would willingly lay down their honoured title of apostles, and assume another less honourable.'[1] To me, on the contrary, I confess the case appears very supposable; and when I take into account the actual circumstances, certainly I cannot see in it, as another Presbyterian writer has done, 'a miracle of voluntary humiliation alike unexplained and unexampled.'[2] For what were the actual circumstances? It is true the first bishops were successors of the apostles in some respects, but in some respects they were not their successors; and whether or no we allow them to have been for the most part 'humble and modest' Christians—a character which both these writers have ventured to deny to them—they could not have been unconscious of the difference, and, unless we will suppose them to have been devoid of truthfulness as well as modesty, not unwilling to acknowledge and avow it by a change of name. But be

---

[1] Dr. Crawford's 'Presbyterianism Defended,' p. 53.

[2] Dr. King quoted, ibid. Is there not an example somewhat similar, not of the motive, but of the result, in the fact that Presbyterians have condescended to surrender the name of *presbyter*, and even of elder, except in the case of lay elders, and to take in exchange for it the name of *minister* (diaconus)?

it so—that, in our want of charity, we are unable to suppose this—what is the alternative? Our uncharitableness must advance a step further; and we who have found it so difficult to believe in the humility which could submit to a change of name, must find it easy to believe in the pride which, together with the change of name, could and did, for its own aggrandisement, accomplish a change—a revolution, in fact —whereby ' Presbyterian bishops rising in their pretensions gradually slid into Prelatical bishops ; ' and to believe also in the universal faithlessness and pusillanimity which could submit to such a change, contrary to the system everywhere authorised and established by the apostles !   This indeed is to believe *a miracle* of unnatural presumption and undutifulness alike unexampled and unexplained ; unexampled, more especially, as shown at a time of persecution and of martyrdom, which would be most sure to fall upon those who were in highest place ; unexplained, because, as we shall presently see, the only testimony which has seemed to offer an explanation is abundantly refuted and contradicted by itself. Moreover the belief of this latter miracle must include a disbelief of those episcopal successions, commenced in some cases before, in others immediately after, the deaths of the apostles ; whereas the belief of the former presumed incredibility naturally implies more or less directly the recognition of those well-attested facts which all ecclesiastical history accepts as such.

It does not appear to be necessary to say more under this head, unless I am to allude to the argument, which has been so often and so vauntingly urged, that we see in the New Testament distinct notice taken of two orders in the ministry, and directions given to them, but no notice taken of, and no directions given to, the supposed highest and most important order.[1] This argument is used partly in forgetfulness of the fact that the writer who gives the directions was himself of that highest order ; and partly upon the assumption, which I have shown to be most unwarrantable, that Timothy and Titus, who received directions from the pen of St. Paul, and the angels of the seven Churches who received directions from Christ Himself by the pen of St. John, are to be regarded as—it matters not what—provided we deny them to have been prelates or bishops of their respective Churches. But more than this. The truth is, that if we were disposed to maintain, as some of our greatest and most learned divines [2] have maintained, that in places of Scripture, such as Phil. i. 1 and 1 Tim. iii. 2, 8, where two denominations only are specified, the three orders may yet be implied [3]—if we were to maintain this, we should be amply justified by similar use of language, both in Scripture itself and elsewhere. How often in the Old Testament do we find the names ' Priests and Levites ' used so as to include the high priest; and therefore to imply the three

---

[1] 'Free Church Catechism,' p. 117; Dr. Crawford's ' Serm.,' p. 27.

[2] Such as Bishop Pearson. See above, p. 149, note.

[3] Upon this supposition, when St. Paul has described a *presbyter* who is *fit* to be made a *bishop*, he has no further occasion to specify the qualifications of a good presbyter, but may proceed at once to speak of the qualifications necessary for a good *deacon*.

orders of the Jewish priesthood! Nay, the word 'priest' is constantly employed even when the high priest alone is intended. Thus, in different passages we read of Aaron the Priest, Eleazar the Priest, Phineas the Priest, Eli the Priest, Ahimelech the Priest, Abiathar the Priest, Zadok the Priest, Jehoiada the Priest, Azariah the Priest ; and yet we know that all these were chief priests, and are so called in other passages. In like manner there would be nothing strange in supposing that either of the two words, πρεσβύτερος, or ἐπίσκοπος, may be used to include, or even to designate, the chief presbyter, the chief overseer. Indeed we find that Irenæus, and some other of the earlier Fathers, have done this, at least in the case of the former of those words.[1] On the other hand, we have an example among ourselves of a twofold denomination, where a threefold is intended, and where not the former but the latter of the two words has the comprehensive application, in the case of the phrase, 'bishops and curates.' Under that expression all the three orders of the ministry are prayed for in our daily service, morning and evening, and again in the prayer for the Church militant. Yet what stranger might not infer from reading those words that the Church of England admits only of two orders, and those two—bishops and deacons—to the omission of presbyters? Moreover, in this use of the word 'curate,' we have another example, similar to that which Bentley produced in the word *imperator* ;—only this is a case

---

[1] See above, p. 99 and p. 116.

of a word having fallen from a higher,[1] that was a case of one having risen from a lower signification. When our Prayer Book was compiled, the word 'curate' signified every clergyman below a bishop, having a benefice or *cure* of souls. Now it *never* means a beneficed clergyman, but only their assistants, whether presbyters or deacons; that is, it is now both lowered and confined to one and that the humblest class of labourers in the ministry.

Let me close my answer to this third objection with one remark. There is a well-known phrase in the Latin language—*verba dare*—literally 'to give words,' but meaning to give words and nothing more, when more was promised or implied; and so, to deceive a person, to impose upon him. And this has been the case (not indeed consciously, but really) in regard to the whole or greater part of the argument, as derived from the New Testament, in favour of Presbyterianism. It has been a 'giving of words,' and nothing more. Let it be understood that the word *presbyterus* was used at first in the Christian Church, as the word ἱερεύς certainly was in the Jewish, comprehensively of the two first orders. Let it be understood that the word *episcopus* was used during the apostles' lifetime in a sense lower than that in which we now use the word *bishop*, as the word *diaconus* undeniably was used in a higher than that in which we now use the word *deacon*; let these simple matters, which every scholar comprehends at once as of ordinary occurrence,

Character of the third objection.

---

[1] Compare the names *parish* and *diocese*. See Bingham, bk. ix. c. ii. 1.

be generally understood, and whatever difficulty may have been felt in regard to the Scriptural application of these terms immediately disappears. And when was this assumed difficulty chiefly taken up and obtruded upon the Church? It was in an age 'which,' according to the testimony of Milton, an unexceptionable witness,

. . . hated learning worse than toad or asp. [1]

The requisite learning in this case would have shown that, however the ancient Fathers and first interpreters of Scripture may be found to differ from one another in regard to the right interpretation of those passages of the New Testament in which the clerical names occur, there is not one of them—no, not even Jerome himself—who does not, in the view of those passages, recognise the *three orders* of the clergy as having existed in Scriptural and apostolic times. [2]

4. In order to complete my notice of the objections which have been raised against the conclusions arrived at in this and my former lecture, it remains to examine the testimony of a few of the Fathers, which appears to be not indeed at open variance, but still scarcely reconcilable with what I have represented as the unanimous consent of patristical authority in favour of the threefold ministry.

4. Objection. Testimony of some of the Fathers quoted on the other side.

The first of these testimonies is the epistle of Clement, [3]

[1] Sonnet xi. See also Twells' 'Life of Pocock,' p. 176: 'In those times of disorder and confusion, the contempt and even *hatred of learning* prevailed to a great degree.'

[2] See Bishop Pearson, 'Vind. Ignat.,' p. 555 sq., and on Jerome, pp. 561–563.

[3] Stillingfleet's remarks upon it are to be seen in 'Iren.,' p. 310 sq., and p. 326 sq.

written from Rome to the Corinthian Church. In this epistle (of which I have spoken in a former part of this lecture) we have, it is true, no positive trace of an episco- See above, p. 139. pate at Corinth ; and yet, it must be confessed, we find a state of things disclosed—a state of unruliness and disorder —in which, had there been a bishop, it is almost certain he would have been mentioned. On the other hand, however, it is to be borne in mind that the writer of the epistle was in all probability himself a bishop at the time—bishop of Rome ; that he appears to have been applied to for his advice and guidance, probably in that capacity ;[1] and that the epistle was written very early[2]—so early, according to the best authorities, as A.D. 69 or 70, i.e. only a year or two after the martyrdom of St. Paul, who himself had found the Corinthians the most ungovernable of all his converts. And to all this it is to be added, that we have certain evidence in the ' History of Hegesippus,' as quoted by Eusebius (iv. 22), that Corinth had received a prelatical ministry before the middle of the second century ; for he mentions ' Primus,' whom he himself had known and conversed with, as the bishop at that time.

2. The testimony to be derived from the epistle of Poly- St. Poly-carp. carp to the Philippians is of the same kind—simply negative. Both *presbyteri* and *diaconi* are mentioned generally (c. v. and vi.), as they were also in St. Clement's epistle, and ex- horted to discharge their respective duties ; and among the

---

[1] St. Jerome says, 'Scripsit ex per-
sonâ Ecclesiæ Romanæ.'—*Catal.*

Script., c. xv. vol. ii. p. 633.
[2] But see above, p. 85, note 1.

presbyteri the chief presbyter or bishop may of course be
included ; but, if he existed, he is not specified. Bishop
Pearson suggests [1] that the see may have been vacant when
Polycarp wrote. At all events, in this case also, we know
that the writer of the epistle was himself a bishop—bishop
of Smyrna—and that he had been appointed by St. John.
Here, too, it is observable that the geographical relations
between Smyrna and Philippi were not unlike to those
between Corinth and Rome ; and, further, in days when the
episcopate led so frequently to martyrdom—one, if not [2] both,
of the writers of these two epistles suffered that glorious
death—we must be prepared to expect that even when there
was a duly ordained bishop, his name would be withheld
from unnecessary publication, as was the case even in our
own Church during the persecution of the last century.

Justin
Martyr.

3. Of Justin Martyr, a Samaritan by birth, and teacher of
philosophy, who, having become a convert to Christianity,
suffered at Rome A.D. 165, the testimony, though sometimes
quoted as unfavourable to the threefold ministry, is still
more inconclusive. It amounts only to this, that in giving
a general description of the Christian assemblies for public
worship in his first apology—a description intended for the
information of the heathen Roman emperor, senate, and
people—having no occasion to specify the three orders, he

---

[1] 'Vind. Ignat.,' p. 551 ; but compare Lightfoot, p. 213, and see
above, p. 102, note.

[2] Clement's martyrdom, though
asserted by Ruffinus in the sixth
century, is questionable. See Tille-
mont, ii. p. 124, and note,

merely mentions ὁ προεστὼς, the person who presided, and the deacons. Of course the former, general, term would be strictly correct as applicable either to the bishop or, in his absence, to the presbyter, who would then perform the chief part of the service.[1]

4. We have now to pass over from the middle of the second to the latter half of the fourth century. That is, all the evidence which is to be found on the other side till we come to the last-named date has now been produced ; and you have seen what it is. It is, in the strictest sense, merely negative. It affords *no sign whatever of the characteristic elements of the Presbyterian system,* of lay elders, of government by presbyteries ; and, instead of exhibiting a clerical parity, it exhibits at least a duality of orders. In short, it amounts to nothing more than an absence of direct proof in our favour, in the case of three writers, the latest of whom died less than seventy years after the death of St. John, viz. in the year 165 A.D. During the 200 years that followed—i.e. from 165 to 365—we have a superabundance of the most express and direct evidence of all kinds, but not one syllable of it is such as to cast, even negatively, a shade of suspicion upon the universality of the institution of the threefold ministry ; not one syllable is such as to indicate the existence—the theory or the practice—of *any other,* as having been either known then, or heard of previously in the Church. But now, at the termination of that long interval of 200 years,

So far the evidence on the other side is only negative.

---

[1] See Bishop Pearson's 'Vind. Ignat.,' p. 569 ; Bishop Kaye's 'Justin Martyr,' p. 98.

we come upon a witness whom it will be necessary to examine more at length, in consequence of the authority which attaches to his name, and to the judgment he has been supposed to pronounce upon this question. The

St. Jerome.

witness to whom I allude is St. Jerome. As in the case of Aerius, his contemporary, whom we have seen universally condemned as a heretic, it becomes important to know something of St. Jerome's history and character, in order

His character and early history.

that we may estimate his evidence at its real worth. A man of vast learning and abilities, but also of a hasty and intemperate judgment, and of an overbearing temper, which made him many enemies, he raised himself, while a sojourner at Rome, so as to become secretary to Pope Damasus, A.D. 382 ; and there is reason to think that, if it was not the avowed object of his ambition, he had at least cherished the secret hope of succeeding him in the bishopric.[1] But in

Like Aerius, disappointed of a bishopric.

this he was disappointed, as Aerius had been, when actuated by the same desire. Upon Damasus' death, in A.D. 385, Siricius was chosen to succeed ; and, to add to Jerome's mortification, the new pope, it is said, refused to continue him in the office of secretary.[2] Upon this, leaving Rome in disgust,[3] he retired into the East, and shortly after fixed

[1] He writes of himself to a Roman lady, as he was leaving Italy for the East, August, A.D. 385, after Damasus' death, 'Omnium pæne judicio dignus *summo sacerdotio* decernebar.' He was then a presbyter. Epist. xlv. ad Asellam. vol. i.

p. 481.

[2] See the Latin life prefixed to his Works, vol. i. p. 54.

[3] He had not spared the Romans, clergy or people, while he dwelt among them, and henceforward, to borrow Dean Milman's words,

himself as a monk in a cell at Bethlehem. He had not been settled there many years before he involved himself in a serious quarrel [1] with his own immediate diocesan, John of Jerusalem, which was kept up between them with great bitterness, at least on Jerome's part,[2] so long as they both lived.

The first work which he composed [3] after he had retired to Bethlehem was his Commentary upon four of St. Paul's Epistles—to the Galatians, Ephesians, Titus, and Philemon. This he wrote at the request, and for the special benefit of two Roman ladies of noble birth, Paula and Eustochium, who had placed themselves under his spiritual guidance; and in order to ingratiate himself still further in their eyes, which he would be tempted to do all the more after the disparaging treatment he had recently experienced, he would naturally be led to magnify his own order in the ministry, which was that of a presbyter (ordained without a title [4]), and, as we have seen, a mortified and disappointed presbyter. Accordingly, in the third of those commentaries—on the Epistle to Titus, i. 5—we read as follows :—

'they became blacker and more inexcusable in his harsher and more unsparing denunciations.'—*West. Christ.*, i. p. 75. In one passage he describes the Roman clergy as 'Pharisæorum Senatus.' 'Præf. ad Libr. Didymi de Spir. Sancto,' vol. ii. p. 102 sq.

[1] According to Fleury, 'the great dispute' with John arose A.D. 392.

See Newman's transl., p. 228, where the causes of it are detailed.

[2] See Clinton, F. R., Append., p. 456.

[3] A.D. 387 or 388. See 'Life,' ut supr., p. 68.

[4] By Paulinus, at Antioch, see 'Life,' ut supr., p. 41, and Newman's note on Fleury, p. 257.

'Let us attend carefully to the words of the apostle, who, pointing out what sort of person ought to be ordained[1] a *presbyter*, says, *If any be blameless*, &c., and adds thereafter, *for a bishop must be blameless as the steward of God.* A presbyter, therefore, is the same as a bishop.' That is the first important statement. He proceeds, 'And before there arose, through the instigation of the devil, factions (studia) in religion, and people began to say, *I am of Paul, I of Apollos*, and *I of Cephas*, the Churches were governed by the common counsel of presbyters.' That is a second important statement. 'But (he continues) after that everyone came to think that those whom he had baptized were his own and not Christ's'—that is a third important statement—'it was decreed in the whole world that one chosen from among the presbyters should be placed over the rest, to whom all the care of the Church should appertain, and so the occasions of disunion should be taken away.' That is a fourth important statement. 'If,' he adds in reference to his first statement, 'anyone imagines that in declaring a bishop and a presbyter to be one and the same—the former being the name of their office, the latter of their time of life—I have stated merely an opinion of my own, and not of the Scriptures, let him read again the words of the apostle to the Philippians—*Paul and Timotheus . . . to all the saints in Christ Jesus which are at Philippi with (the) bishops and deacons.* Philippi is a single city of Macedonia, and cer-

---

[1] The word in the original properly means to 'place' or 'appoint.' They might have been *ordained* presbyters already. See p. 157, note 3.

tainly in one city there could not be several bishops, as
they are now called (or reckoned).[1] But because at that
time they called "bishops" those whom they also called
"presbyters," therefore he speaks of bishops as of presbyters
without any difference. Some one may perhaps still think
the point doubtful, unless I prove it by another testimony.
It is written, then, in the Acts that when Paul had come to
Miletus, he sent to Ephesus, and summoned the presbyters
of that Church ; to whom, among other things, he said, *Take
heed to yourselves and to all the flock over the*[2] *which the Holy
Ghost hath made you bishops,* &c. Here, also, observe carefully how calling together the presbyters of that one city,
Ephesus, he afterwards styles the same persons "bishops."
Again,'—he is now to produce proof in support of his third
statement—'whosoever will receive[3] the epistle which is
written in the name of Paul to the Hebrews, there, too, the
care of the Church is divided equally among several : for he
writes, *Obey them that have the rule over you.* And Peter, in
his epistle, speaks (in the same way) as follows :—*The presbyters which are among you I exhort, who am their fellow-
presbyter, feed the flock of God which is among you,* &c.

---

[1] There is a variation in the MSS.
between 'nuncupantur' and 'nunc
putantur.'

[2] Literally '*in* the which.' Jerome
has 'in quo,' which the Greek requires.

[3] It is important to observe this
statement. It shows that if we are
to listen to doubts respecting the
true constitution of the Christian
ministry—notwithstanding the abundant evidence upon which it rests—
because an author like Jerome, in
the fourth century, chooses to cast
a slur upon it, we have the same or
greater reason to entertain doubts
respecting the Canon of the New
Testament. See above, p. 143.

(1 Pet. v. 1, 2). My design,' he adds, 'in all this, is to show that among the ancients presbyters and bishops were the same; but that *by degrees* [1] the whole care and charge was committed to one, in order that the dissensions which were growing up (dissensionum plantaria) might be eradicated. Therefore,' he concludes—with a suitable admonition to all his superiors in the ministry—' as the presbyters are well aware that it is the custom of the Church which makes them subject to him who has been set over them, so let the bishops know that it is the same custom of the Church rather than any reality of a divine appointment which has made them greater than the presbyters; and that it is their duty, while they govern the Church for the good of all (in commune), to imitate Moses, who, when he had it in his power to rule the people of Israel by himself alone, yet chose seventy persons to assist him in his jurisdiction (Numb. xi.).'

I have sometimes fancied that the main ideas of this passage may have been set down by Jerome (in a fit of spleen against bishops—his own bishop in particular) from recollection of what he had heard respecting the teaching of Aerius.[2] But be this as it may, the passage itself contains,

---

[1] 'Paulatim.' Stress has been laid upon this expression, as tending to show that Jerome did not mean a formal decree, but the gradual upgrowth of a custom. See 'Irenicum,' p. 281. But the gradual upgrowth was *during apostolic times.* See 'Comment. in Ep. ad Gal.,' i. 19, for a similar use of 'paulatim,' vol. vii. p. 330.

[2] Aerius was alive when Epiphanius wrote his work against Heresies, A.D. 376 (see Clinton, 'Fast. Rom.,' Append., p. 445), and Jerome, though he was considerably younger, knew Epiphanius well.

as you have seen, four important statements; and it is now The passage contains four important statements. our concern to mark how far the author of those statements has proved, or attempted to prove them. It is evident he was desirous to prove them as far as he could, under a consciousness that what he had stated might be supposed to be not the teaching of Scripture, but only an opinion or fancy of his own. If, therefore, he has failed in this respect, it may fairly be concluded that, from some cause or other, he had been carried away into assertions which he could not justify.

1. First, then, he has stated that, according to Scripture, 1st statement of St. Jerome examined. a presbyter and a bishop are all one, not in name only, but in degree.

This he has attempted to prove by the fallacy of which I have before spoken, and which consists in the use of two ambiguous terms, *presbyter* and *episcopus*; while, at the same time, he has studiously kept out of view the position and authority of the apostles themselves and of apostolic men, such as James at Jerusalem, Timothy, Titus, the angels of the seven Churches, and the first beginners of the suc-

See below, p. 173. Dupin observes that Jerome was in the habit of adopting into his commentaries, without acknowledgment, the views and expositions of others; and this even when he did not approve of them. Vol. iii. p. 103; and comp. 'Irenicum,' p. 278, where Stillingfleet (in making the same disparaging remarks founded upon Jerome's own confession in a letter to St. Augustin) appears to have forgotten how much more his own side of the argument is dependent upon one of the commentaries (viz. on Ep. to Titus) than the other side is upon all the rest of the commentaries put together.

cession at Rome, and Antioch, and Alexandria, all of whom, as we shall presently see, he himself has elsewhere reckoned to have been bishops not in the presbyteral but prelatical sense.

2nd state-
ment of
St. Jerome
examined. 2. Secondly, he has stated that Churches were originally governed by the common counsel of the presbyters. Of this he has offered no better proof than the apostolical injunction addressed to the Hebrews in all parts of the world, *Obey them that have the rule over you,* &c. ; as if the use of such language must necessarily imply that in every separate Church or congregation there must be several rulers to be obeyed, and not that each was to obey its own ruler; or as if, among several rulers, there might not be different degrees of rule, each to be obeyed according to his own degree, the bishop as bishop, the presbyter as presbyter, the deacon as deacon; which, in truth, is the very lesson St. Ignatius has expressly taught. And to this Jerome has added another testimony which, if possible, is weaker still; viz. from the injunction of St. Peter, also addressed to Jewish Christians dispersed abroad, where he exhorts *the presbyters, as their fellow-presbyter, to feed the flock of God* ; as if that apostle might not be speaking there with the humility and self-abasement which his Divine Master had prescribed especially to one who would be first of all; and as if the higher order of the apostle did not include the lower order of the presbyters, according to the well-known maxim, ' Omne majus continet suum minus.' [1]

---

[1] Comp. below, p. 176, p. 191 sq., and above, p. 116.

3. Thirdly, Jerome has stated that the primitive Chris- 3rd statement of St. Jerome examined.
tians, and especially the clerical portion of them, were
everywhere quarrelsome, and actuated by party spirit. Of
this he offers no proof at all.   Only we see that he had the
Church of Corinth in his eye ; and from this single instance
he draws a universal conclusion ! We also see from the
same reference that the time to which his remarks are meant
to apply was the very earliest time in the Church's history ;
a time about which (living when he did) he could know no
more than we all know from Scripture itself; the time
when St. Paul and St. Peter and St. John and other apostles
were still alive, and governing the Church.[1] This, I say,
we see, if not from the expression *I am of Paul,* &c., which
may be interpreted, perhaps, more generally and with greater
laxity, yet from the allusion to the circumstance of the bap-
tizers claiming to themselves those whom they had baptized,
a circumstance which comes to us authenticated in no other
way but from the experience and the testimony of St. Paul
himself.[2]

4. Fourthly, Jerome has stated that as a remedy for the 4th statement of St. Jerome examined.
universal quarrelsomeness which existed (so far as appears)
only in his own imagination, a change was decreed, and
gradually effected, still more imaginary, whereby the Churches

---

[1] See Bilson, p. 291 sq.

[2] See Dodwell in Churton's edit.
of Pearson's M. T. Works, ii. p. 389.
The time of the supposed change is
also proved to be apostolical from
the epistle to Evangelus. See below,
p. 177.   Comp. Pearson, 'Vind.
Ignat.,' p. 318, ' Originem tantum
spectat,' and p. 562, ' seris apostolorum temporibus, vel paulo ante
obitum Petri et Pauli, vel certè ant
mortem Joannis.'

everywhere ceased to be presbyterian and became prelatical; from which it is inferred that the result of the change, viz. prelacy, did not rest upon any divine provision, but only upon the received custom of the Church. But of all this, also, utterly at variance as it was with his own experience, and removed altogether from his own cognizance, he offers no proof whatever. *Where, when,* or *how* a decree of such vital consequence was passed, and thenceforth became the universal law not only of every portion of the Church, but of every sect of heretics (for, as I have before observed, the threefold ministry prevailed in the early heretical bodies not less than in the Church); and again, whether or no the supposed alteration was effected with the sanction of the apostles (if with their sanction, they must have repented of their original design)—nothing of all this does he condescend to explain. And the truth is, it did not admit of explanation.[1] Not only is there no mention in the New Testament of any such decree, of any such change, but there is not a syllable to suggest the faintest surmise of such an occurrence; no, nor in any other primitive record of any kind. Well, indeed, might Chillingworth declare[2] that he would sooner believe all the transformations of heathen mythology which Ovid describes than he would credit this fable—this dream—which the wounded vanity of Jerome attempted to impose upon his two female devotees, and through them upon the

See above, p. 121.

[1] Stillingfleet's remarks upon the passage may be seen in 'Irenicum,' pp. 278–283.

[2] Vol. i. p. 485. And yet, see Dr. Cunningham's 'Church Hist.,' i. p. 66.

Church ! He does not, however, need to be rebuked by us for these wild imaginations. In the person of the heretic **Aerius, he was** abundantly rebuked, while alive, by the venerable metropolitan of Cyprus, Epiphanius,[1] who had been his friend and patron, and whom he himself has styled 'patrem pæne omnium episcoporum, et antiquæ reliquias sanctitatis ;'[2] nay, he was afterwards rebuked even by himself when he severely condemned his own bishop, John of Jerusalem, for using language only too similar to that of his own Commentary.[3]

But, after all, wild and fanciful as those statements of Jerome are, taken as a whole, what is the kind of shelter which they afford to the opponent of prelacy? On the one hand, if he is to claim the benefit of those statements, he must, *ipso facto*, admit that the parity which he advocates has been introduced in contravention of a decree of the Universal Church—a decree passed in the very earliest times, and adopted as a necessary remedy for the very evils of which we have now so much reason to complain, and the existence of which must at least go to prove that the said decree ought never to have been violated, and needs now to be

The statements of Jerome, as a whole, of no real value to anti-prelatists.

---

[1] Epiphanius calls it 'a mad assertion,' to say that a bishop and presbyter are equal ; and again 'to every sensible man it is manifest that nothing could be more foolish.' Vol. i. pp. 906, 908 ; comp. above, p. 125. There is an absence of critical power in the writings of Epiphanius, or he would probably have seen that, instead of using strong language, it would have been better to have exposed the *verbal fallacy.*

[2] Vol. ii. p. 365 ; comp. Fleury, ut supr., p. 228.

[3] See below, p. 183 ; and comp. Bilson, p. 358.

reinforced. On the other hand, what was it that Jerome himself would have as the practical result of those statements? Does he suggest that bishops, if they would do their duty, and be content with the position which the Scripture has assigned to them, should surrender their pre-eminence, and allow the Churches to be governed by a parity of ministers? No! He wishes bishops to do as Moses had done; not to cease to govern, but to admit the presbyters to partake of their authority and assist them in their charge; a sound and just determination—however visionary the premises upon which it rests—and one which no bishop, who understands either his duty or his interest, will ever venture to neglect.[1]

St. Jerome's epistle to Evangelus So much concerning this famous passage of St. Jerome's Commentary, which has probably produced more mischief in the Church than any other that was ever penned. There is, indeed, a companion to it,[2] though somewhat less mischievous, in one of his epistles—the well-known epistle to Evangelus (or Evagrius),[3] which appears to have been written about the same time.[4] His object in writing it

---

[1] See 'Irenicum,' pp. 335, 354, sqq., for examples of the practice of primitive bishops, and other testimonies to this effect.

[2] Both passages are quoted by Professor Lightfoot, p. 204, who derives from them the remark: 'To the dissensions of Jew and Gentile converts, and to the disputes of Gnostic false teachers, the development of

episcopacy may be mainly ascribed.' But is not this to attribute too much to mere secondary causes?

[3] As it used to be quoted. See vol. i. p. 1192, and comp. p. 676, note.

[4] According to Dupin, vol. iii. p. 93, 'about A.D. 387,' i.e. the same year. There is also an epistle of Jerome to Oceanus, supposed to

was to express his indignation (and he does express it!) at the presumption of the Roman deacons, who, being confined to 'seven,' in imitation of the number in the Acts, by a fanciful species of abuse, became men of wealth and consequence; more so in some respects than the presbyters, who were far more numerous, and whom they presumed to regard as their inferiors.[1] So that, whereas in his Commentary, Jerome's object had been to elevate presbyters in order to depress the episcopate, he now, in this epistle, endeavours to do the same, in order to depress the diaconate.[2] I need not quote the passage in full. Except that it says nothing of the Church being governed by the common counsel of presbyters, it repeats substantially the same statements—that presbyters and bishops, according to Scripture, were originally the same; but that afterwards, when there was a fear lest the Church should be torn in pieces by each of them attracting followers to himself, one was chosen to be placed above the rest as a remedy against schism. Again, however, we have no proof of this latter statement. In support of the former—the original equality of bishops and presbyters—the same texts are produced as in the Commentary; viz. Acts xx. 18, Phil. i. 1, 1 Pet. v. 1, 2; except that instead of

---

have been written ten years later, i.e. about A.D. 397, in which he repeats the statement that 'apud veteres iidem episcopi et presbyteri fuerunt, quia illud nomen dignitatis est, hoc ætatis.' (Ep. lxix. vol. i. p. 656.)

[1] See Euseb. 'H. E.,' lib. vi. c. xliv.

[2] Comp. the author of 'Quæst. Vet. et Nov. Test.' 'De jactantiâ Romanorum Levitarum.' St. Aug., vol. iii. p. 2939.

the passage from the Hebrews before quoted, now (besides
2 John 1 and 3 John 1, which add nothing to the text of
St. Peter) Jerome alleges also 1 Tim. iv. 14, respecting
ordination '*with* the laying on of the hands of the presbytery ;' and from 1 Tim. iii., Titus i. (where St. Paul gives
directions about persons to be ordained, and in so doing,
proceeds at once from the *bishop* to the *deacon*), he draws
the remark : 'St. Paul says nothing at all about presbyters,
because in the bishop the presbyter also is contained'—a
remark which is perfectly just, if properly understood ; for,
as I before observed, that which contains must be something
more and greater than that which is contained by it.[1]

See above, 170.

Admissions contained in that epistle.

I have called this letter less mischievous than the Commentary on account of the admissions which we find in it.
For instance, it admits that only bishops have the right to
ordain ; stating, however, at the same time that this is their
only legitimate distinction from presbyters :[2] and yet St.
Jerome elsewhere testifies that, by the universal practice of
the Church, bishops also alone administered confirmation.[3]
It declares expressly that bishops, besides being all equal in
office, whatever the size or dignity of their respective sees,

---

[1] Elsewhere he says that St.
Paul in Titus c. i. is giving directions for the 'princeps' and 'ponti-
fex' of the Church. See 'Comment.'
in loc., vol. vii. p. 567 ; and ' Adv.
Jovin.,' vol. i. p. 35; vol. ii. p.
258.

[2] This remark appears to have

been borrowed from Aerius. See
Epiphanius, vol. i. p. 908. And St.
Chrysostom, who repeats it on
1 Tim. iii., Hom. xi., may have
borrowed it from Jerome. Compare below, p. 192, note 3.

[3] 'Contr. Lucif.,' c. ix. vol. ii. p.
164 sq.

are also all successors of the apostles ; and it does not declare the same of presbyters.[1] It recognises the typical parallel of the high priest, priests, and Levites, with the bishop, presbyters, and deacons ; and, as regards the latter, it avows that parallel to be an 'apostolical tradition' taken from the Old Testament ; and finally it concludes, 'What Aaron and his sons and the Levites were in the Temple, that let bishops and presbyters and deacons claim to themselves in the Christian Church.'[2] The epistle is also more valuable to us than the commentary in this discussion, because it marks more distinctly the time at which Jerome imagined the change which he specifies (from presbyterian to episcopal regimen) to have taken place. It must have been while the apostles were still alive—and the change, if made at all, must have been made by apostolic authority, or, at least, with apostolic sanction—because he exemplifies his statement by the case of St. Mark as one whom the change in question had raised to be the first bishop at Alexandria.

' It is true, this last statement is expressed in such a way that

---

[1] It must be admitted, however, that elsewhere ('Epist. ad Heliod.,' vol. i. p. 352) he has spoken of the clergy generally as 'Apostolico gradui succedentes,' in opposition to monks, who could boast of no such distinction. Comp. 'Iren.,' p. 308. But this need imply no more than that a portion of the clergy enjoyed a privilege which no portion of the monks enjoyed.

[2] See Bilson, p. 309. Young Stillingfleet's attempt (against Pearson) to explain away this passage of Jerome may be seen in his 'Irenicum,' pp. 265 sqq., 283. He does not seem to have been aware that Jerome (after St. Clement) repeats the same comparison in other passages. See below, pp. 182, 183.

the opponents of prelacy have attempted to discover in it a primitive usage on the part of presbyters, not only to appoint their president or bishop out of their own body, but even to ordain him. The words are these : ' At Alexandria, from Mark the Evangelist [1] down to the bishops Heraclas and Dionysius [the 13th and 14th in the succession ; the date of the latter is A.D. 249], it was the custom for the presbyters to choose one out of their own body whom they placed in a higher grade and called bishop ; in the same way as if an army were to make its own general, or deacons to choose from among themselves one whom they knew to be diligent and call him archdeacon.' It is quite possible that what St. Jerome here states may have been the practice at Alexandria ; but the statement, if correct, while it proves, as I have said, the primitive institution of prelacy in the case of St. Mark, or, at least, at Alexandria immediately after St. Mark's death, it proves nothing in regard to ordination by presbyters.[2] On the contrary, in the very next sentence of the letter we read : ' For what is there that a bishop does which a presbyter may not do, *except ordination* ? ' It is certain that Jerome would not have made this exception if he had meant to say that the Alexandrian presbyters, down to A.D. 249, had been accustomed not only to elect but to consecrate their bishop. It is true that the spurious Ambrose, of whom I shall have occasion to speak presently, tells us that ' In Egypt

[sidenote: Practice of the Church of Alexandria according to St. Jerome,]

[1] See above, Lect. i. p. 37.

[2] See Pearson, ' Vind. Ignat.,' pp. 284. 289 sq.; Bingham, book ii. c. vi. sect. 3, vol. i. p. 87 ;

Elrington's ' Life of Ussher,' p. 257; and Bright's ' Church Hist.,' p. 20, note.

the presbyters *consignant,*' i.e. administer confirmation, 'if a bishop be not present ;' and in the anonymous work, entitled 'Questions upon the Old and New Testament,' now commonly supposed to have been written by the same author, we find a similar statement, but with a various reading in the text, which renders it uncertain whether *confirmation* or *consecration* (whatever the latter word may [1] mean) is intended to be ascribed to the Egyptian presbyters.[2] It is also true that more than four centuries afterwards, Eutychius, who was then (A.D. 933) patriarch of Alexandria, in a preserved fragment of his historical work upon the antiquities of his Church, does actually assert as follows :—' The evangelist St. Mark appointed Hananias the first patriarch of Alexandria ; and together with Hananias he also appointed twelve presbyters, who should remain with the patriarch, so that, when the see should become vacant, they might choose one of their body, upon whom the remaining eleven might lay their hands, and bless him, and create him patriarch. And this

and the author of 'Questions on the Old and New Testament.'

Statement of Eutychius.

---

[1] See Bingham, book xii. c. ii. sect. 2. He does not even mention the meaning of ordination.

[2] The words are : 'In Alexandriâ et per totam Ægyptum, si desit episcopus, consecrat (v. l. consignat) presbyter.' See in St. Augustin's Works, vol. iii. Append., p. 2941. Valesius in Euseb. 'H. E.,' vi. 43, p. 313, reads 'consignat,' and interprets it of confirmation, in both passages. Selden, 'Comment. on Eutychius,' p. 509, also reads 'consignat,' and is inclined to understand by it both ordination and confirmation. On the contrary, Professor Lightfoot reads 'consecrat' in both places, and supposes it may mean not only ordination of presbyters, but consecration of a bishop. P. 229.

practice continued to be observed at Alexandria to the time of the patriarch Alexander, A.D. 318, who ordained that, upon the vacancy of the see, the bishops should convene to consecrate a successor, and that the power of election was to be in their hands, without confining themselves to the twelve presbyters.'[1] And further, he states that ' whereas there had been no other bishop in the provinces of Egypt down to the time of Demetrius, that patriarch, the eleventh of the succession, ordained three.' It would take me too far from the point before us if I were to enter now into the merits of this last testimony, but I promise to do full justice to them when these lectures shall appear in a printed form.[2]

Evidence of St. Jerome as collected from his other works.

We return, therefore, to Jerome and his letter to Evangelus. The admissions which escape from him in that letter form a very small portion indeed of the evidence which he has given us of a similar kind, and which it would puzzle the most ingenious disputant to reconcile with his dream first told to Paula and Eustochium. The truth is, there is no one author who helps us so much as Jerome does, to establish the true constitution of the Christian ministry, as of Scriptural and apostolical authority; there is no author who enables us so thoroughly to confute his own wild and fanciful theory ; and this, for the most part, in works which he wrote at a later period of life, and when the unfortunate

---

[1] See Selden's Works, vol. ii. p. 422, who first published the fragment in Arabic, with a Latin version.

[2] A.D. 1642. See supplement at the end of this lecture.

bias to which he had been previously subject would be likely to operate less forcibly upon his mind. You will be able to judge for yourselves of the truth of the remark which I have now made, if I simply lay before you a summary of the several statements bearing upon this question which are to be gleaned from the various writings of Jerome, arranged according to their contents, under four general heads, and with the date of publication, so far as it can be ascertained, affixed to each :—

I. In his book of 'Biographical Sketches'—'De Viris Illustribus'—written A.D. 392, in his sixty-first year,[1] he records :— 1. Biographical sketches.

1. That Peter was bishop of the Church of Antioch, and afterwards became bishop of Rome. C. i. and v. vol. ii. p. 607.

2. That James 'the Just,' called the Lord's brother, was ordained bishop of Jerusalem by the apostles, immediately after the passion of our Lord, and remained bishop for thirty years. C. ii.

3. That Mark as bishop of Alexandria was succeeded by Annianus. C. viii.

4. That John wrote his Gospel at the request of the bishops of Asia. C. ix.

5. That Clement, St. Paul's fellow-labourer, was bishop of Rome C. v. and xv.

6. That Ignatius, who suffered martyrdom A.D. 115, was the third bishop of Antioch. C. xvi.

---

[1] He was born A.D. 331, and died A.D. 420.

7. That Polycarp was ordained bishop of Smyrna by St. John. C. xvii.

8. That Papias, a disciple of St. John, was bishop of Hierapolis. C. xviii.

9. That Quadratus, a disciple of the apostles, was bishop of Athens, in succession to Publius, who had suffered martyrdom. C. xix.

2. Epistles.

II. In his Epistles :—

1. He speaks of St. Mark as first bishop of Alexandria, as before quoted. To Evangelus, A.D. 387 (?), vol. i. p. 1194.

2. He asserts that bishops occupy the place of the apostles. To Marcella, A.D. 384. Ibid., p. 476.

3. He describes the Christian ministry as consisting of bishops, priests of the second order, and Levites. To Eustochium, A.D. 404. Ibid., p. 904.

4. He compares the bishop, presbyters, and deacons to the high priest, priests, and Levites ; speaking of the parallel, on the part of these latter, as 'an apostolical tradition derived from the Old Testament.' See above, p. 177. To Evangelus, as before. And again, in another letter, he writes, 'We should know the bishop and his presbyters to be what Aaron and his sons were.' To Nepotianus, A.D. 394. Ibid., p. 534.

5. He specifies the directions given by St. Paul to deacons, I Tim. iii., as directions 'to the third order'—*tertio gradui*; thereby alleging Scriptural and apostolical authority for the

threefold ministry. To Heliodorus, A.D. 373. Ibid., p. 352. Comp. 'Advers. Jovin.,' lib. i. c. xxxiv. vol. ii. p. 258.

III. In his controversial Treatises :—

3. Contro-versial treatises.

1. He repeats the parallel of the three orders as existing equally in the Old and New Testament : therefore they are equally of Scriptural and divine authority. 'Adv. Jovin.,' lib. ii. c. xxviii. A.D. 393. Vol. ii. p. 325.

2. He asserts that neither presbyter nor deacon has the right of baptizing without authority of the bishop ; as Tertullian[1] had asserted nearly two — and Ignatius[2] nearly three—centuries before. 'Advers. Lucif.,' c. ix. A.D. 379. Ibid., p. 165.

3. He regards the Ark, with its measurement of thirty cubits, as typical of the Church ; which 'multis gradibus consistens, ad extremum diaconis, presbyteris, episcopisque finitur.' Therefore the type having been of divine institu- . tion, the antitype must be the same. Ibid., c. xxii. p. 176.

4. He states that Clement was bishop of the Church of Rome. 'Apol. adv. Libros Ruffini,' lib. ii. c. xvii. A.D. 402. Ibid., p. 439.

5. He tells John, the bishop of Jerusalem, that he had made 'a grievous blunder at starting,' *in portu naufragium*, when in a spirit of undue condescension and mistaken courtesy he had spoken of there being *little or no difference between a bishop and a presbyter.* 'Contr. Joann. Hierosol.,' c. xxxvii. A.D. circ. 400. Ibid., p. 390.

---

[1] 'De Baptismo,' c. xvii.   [2] 'Ep. ad Smyrn.,' c. viii.

6. Above all, he declares that the safety and well-being of the Church depend upon the dignity of the bishop—*summi sacerdotis*—and that if some special and pre-eminent authority be not given to him, there will be caused as many schisms in the Churches as there are priests—*sacerdotes.* 'Adv. Lucif.,' c. ix. vol. ii. p. 164.

IV. In his Commentaries :—

1. He asserts that Clement was bishop of Rome as Peter had been before him. 'In Isaiam,' c. liii. A.D. 410. Vol. iv. p. 504 sq.

2. He considers the episcopate the fulfilment of prophecy. Ibid., c. lx. and lxi. pp. 596, 601.

3. He speaks of the three degrees of the ministry as being all worthy of honour. 'In Mich.,' c. vii. A.D. circ. 390. Vol. vi. p. 1220.

4. He states that the apostles ordained in the different provinces presbyters and bishops. 'In Matt.,' c. xxvi. A.D. 398. Vol. vii. p. 188.

5. He mentions James, the Lord's brother, as having been the first bishop of Jerusalem. 'In Ep. ad Gal.,' lib. i. c. i. A.D. 387. Vol. vii. p. 230.

6. He does not appear to doubt what he records as the received account, that Peter was the first bishop of Antioch, and was from thence translated to Rome; although, he observes, St. Luke has omitted to mention these circumstances in the Acts. Ibid., lib. i. c. ii. p. 341.

I make no use of the many important testimonies contained in the 'Chronica' of Eusebius, because, though that

work was translated by Jerome, and therefore, we may conclude, was considered by him to be generally trustworthy, in
regard to any particular statement, it would not be fair to
impute him a responsibility which he has himself declined.
(Præf., p. 39.)

Now, in reference to the various passages [1] I have quoted
from Jerome's works, it is important to observe that many
have consisted of simple statements of fact, commonly
received as such in the history of the Church, and as such
accepted by him; whereas the two previous quotations—

Character of
these admis-
sions made
by Jerome.

[1] Most of them have been quoted
by Hammond, 'Diss. Sec.,' cap.
xxix.; and by Bishop Pearson,
'Vind. Ignat.,' pp. 318–323, and
p. 561 sq. Stillingfleet, 'Irenicum,'
p. 278, attempts to depreciate the
testimony of Hammond's quotations, as being 'occasional and
incidental,' in comparison with the
other two, which he describes as
'designed and set discourses.' I
mention the remark, and leave the
reader to judge of its fairness and
accuracy.

Blondel's 'Apology for the
Opinion of Jerome' on the primitive
equality of bishops and presbyters,
written at the request of the Westminster Assembly, and published
1646, in a thick closely printed
volume, has been answered, *so far
as it went*, by Hammond (1651 and
1654), Pearson (1672), Samuel
Parker (1683), Hughes (1710). I
say 'so far as it went,' for at p. 8,
the author announces that 'he
hopes to explain in its proper place,
infrà sect. vi., the last part of
Jerome's "Epistle to Evangelus," in
which he speaks of *promotion from
a less degree to a greater*, of *apostolical traditions*, and of *the dis-
parity between Aaron, his sons, and
the Levites.*' But Blondel's work
consists of only *three* sections, and
there is *no other evidence* that he
ever intended to continue it. At
all events, the said statements of
Jerome remain *unexplained.*

The same has happened also in
the case of Salmasius, who, as
'Walo Messal.' (1641), made a
similar promise, p. 467, which has
never been performed.

See Hammond, Ibid., p. 124;
Pearson, Ibid., p. 321.

from the Commentary on Titus, and from the **Epistle to** Evangelus—presented nothing more than a theory of his own ; a theory purporting indeed to be deduced from Scripture, but unsupported by any evidence, and appealing to no knowledge not accessible to **ourselves,** and for the most part inconsistent with the statements which he himself has made **elsewhere.** And well may it be asked, Are we to believe in Jerome when he indulges his own fancy, or his own spleen, and disbelieve him when he records historical facts, or testifies to the practice of the universal Church?

Thus, then, we have not only examined, but cross-examined, this important witness ; and the result is, that the story, which he told at first, so far as it may have been designed, as it certainly has been employed, to impair the authority of the threefold ministry, has entirely broken down. Called, as it were, to curse, he has blessed it altogether. For what are the conclusions to which the evidence which you have heard, taken as a whole, indisputably leads ? They are these :—

Summary of St. Jerome's evidence.

1. That the episcopate, in Jerome's opinion, was an order distinct from and superior to the presbyterate ; and the presbyterate an order distinct from and superior to the diaconate.

2. That, accordingly, he recognised the three orders of the ministry, bishops, priests, and deacons.

3. That he regarded the three orders as necessary, and laid especial stress upon the highest order.

4. That he considered the three orders to be derived

not only from apostolical times, but from the apostles themselves.

5. That he held them to be Scriptural, and the episcopate the fulfilment of prophecy.

6. That bishops alone have the right of ordination.

7. That all bishops, whatever may be the size or dignity of their respective dioceses, are equally successors of the apostles.

Hence, then, it appears that one who has been brought forward as a leading and all-important witness by those who are commonly wont to pay little or no regard to the testimonies of antiquity, has not only failed to substantiate a single point in their favour, but has given against them manifold evidence of the strongest kind. And I am persuaded that had they been sufficiently aware of the general tenor and character of his works, he would never have been called into court. Notwithstanding his vast learning and unquestionable ability, he is sometimes very inaccurate, and this too when writing without personal bias, and with no apparent cause to disturb his judgment. To give but a single instance, which may suffice to show that in regard even to Scriptural matters, and such as are obvious to the most ordinary reader, he is not always to be trusted. He tells us that St. John founded (ἐθεμελίωσε) all the Churches of Asia,[1] whereas we know from the New Testament that Ephesus and many others were founded by St. Paul.[2]

---

[1] 'De Vir. Illustr.,' c. ix. vol. ii. p. 626.

[2] Irenæus, iii. 3 (quoted by Eusebius, iii. 23), says expressly

Ambrosiaster's 'Commentary on St. Paul.'

There is still one other witness to be examined, who, though of much inferior authority, occupies a position upon this question somewhat similar to that of Jerome. I allude to the anonymous author of the ' Commentary on St. Paul,' which was formerly attributed to St. Ambrose, and is still printed as an appendix to his works, but which is now universally believed to have been compiled and partially written, either by Hilary, the Roman deacon (who was engaged in the Luciferian schism [1]) or by some later author. He, too, whoever he was, like Jerome, has dreamed a dream ; a dream which imputes the first institution of our present episcopacy not (as Jerome's did) to the quarrelsomeness, but to the general unworthiness of the senior presbyters ; [2] but as (though living so late as the end of the fourth [3] or beginning of the fifth century) he has offered no authority whatever for the statement, we may safely leave it, like other dreams, to be told and forgotten. And all the more because, in his waking moments, the same author has said all, or nearly all, that

that the Church of Ephesus was founded (τεθεμιλιωμένη) by St. Paul.

[1] See Dupin, Cent. v. p. 189.

[2] On Eph. iv. 12, p. 241. At first, he says, the senior presbyter *succeeded* to a kind of prelacy; 'sed quia cœperunt sequentes presbyteri *indigni* inveniri ad primatus tenendos, immutata est ratio, prospiciente concilio, ut non ordo (seniority) sed meritum crearet episcopum.' See Bilson, pp. 283, 286, 310 ;

Heylyn, p. 216 ; and comp. Stillingfleet, ' Iren.,' pp. 312, 330 sq.

[3] The author himself says that he wrote ' sub Damaso,' who died A.D. 384 ; but the words have been thought to be an interpolation. Bishop Pearson supposes that he wrote before Chrysostom and Jerome, 'Vind. Ignat.,' p. 560 sq.; and comp. Clinton, Append., p. 437. He has borrowed largely from the spurious Jerome, or *vice versâ.*

we could desire ;[1] though perhaps not without a lurking tendency to depreciate the episcopate, which, if we knew who he was, and the circumstances of his life, we might be better able to account for.

For example :—

1. He says that when St. Paul wrote to the Corinthians, governors in the several Churches were not yet ordained (1 Cor. i. 1, p. 112. . Ibid., vi. 5, p. 129). Consequently, the constitution or management of the Churches then was not in all things the same as it is now, in their complete and settled state. On Eph. iv. 2, p. 241.

2. He says that the angels of the seven Churches in the Book of Revelation were bishops. On 1 Cor. xi. 8, p. 147.

3. He says that because all things are from God the Father, therefore God decreed that each Church should be governed by its own bishop. Ibid., xii. 28, p. 153.

4. He says that 'the apostles were bishops ;' that in the bishop all the orders are contained, because he is the first priest (sacerdos), that is, the 'chief of the priests' (*princeps sacerdotum*) and *prophet* and *evangelist.* Eph. iv. 11, p. 241.

5. He says that St. Paul wrote to Timothy and Titus, as individuals, because they had been made by him bishops respectively of Ephesus and Crete. Phil. i. 1,[2] p. 251. Comp. Prolog., pp. 290, 314.

6. He says that St. Paul (1 Tim. iii.), 'after speaking of the bishop, goes on to treat of ordination to the dia-

---

[1] See Pearson, 'Vind. Ignat.,' pp. 560, 574, where some of the following passages are quoted.

[2] He interprets 'with bishops' in that verse so as to refer the title to Paul and Timothy, 'qui utique episcopi erant.'

conate, because the ordering (ordinatio) of bishop and presbyter is one ; for either is a priest (sacerdos), yet the bishop is first ; so that though every bishop is a presbyter, yet every presbyter is not a bishop ; for the bishop is he who is the first among the presbyters.' [1]

7. Lastly, he signifies that 'Timothy was an ordained presbyter ; but, because he had no one before him, he was a bishop. Wherefore, also, St. Paul shows him how he is to ordain a bishop ; for it was not allowable, nor indeed possible, that the less should ordain the greater. For no one is able to give what he has not received ;'—a confused statement, from which it is not altogether easy to discover whether the author considered that a third ordination was necessary or not ; only it would seem that he did *not* consider ὁ ἐπίσκοπος (with the article) as used by St. Paul to be altogether synonymous with πρεσβύτερος.　1 Tim. iii. 8, p. 295.

Reflections on this evidence and on Jerome's.

And now, in parting from this witness, whose evidence, whatever else it may be good for, is certainly of no value (taken as a whole) to the presbyterian cause, there is one remark which must, I should imagine, occur to all our minds.　Is it not obvious that a due feeling of reverence should have led him—and should have led Jerome also—to assume that the apostles, being under the guidance of the Holy Spirit in matters of far less importance, would not—could not—have been left without direction in regard to so vital a point as the constitution of the Church's ministry ; a

---

[1] Quoted by Lightfoot, p. 227.

point which, above all others, would be liable to cause among their converts jealousies and disputes, if known to be contingent upon their own choice? But, as God had given to Moses a pattern of the future tabernacle (Heb. viii. 5) ; as He had given to David, by inspiration, a pattern of the future **Temple** (1 Chron. xxviii. 12, 19) ; so was it not to be expected that the apostles would likewise receive their plan, **duly** prearranged and settled, upon which to work?[1] Had our two critics considered this as they ought to have done, they would have abstained from the indulgence of their own fancies, and would have piously concluded that what they saw and knew to be everywhere the uniform and well-ordered result, had been from the beginning the divinely-revealed and foreordained **design.**

I know of no other testimony that remains to be noticed, unless I am to allude to expressions of condescension, or of compliment; such as **those** in which St. Cyprian, imitating the humility of St. Peter and **St. John,**[2] addresses clergy of

Expressions of condescension afford no evidence.

---

[1] It is no proper answer (see Stillingfleet's 'Iren.,' p. 177 sq.) to this question that *ceremonial details* were settled under the Law which are not settled under the Gospel. All that is pleaded for is that if *sufficient guidance* was given under the Law, *being such as it was*, we may conclude that sufficient guidance would be given under the Gospel, *being such as it is*; but without fundamental direction concerning the form of ministry (though not concerning ritual), the guidance would be insufficient, as I have argued , young Stillingfleet, however, argued otherwise, p. 179. Comp. **above, Lect. i. p.** 18, note. It is further to be observed, that in the pattern of the Temple, delivered by David to Solomon, there was a constant reference made to the pattern of the Tabernacle delivered by God to Moses. See Bishop of Lincoln on **1 Chron. xxviii. 18.**

[2] 1 Pet. v. 1 ; 2 John 1 and 3 John 1. But in all those passages there may be a reference to age.

the second order as his 'fellow-presbyters;'[1] or in which
St. Augustin, though a bishop, tells a great scholar and
divine like **Jerome, though only** a presbyter, that **'notwith-**
standing the superior titles **of respect** which it is customary
to **give to** bishops, in many things Augustin is inferior to
Jerome.'[2] Nor, again, **will it, I think, be** worth our while
to lay stress upon occasional language which the supposed
necessities of a lax or inaccurate criticism of the sacred
text may have led even an author like St. Chrysostom to
use ;'[3] when we consider that long before his time the dis-
tinction between the first and second orders of the ministry
was unquestionably as strongly marked as it has been **at any**
subsequent period in the history of the Church.

   And let it not be supposed that there is any inconsistency
between this whole argument and those sayings of our **Lord**

---

[1] See above, pp. 170, 176. In like
manner St. Paul speaks of many
who were not apostles as his 'work-
fellows.' Rom. xvi. 3, 9, 21, and
elsewhere. Nay, our Blessed Lord
Himself, being the Son of God,
preferred to call Himself the Son
of Man.

[2] Epist. lxxxii. 34, vol. ii. p.
303. 'Quanquam secundum hono-
rum vocabula, quæ jam ecclesiæ
usus obtinuit, episcopatus presby-
terio major sit, tamen in multis
rebus Augustinus Hieronymo minor
est.' He could not have meant
to imply that the episcopate was
greater *only* in titles of respect.

Comp. Lightfoot, p. 228.

[3] See, for example, on Tim. iii.
8, Hom. xi. vol. xi. p. 666 (upon
which passage Dr. Cunningham has
remarked, ' Even in the beginning of
the fifth century Chrysostom and
Jerome could assert the primitive
equality, or rather identity of the
bishop and presbyter.' 'Church
Hist.,' vol. i. p. 66), and the
spurious Jerome on the same text in
Jerome's Works, vol. xi. p. 880,
'Episcopos presbyterorum nomine
comprehendit, quia secundus, immò
pæne unus, est gradus.' Compare
above, p. 176.

when, on more than one occasion, He rebuked the ambitious rivalry of His disciples (Mark ix. 33–37, Luke ix. 46–48, Matt. xx. 24–28, Mark x. 41–45, Luke xxii. 24–27), or when He admonished them that as they were to call no man their father upon the earth, so neither should they themselves, like the scribes and Pharisees, seek to be called of men Rabbi, Rabbi (Matt. xxiii. 1–12). It is evident that our Lord's intention on these occasions was not to condemn pre-eminence as such (which He expressly sanctions on the part of all the twelve), but the undue desire and ambition of pre-eminence;[1] and, at the same time, to teach that among themselves there was to be an equality of rank, which, while it justifies the order of bishops as coequal fathers and governors of the Church, would seem to denounce by anticipation the exorbitant supremacy which has been claimed by one.[2]

Such, then, is the evidence, Scriptural and historical, upon this great question—the question of the right constitution of the Christian ministry; and such the objections which have

---

[1] See Blondel, Præf., p. 49 sq.; and Hammond, ' Diss. Tert.,' cap. ii. pp. 139–141.

[2] 'The bishop of Rome has not been content with the precedence of an elder brother in the see of St. Peter, but has claimed that of *a master* and *father*; and this command of our Lord (Matt. xxiii. 8) being broken, the unity and strength of the Church has been lost. But it may be asked, Does not this command militate against the authority of individual bishops over their flocks altogether? It will be found on consideration that it does not do so; on the contrary, that *this divinely commissioned authority is the only remedy against the ambition which breaks up society.*'—Williams' *Holy Week*, p. 216 sq. See the whole passage.

been raised to invalidate its force. I venture to think that
the objections have been shown to rest upon no solid foundation ; that the evidence is conclusive. I venture to
believe that if the case were to be submitted to the judgment
of any competent tribunal in this country—simply upon the
matter of fact and of constitutional right—there would be no
hesitation as to the verdict which would be pronounced. I
venture to maintain that there is nothing of the same importance in the world's history which stands upon stronger
testimony; and that, whatever there may be of doubt or
difficulty concerning it, which has not been manifestly caused
by human failings or excesses on the part both of governors
and governed, is no more than was to have been expected,
to try our faith and obedience in accordance with God's
dealing with us for our moral probation in other instances.

Summing
up of argu-
ment from
Scripture
and history.
And now, having laid this evidence before you, I ask for
nothing but a patient and impartial examination, such as
may lead to the discovery of the truth ; and that, when the
truth is discovered, justice may be done accordingly. In a
word, we ask from you what John Knox asked from the
opponents of the Reformation. Shall we ask in vain, as he
did? Speaking for his brethren and fellow-reformers, as
well as for himself, 'We are content,' he said, 'not only that
the precepts and rules of the New Testament, but also the
writings of the ancient Fathers . . . decide the contest.'[1]
And again : 'Let God speak by His law, by His prophets,

---

[1] 'First Petition to the Queen Regent' in 1558. Knox's Works, i. p. 305.

by Christ Jesus, or by His apostles, and so let Him pronounce what religion He approveth : . . . and if my adversaries think to have advantage by their councils and doctors,
this I further offer, to admit the one and the other as witnesses in all matters debatable.'[1]   We continue that appeal
against the usurpations and corruptions of the Church of
Rome ; but we repeat it also with equal confidence in
favour of a system such as can be proved to rest upon
Scripture and upon the example of the Primitive Church.
Are we unreasonable in this ?   Will you reject our petition ?
Will you oblige us to continue in apparent separation ?   I
address myself now more especially to those who represent
the Church established in this country—will you oblige us
to continue separated and excluded from the national embodiment of our common Christianity, because we cannot
consent to separate ourselves from the only system which
the Universal Church has recognised, and which is established in the sister country ; from the system which rests, as
I have said, and as you yourselves have seen, upon abundant Scriptural and apostolical authority, and which, even
though it rested upon no better sanction than the primitive
decree throughout all the world which Jerome dreamt of,
ought not to be abrogated without a decree of equal authority to justify the change?   Will you persist in your determination—as it stands now expressed in the ordination-promise
required of all your ministers and elders [2]—to say to us for

Appeal to
members of
Established
Church of
Scotland.

---

[1] 'Appellation to the Nobility,'   [2] Elders are required to declare
vol. iv. p. 518 sq.; see also p. 446.   that they 'own and acknowledge

all time to come :—' Brethren though you are, and with title-deeds to show far more ancient than our own, yet you shall have no portion, no inheritance with us, in the Church of your fathers, unless you will consent to adopt and maintain exclusively those standards of doctrine and of worship which owe their origin to a period not of religious reformation, but of political turbulence and civil war?' If on these accounts our exclusion is to be continued; if on these accounts a division is to be kept up, and the ecclesiastical concord which we crave is to be denied; I will urge you no further. I will not ask, Is not this harsh? Is not this unbrotherly? Is not this unchristian usage? But I appeal to a higher tribunal. The Lord judge between us and you!

The third and last head of the main argument—viz. that which arises from consideration of consequences—remains to be treated of in my next and concluding lecture.

Presbyterian Church government, now settled by law to be the only government of this Church, and that they will submit thereto and concur therewith, and *never directly or indirectly endeavour the prejudice or subversion thereof.*' To which ministers and probationers are required to add that they are 'persuaded that the Presbyterian government of this Church is founded upon the Word of God and agreeable thereto.'

SUPPLEMENT TO LECTURE II.

On the Testimony of Eutychius, &c.

(See above, p. 179.)

THE value of the testimony of this mediæval patriarch has been keenly contested on both sides ; because *if accepted* it appears to afford at least one conclusive proof that ordination, or rather, what is more, consecration, by presbyters, was allowed from the beginning in the primitive Church, and continued, if nowhere else, yet in so important a see as Alexandria, even to the early part of the fourth century.

It was, as I have said above, the learned John Selden, who, in 1642, the year before the meeting of the Westminster Assembly—*of which he was himself a prominent member*—first gave to the world, from an Arabic MS., the fragment of Eutychius' historical work which contains the testimony in question ; claiming at the same time for the author of it a character not less trustworthy than that of our own Bede (Works, ii. 418). And probably the appearance at such a time of such a testimony may have produced an effect prejudicial to episcopacy [1] not inferior to that which the appearance of 'Eikon

Fragment of Eutychius, first printed by Selden in 1642.

---

[1] 'That learned man (Selden) having been censured by the High Commission for some offensive passages in his "History of Tithes," became not a little displeased with some bishops of the Church of England ; and the resentment of that former usage lay deep in his

Basilikè seven years afterwards produced in favour of the restoration of the monarchy and of the Church.   The entire work[1] of Eutychius was not long after, viz. in 1658, published at

E. Pocock.   Oxford by the celebrated Oriental scholar Dr. E. Pocock, who had undertaken it at Selden's request, but who felt no sympathy with his opposition to episcopacy, and who also entertained a much lower opinion of the general trustworthiness of the patriarch's performance : and, as it would appear, not without reason, both from internal evidence (for example, the writer states that 2,048 bishops were present at the Council of Nice, and he makes a bishop of Origen, and places him in the middle of the sixth century !), and from the fact (which Pocock himself discovered from another Arabic work which he afterwards published) that the archives of the Church of Alexandria, from which Selden 'had no doubt' that Eutychius had derived much of his annals, were all destroyed by fire when the city was taken by the Saracens, A.D. 638, three centuries before.[2]   In short, it seems to be now agreed that the general character of the work is not unfairly described in the words of Du Pin : ''Tis full of fables and very vulgar stories.'[3]

But to return to the testimony itself.   It was first made use

D. Blondel.   of by Blondel, in his famous 'Apologia pro sententiâ Hieronymi,' 1646 ; see Præf., pp. 17-20.   The first answer was from the

H. Thorn-   pen of Thorndike, 1649 ; see 'The Right of the Church in a
dike.

mind, and was at length sufficiently discovered by him.'—Twells' *Life of Pocock*, p. 225 sq.   See also Walton's 'Proleg., xiv. 10 ; but comp. Aikin's 'Life of Selden,' p. 122.

[1] It consists of annals from the beginning of the world to A.D. 900.

[3] See Twells, Ibid., p. 228, and

Hughes in Hickes' 'Treatises,' vol. iii. p. 49.   The Arabic work alluded to is the 'Oriental History of Gregory Abulpharagius,' primate of the Eastern Jacobites, A.D. 1266.

[2] 'Eccles. Hist.,' vol. viii. p. 4. Cave, 'Hist. Lit.,' vol. ii. p. 96, speaks of it in the same way.

Christian State,' pp. 498–500. This was followed two years afterwards (1651) by Hammond in his fourth Dissertation against Blondel (c. x. pp. 177–179). Both decline to believe the assertion of Eutychius, that before Demetrius there were no bishops in the whole of Egypt besides the patriarch of Alexandria ; and consequently 'cannot admit his relation to be historical truth.' But Dr. Bryan Walton, four years later, in the Prolegomena to his celebrated Polyglott, 1657, not only rejects the statement as incredible, but speaks of the author in the most contemptuous terms (c. xiv. sect. 10). Again after two years, viz. in 1659, appeared young Stillingfleet's 'Irenicum,' who professes to answer Hammond (p. 273 sq.), and wishes to know ' who and where those bishops in Egypt were who did consecrate and ordain the bishop of Alexandria after his election by the presbyters, especially while Egypt remained but one province, under the government of the *Præfectus Augustalis.*' The work of Abraham Echellensis, a learned Maronite, who took up the opposite side of the question, at Rome, in 1661, I have not seen ; but probably it contains nothing of importance which has not been urged at least equally well from the same point of view by Bishop Pearson (who refers to it, pp. 290, 303, sq.) in his 'Vindiciæ Ignatianæ,' 1672, where he elaborately discusses the whole question (Part i. c. xi.). He begins by noticing the inconsistency between Jerome's statement and that of Eutychius ; the former asserting that the practice of the Alexandrian presbyters to choose their bishop ended with Heraclas and Dionysius, in the earlier part of the third century ; the latter that it ended with Alexander, nearly a whole century later (p. 283). He considers it incredible that the consecration of the patriarch was made without bishops ; and he remarks that had Jerome known of any such custom, he would certainly have mentioned it in his letter to Evangelus (p. 286). He points out that in the 'Apostolical Constitutions,' book vii. c. xlvi. sect. 4

H. Hammond.

B. Walton.

Stillingfleet.

Abraham Echellensis.

Pearson's arguments.

(where see Coleterius' note) Avilius, or Abilius, the second bishop of Alexandria, is said to have been ordained by St. Luke (p. 289). He rejects the statement of Eutychius as to the non-existence of bishops in Egypt before the time of Demetrius (about A.D. 190) ; repeating the fact respecting the destruction, long before, of the Alexandrian archives (on which see Archdeacon Churton's note in answer to Gibbon) as a ground for refusing credit to an annalist of the tenth century, whose inaccuracy at the same time he exposes upon other points (pp. 292–296) ; and in regard to the matter stated, he shows by various proofs,[1] that Egypt was not without bishops before the end of the second century ; and he infers the same from the circumstance (for which see Athanasius' ' Hist. Tracts,' p. 300) that in A.D. 324 nearly a hundred bishops of Egypt and Libya met together at the call of Alexander, then patriarch of Alexandria, to condemn Arius and his supporters (pp. 296–303).

Gibbon. But notwithstanding all this, Gibbon, in the notes to the fifteenth chapter of his Roman History, has not failed to let us know, more than once, that he is not persuaded by it. His words are (vol. ii. p. 332): ' The ancient state, as it is described by Jerome, of the bishop and presbyters of Alexandria, receives a remarkable confirmation from the patriarch Eutychius, whose testimony I know not how to reject, in spite of all the objections of the learned Pearson, in his " Vindiciæ Ignatianæ." ' And again, he states in his text (Ibid., p. 363): In Egypt, ' the progress of Christianity was for a long time confined within the limits of a single city, which was itself a foreign colony (Alexandria) ; and till the close of the second century, the predecessors of Demetrius (the Alexandrian patriarch) were the only prelates of the

---

[1] Dr. Neale, however, admits that none of those proofs can be considered decisive. ' Hist. of the Church of Alexandria,' vol. i. p. 11, note.

Egyptian Church. Three bishops were consecrated by the hands of Demetrius, and the number was increased to twenty by his successor **Heraclas.'** And then he adds in a note : ' This curious fact'—if he means the latter statement, it certainly is *most curious and utterly unexampled* in the history of the Church that one single bishop should appoint twenty—' is preserved by the patriarch Eutychius, and its internal evidence would alone be a sufficient answer to all the objections which **Bishop** Pearson has urged in the " Vindiciæ Ignatianæ."' For my own part I can see no 'internal evidence' in the passage, or in the context as given by Selden, to justify this description. On the other hand, **Professor Lightfoot, though he follows on** the same side, does so out **of regard not** to internal but external evidence. **He remarks : ' The authority of** a writer so inaccurate as Eutychius, *if it had been unsupported,* would have had no great weight ; **but, as we have seen, this** is not the case ' (p. 229). **What, then, has been 'the support'** which the Professor refers to ? **I can see none but** that of Jerome and of the spurious Ambrose (as above quoted, p. 178 sq. and note 2) ; the former of whom could not, as we have shown, have meant to imply *ordination* by presbyters, even at Alexandria, and the latter must be regarded as at best an insufficient witness so long as his text and the meaning to be assigned to it **are** both uncertain. **Be** this, however, as it may, it is evident that Dr. **Lightfoot** accepts the Eutychian statement of the non-existence **of bishops in** Egypt till the time of Demetrius in **all its breadth.** He writes : ' At the close of the second century, when every considerable **Church in Europe and Asia** appears to have had its bishop, **the only representative of the** episcopal **order in** Egypt was the **bishop of** Alexandria. **It was** Demetrius **first** (A.D. 190–233), as Eutychius informs us, who appointed three other bishops, to which number his successor **Heraclas** (A.D. **233-249)** added twenty more.' And **further he remarks :** ' This

Professor
Lightfoot.

extension of episcopacy to the provincial towns of Egypt paved the way for a change in the mode of appointing and ordaining the patriarch of Alexandria. But before this time it was matter of convenience and almost of necessity that the Alexandrian presbyters should themselves ordain their chief' (p. 230).

J. M. Neale.   It only remains to lay before the reader the opinion of the late learned Dr. Neale, in his valuable 'History of the Alexandrian Church.' He begins (vol. i. p. 9) by remarking that though the statement of Eutychius has been repeatedly noticed and *confuted*, a history of the Church of Alexandria would be incomplete without an examination into its truth. Taking the story as it stands, he considers it impossible to believe 'that the second see in the Catholic Church was for the space of one hundred and fifty years governed by arch-priests; that these men, during that period, refrained from the ordination of other bishops, though presuming to lay hands on priests [1] and the inferior order of the hierarchy; that the eleventh patriarch asserted his claim to consecrate bishops; and that six of his successors (i.e. between Demetrius and Alexander), for nearly a hundred years, persevered in this practice,[2] without a remonstrance from, and enjoying communion with, every other branch of the Church.' He admits indeed that some foundation for the story is to be found in Jerome's statement; at least so far as to forbid us to treat it as a mere fabrication of Eutychius; but he considers that the words of the latter, though apparently so much stronger, no more really imply ordination than those of

---

[1] This does not follow necessarily from Eutychius' statement. The patriarch might have ordained them; though this, of course, would add nothing to the validity of ordination, if he himself had been ordained only by presbyters.

[2] This appears to mean, the practice of being consecrated by presbyters. The only patriarchs who are said by Eutychius to have consecrated bishops, are Demetrius and his successor Heraclas.

the former. He writes : 'It may well be asserted that the
words of Eutychius refer to the election, not the consecration of
the bishop. It was the custom in the early Church that not
only presbyters but even laics laid their hands on the heads of
the party so chosen ; and this was the case more especially in
the Coptic Church, as writers, both Catholic and Jacobite,
allow. And Echellensis has clearly proved that in many
instances at least a triple imposition of hands took place ; of the
people voting, of the presbyters electing, of the bishops conse-
crating. At the same time the presbyters of Alexandria had
certain privileges which the presbyters of other Churches did not
enjoy ; [1] and these two facts coming together to the knowledge of
an ignorant writer like Eutychius, may have occasioned the
fable to which the unhappy consequences of the Western Reformation have given such undue celebrity.' To this explanation he
adds the following : Prepared to grant that the patriarch may
have been really ordained by those twelve (eleven) presbyters,
he infers that, if so, they must have been 'an episcopal college,
retaining the name which in the primitive Church was used
synonymously with bishops.' He considers that either of these
explanations is 'perfectly satisfactory' (pp. 10-12).

[1] More especially provincial letters were addressed in their name con- jointly with the patriarch's. Ibid., p. 12.

LECTURE III.

IT has been shown in my two former lectures, first, that a ministry, uniform and of a particular character, was antecedently to have been expected in the Christian Church; and, secondly, that such a ministry existed from the beginning, and continued everywhere to exist (though in the West, for many centuries, in a corrupt and exaggerated form, through the undue influence of the Church of Rome) till the period of the Reformation; and that it still exists, reformed or unreformed, over by far the largest portion of Christendom—east and west, north and south—at the present day.

Argument from evil consequences due to disregard of foregoing conclusion.

I have now to ask your attention to several considerations, which will appear in the form of consequences; some of them tending more or less directly to justify and confirm the conclusion which the two preceding lines of argument have led us to adopt; while others, I am conscious, will add nothing in the way of proof, and are only valuable as giving force to this appeal, upon the *assumption* that the point in question has been already proved.

1. In the first place, then, it will not be denied that a

disregard of the position which I have sought to establish, is calculated to lead, and has actually led, to the practice of separation, and to a growing indifference to that practice. In saying this, I do not mean to imply that the acceptance of that position has been,[1] or ever will be, found sufficient of itself under all circumstances to secure us against separation. All I intend—and would maintain—is, that the apostolical institution of one uniform system of the ministry, and a firm belief in that institution, supposing it to be proved, cannot but be powerful instruments to deter us from divisions, and to assist us in keeping or recovering unity. Now, whatever ideas we may severally entertain of the duty of union, and communion among Christians, as prescribed in Scripture, I think we shall all admit [2] that our present

First evil conse-quence :—Indifference to unity, though taught in Scripture ;

---

[1] St. Irenæus taught that all who belong to the Church 'preserve the same form of ecclesiastical constitution,' or 'ordained ministry.' Book v. c. 20. And yet there were even then many heretics who became also schismatics. Nevertheless, we know the remark of St. Cyprian, and even of St. Jerome, and we do not doubt that it contains truth. 'Neque enim aliunde hæreses obortæ sunt, aut nata sunt schismata, quàm inde quod sacerdote Dei non obtemperatur.'—Cyprian, Epist. liv. (or lix.) *ad Cornel.*, vol. iii. p. 802. And again Epist. lxviii. (or lxvi.) ad Florent. Papian. : 'Inde enim schismata et hæreses obortæ sunt et oriuntur, dum episcopus, qui unus est, et ecclesiæ præest, superbâ quorundam præsumptione contemnitur.'—Vol. i. p. 403. 'Ecclesiæ salus in summi sacerdotis dignitate pendet ; cui si non exsors quædam, et ab omnibus eminens detur potestas, tot in ecclesiis efficientur schismata, quot sacerdotes.' —Jerom. *Dial. contr. Lucif.*, vol. ii. p. 165.

[2] This has been admitted by ministers of the Established Church, such as Dr. Bisset, in his Moderator's Address for 1862, and of the Free Church such as Dr. Guthrie, in his speech at Blair-Atholl, of the same year—both quoted in the

condition is not what it ought to be in this respect. Most of us, it is to be hoped, would be glad to see somewhat less of inconsistency between the actual relations in which fellow-Christians, especially of the same country, the same language, the same neighbourhood, now live as such, and the plain requirements of the Word of God.[1]

and in-tended and desired by Christ.

We have been told indeed that 'the average Presbyterian does not deem it necessary to attend to antiquarian and Scriptural arguments,' such as have been brought before you in my former lectures, ' because they seem to him to be attempting to prove what cannot be true ; inasmuch as God cannot be conceived to have spoken miraculously on a mere matter of detail and convenience like Church government.'[2] But surely it is not inconceivable that God should have done under the Gospel what it is certain He did under the Law. And, still more is it conceivable that the Divine Founder of the Christian Church should desire to preserve from disorganisation the Society which He instituted ; and if 'a matter of detail and convenience, such as Church

author's 'Bicentenary Lecture' delivered at Kidderminster, 1862, pp. 31-40. 'We are beginning to feel the *inexpediency* of schism ; we shall next feel its *sinfulness.*'—Rev. P. Grant, of Tenandry, at a meeting of the presbytery of Dun-keld, April 26, 1870. Since the year of Dr. Bisset's Address, almost every moderator of the Established Church has spoken, more or less, *on the evils of separation.*

[1] 'There are at the present moment in Scotland fourteen distinct Churches, or complete Christian organisations, competing for the attachment of the nation.'— Dr. R. Wallace, in 'Recess Studies,' p. 187.

[2] Ibid., p. 204 sq.

government,' would be calculated, as certainly it would, to assist in this, then so far from pronouncing it inconceivable, we should certainly expect Him, in His goodness, to afford such assistance. I repeat therefore that, if we desire to please God, and to obey His commands in regard to unity among fellow-Christians, we shall (among other means for producing that result) endeavour to ascertain the divine intention in regard to the constitution of the Church's ministry. If episcopacy be in accordance with that intention (as, I think, I have shown it is), then, as one way towards diminishing our separations, let us add to our presbyterianism what it now improperly wants. If presbyterianism be in accordance with that intention—and can be proved to be so by fair argument—then let it be asserted as such. If it can be proved only to be ' defensible,' then I cannot see what claim it has to be established, to the entire exclusion of other systems also, upon that theory, granted to be defensible ; and sure I am, it never would have been established, to the exclusion of a reformed episcopate, if, in the first instance, it had been content to rest upon such a plea. But the point which we have to keep in view is this. The theory that a Church which is accepted and established as national, is merely defensible, or even is merely preferable, has a direct tendency to cause indifference to separation ; and so tends, indirectly at least, to produce it. Let us not then be told of established presbyterianism (nonestablished presbyterianism will often hold a bolder and more consistent tone), that, having thrust itself into the place

The course to be taken by all lovers of Christ, and of His truth.

of authority and of privilege, in which God's truth alone
should be enthroned, it now ' detests proselytising ;' it now
declines to assert that truth ; and that being lawfully settled
in the sole possession of the national kirks and manses, it
now only desires to leave alone and be left alone. And
yet not altogether to leave or be left alone ; for it seeks and
even claims [1] support for new endowments, and augmented
stipends, upon the plea of its established position, from the
descendants of those whose forefathers, because it pronounced them to be in error, and avouched itself to be the
truth, it unmercifully dispossessed of all privilege and all
endowment !   Or, once more, if popery be in accordance
with the divine intention, and can be proved to be so, then
let us not only accept a national episcopate, in addition to
our presbyterianism, but let us further add the authority
of a foreign autocrat ; let us submit ourselves, one and all,
to the spiritual supremacy of the bishop of Rome.   But let
us not go on any longer in this pitiful, this most miserable
bewilderment ; as if, upon so great a matter as the constitutional ministry of the Christian Church, there were no such
thing as truth or untruth, right or wrong ; or at least, if
there be, that we, for our part, are unable to discover them !
I was asked the other day, by a most excellent lady, to
subscribe to a charitable institution for imbecile children,
and I did so, though not without some misgiving ; for upon

---

[1] See the speeches delivered at
the public meeting, held at Glasgow, in behalf of ' the Church of
Scotland Association for Augment-
ing the smaller Livings of the
Clergy,' December 1866.

enquiry respecting the religious training of the children, I found, from the printed report which was put into my hands, that all difficulty had been amicably smoothed over by the boys being taken to the Established, and the girls to the Free Church ! Are we not, most of us, upon this great question, in such a state of childish imbecility, that we should be no unfit inmates for such an institution ?

This, then, is the first evil consequence which flows in part at least from our non-acceptance of the truth,[1] that there is a right constitution of the Christian ministry, and that we may ascertain it if we will. The Word of God did not mock at the poor and the unlearned when it told them to 'avoid those who cause divisions' (Rom. xvi. 17) ; and when it reckoned 'separations' among 'the works of the flesh,' and assured us that 'they who do such things shall not inherit the kingdom of God' (Gal. v. 20, 1 Cor. iii. 3). It did not mock at the poor and the unlearned when it bade them to be 'all of one mind' (1 Pet. iii. 8, Phil. ii. 12, Rom. xii. 16, xv. 5) and to 'live in peace,' and that so 'the God of love and peace would be with them' (2 Cor. xiii. 11), or when it besought them all 'to speak the same thing,' and that there should be 'no divisions (or schisms) among them'

Scriptural proof of God's will in regard to unity.

---

[1] Let me explain, once for all, that I have no wish to enforce this word, as so used, in its highest sense, upon the consciences of others, whatever may be my own opinion concerning it. I am quite content that it should be understood to imply no more than some suppose (though not, as I think, correctly) Hooker intended, viz. 'a divine expediency ;' or than Mr. Matthew Arnold contends for, viz. 'a true development.' See 'St. Paul and Protestantism,' pp. 174-178.

P

(1 **Cor. i. 10, xii.** 24, 25, Rom. xii. 5) ; when it exhorted
them to ' be like-minded one towards another,' for this end,
that they might not only ' with one mind,' but also ' with
one mouth glorify God ' (Rom. xv. 5, 6 ; comp. Phil. i. **27,**
Heb. x. 25, Acts ii. 42). Once more, the Word of God did
not mock at the poor and the unlearned when it taught
them to **'obey those** who have,' i.e. have rightly and legitimately, '**the rule over them**' (Heb. xiii. 17), and again, to
'know those who are over them in the Lord and admonish
them' (1 **Thess. v. 12**). No; it did not mock at them, when
it bade them to observe and to do all these things. **But is**

Our duty
towards the
poor and
unlearned.

it not true that *we* mock at the great mass of the poor and
ignorant when we put the Bible into their hands, to be their
rule of life, and at the same time virtually tell them that there
are no such things as *divisions* to be avoided ; no such persons
to be *known*, who can claim to *admonish*, to guide, to *rule*, to
watch for their souls, as being *set over them in the Lord* ;—
except so **far as** they themselves (in **their** poverty) may
make, **or (in** their ignorance) **may** *choose* such an one for
themselves? I speak, you will observe, more particularly of
the poor and the unlearned ; because it is the will of **God**
that they, and such as they, should ' never cease out of the
land,' **and because it is the will of** Christ **that to** them, and
to such **as they, more** especially the Gospel should be
preached. **But who is** to be their preacher? And how can
he preach except he **be sent?** [1] And who is to have authority to send him? A weighty question, my friends ; one of

----

[1] Rom. x. 15.

the weightiest that can be asked in this world, because if it is to receive no answer, then what limit can there be to divisions, and to confusion of every kind in the Church of Christ? And yet it is impossible to **give** any sufficient or satisfactory answer to it, until we have determined what is the right and true constitution of the Christian ministry. To that question, therefore, I shall next proceed. **In the meantime** I will only remind you what is the sum and substance of the remarks which have now been made. As we **had** been led from various considerations to conclude *à priori* that a definite system of the Christian ministry would be provided by the Divine wisdom and goodness; so we have been brought to the conclusion, *ex consequente*, that such a system must have been provided, and can be ascertained, and ought to be observed by us, in order that we may obey God's plain, repeated, and most strict command of Christian unity—a command in which the highest and most important interests of the poor and ignorant are especially concerned. **At present**, need I say? we are living in the most careless and most flagrant violation of that command. And what if it should be the will of God that the poor and ignorant should **ere long** become the instruments to take His vengeance upon those who are comparatively rich, and who are, or might be, better informed, unless we will seek to enter upon some sounder, **more obedient, and** more Scriptural course? And let us not be told **that** having gone on for so long in our present path, **it is now** hopeless to escape from it; or that **bad as** our existing separations are, we **must** be content to make the best of them. Let us rather assure ourselves that no duration of time can give a prescriptive right to what is wrong in the sight of God. The whole history of the Jewish people, for upwards of a thousand years, is a continued proof that God is willing and waiting to be gracious to nations that will repent and walk in the ways which He has appointed for them to walk in ; and that if they will not do so, their degradation, if not their utter ruin, is eventually inevitable.

Second evil consequence: —Undue assumption of the right to Ordain.

2. **The second evil consequence** of our present state, or, in other words, of our disregarding the principle of a uniform Christian ministry, is one which if consciously admitted, would involve a still graver offence against the divine law ; viz. the offence not of discord and division only, but of injustice, of usurpation. For is not this offence committed when the power of Ordination is assumed otherwise than according to the ' authoritative example ' which we find in the New Testament, and to the unquestionable rule, and standing practice— for fifteen centuries, as we think, the invariable practice— of the universal Church, which assigns that power to the highest order of the threefold ministry ? Again and again the opponents of prelacy have been challenged to show the record of a single authentic and indisputable instance of non-episcopal ordination in the entire history of the Church *before the Reformation* ; and—must it not be said ?—no *such* [1]

---

[1] On the several *disputed* instances which have been produced—viz. (a) of Ischyras, ordained by Colluthus, but deposed; (b) of the abbot Daniel ; (c) of the Goths and Scots; (d) of the power of the chorepiscopi ;—see Bingham, book ii. c. iii. 7, and c. xiv. 6 ; Potter ' On Church Gov.,' p. 265 sq.; Hughes, in Hickes' ' Treatises,' vol. iii. pp. 339-355 ;

instance has been produced. I will not undertake to say that no weight whatever is to be attached to the negative evidence which may be derived from the Epistle of Clement to the Corinthians, or of Polycarp to the Philippian Church; or again to the positive statements—such as they are—of Jerome at the end of the fourth, or of Eutychius, at the beginning of the tenth century; all of which have been referred to in my last lecture. But I cannot admit that these few particles of evidence, taken even at their highest estimate, deserve to be placed for a moment in comparison with the overwhelming mass of authority which is to be reckoned on the other side. I am also aware that *for more than a century after the Reformation,* i.e. down to the Restoration in 1660, even in England—to say nothing of this country, in which some of our leading reformers were not ordained at all—cases occurred in which presbyterian ordination, received abroad (where no Reformed bishops [1] were to be found), was recognised and admitted as sufficient by individual bishops, though not, I believe, by any law or action of the Church itself.

See above, p. 161 sq., and p. 164 sqq.

Thorndike, 'Right of Church,' &c., vol. i. pp. 493-500; 'Irenicum,' pp. 379-382. See also Lightfoot, p. 230 sq.; and add the case of Liudger, the Saxon missionary, mentioned by Hardwick, 'Church Hist.,' p. 26, note.

[1] In all such cases therefore there had not been any conscious or intentional preference of presbyterian ordination, and still less any intentional opposition to Reformed episcopacy. Only more stress had been laid upon emancipation from papal error and usurpation than upon the strict observance of ceremonial regularity. This important consideration is too often overlooked. See an article by Principal Tulloch in the 'Contemporary Review,' January 1872. Compare below, p. 222, note 3.

But before we enter further upon the Church's witness in regard to this most solemn and important matter, which St. Chrysostom has justly called τὸ κυριώτατον πάντων, *the most sovereign instrument of all for maintaining the unity of the Church,*[1] let us enquire what is the guidance and authority concerning it which we may derive directly from the Word of God.

Scriptural evidence concerning Ordination.

First, then, we see that the apostles ordained 'the seven,' supposed deacons (Acts vi. 6). Next, we see that the apostles **Paul and** Barnabas ordained presbyters (xiv. 23). Then, we see that Paul ordained Timothy *with*, but not[2] *by*, the laying on of the hands of the presbytery ; just as bishops now ordain presbyters, admitting other presbyters to lay on their hands simultaneously (2 Tim. i. 6, 1 Tim. iv. 14). Moreover, we see that Timothy himself, as supposed bishop of Ephesus, is empowered to ordain presbyters and deacons ; but we do not see that the Ephesian presbyters had any **such power of themselves,** however they might have been **permitted** to join in that solemn action (1 Tim. v. 22, iii. **1–10). In like** manner **we see that** Titus, as supposed bishop of Crete, is empowered to ordain ;[3] but we do not see that a Cretan presbytery had **any** such power (Tit. i. **5–7).**

---

[1] In Ep. i. ad Tim., Hom. xvi. vol. xi. p. 691.

[2] Stillingfleet, 'Irenicum,' p. 271, has fallen into this mistake. Comp. p. 275, where he asks, 'If the presbytery had **nothing to do,** to what purpose were their **hands laid** upon him?' We answer, they had something to do—in **the** way of dutiful concurrence **and** brotherly recognition, but **not** of primary action or direct authority—as they still have in **our own** ordinal. See the bishop of Salisbury's ' Bampton Lect.,' p. 209 sq.

[3] But see **above,** p. 166, note.

Lastly—and this is the only other remaining instance of ordination recorded in the New Testament—we see that among five so-called 'prophets and teachers' at Antioch— Barnabas, Simeon or Niger, Lucius, Manaen, and Saul—the first and last were ordained, in consequence of a special revelation and command of the Holy Ghost to that effect, by the other three (Acts xiii. 1–3). But this was a case so special and extraordinary that they are said to have been 'sent forth by the Holy Ghost' (Ibid. 4), and St. Paul expressly declares that he was an 'apostle,' or one sent out, '*not* by man, but by Jesus Christ and God the Father' (Gal. i. 1 ; comp. Acts xxvi. 17). The whole proceeding, I say, plainly belongs to those extraordinary ministrations in which the Holy Spirit, during the infancy of the Church, manifestly interposed so as to supply what was afterwards to be obtained by the regular action of the ordinary ministry. And may we not suppose that though the form of ordination, in order to mark its obligatory character, was not to be omitted even in a privileged case like that of St. Paul—as it had not been omitted by our Lord Himself in the no less privileged case of 'the traitor'—there was a special intention in giving to the great *apostle of the Gentiles* a sanction which should be at once equally divine, and, so far as it was primary, altogether independent of the *apostolate of the Jews,* 'the Twelve,' as we know, being all of that nation ?[1]

---

[1] The election (by lot, before the day of Pentecost) of Matthias into the place of Judas, indicated the *necessary continuation of the apo-* *stolic office.* This appointment of Barnabas and Saul (who are thenceforth also called apostles), after James, the brother of John, had

Such, then, is the guidance which we receive **from** Scripture itself. There is no text which gives any direction or authority to presbyters to ordain ; but direction and authority to that effect are given to two several individuals—to Timothy and to Titus—who we know had presbyters under them ; and as, it appears, the authority in question was **not** given to presbyters, so neither, so far as we read in the New Testament, did they attempt to exercise it.

Nor is there, as I have already said, any well-authenticated instance in the history of the Church of their being allowed so to do till the time of the Reformation. Hooker—whom no one will accuse of speaking either ignorantly or at random—declares expressly : ' No man is able to show either deacon or presbyter ordained by presbyters, and his ordination accounted lawful, in any ancient part of the Church.' [1]

<hr />

been slain by **Herod (Acts** xii. 2), indicated not **only its necessary** continuation, **but** its *necessary extension in number beyond twelve :—* thus pointing **to an enlargement** which would eventually be co-extensive **with the** universal episcopate. A fundamental act of this kind in **the** constitution of **the Church,** coupled **as it** was with the first great mission **to the Gentiles,** might seem to require **the** same direct sanction of divine authority, **in the person of** the Holy Spirit, **as that which** Christ Himself had **exercised in His** own person upon **earth in the ap**pointment of the original twelve, **and** as He afterwards exercised less directly (through lot) in the appointment of Matthias.

[1] **Book vii.** c. vi. sect. 5, vol. iii. **p. 170. See** also Overall, ' Convoc. **Book,' pp.** 150, 156 ; Pearson, Minor **Theol.** Works, i. pp. 274, 289 ; ii. p. 75, 232. Compare 'Irenicum,' p. 382, **and** Professor Lightfoot, p. 231 : ' As a general rule, even those writers who maintain a substantial identity in the offices of bishop and presbyter, reserve the **power** of ordaining to the former.'

And Gibbon, who may be trusted upon the matter of fact, thus writes concerning the age of Constantine, that is, the early part of the fourth century : ' The Catholic Church was administered by the spiritual and legal jurisdiction of 1,800 bishops, of whom one thousand were seated in the Greek, and eight hundred in the Latin provinces of the empire ; ' and he adds, in his usual style of ill-disguised irreverence when he has occasion to speak of religious matters: ' the bishops alone possessed the power of spiritual generation ' (c. xx.)—meaning that the ordination of clergy was confined exclusively to them.[1]

How came it, then, to pass that this universal practice of the Church was first interrupted in some parts of Western Christendom (in the East it has never been interrupted) at the time of the Reformation ? It came to pass, if we are to believe no less an authority than Hallam, because ' the foreign reformers had neither *the wish,* nor possibly the means, to preserve ' an episcopal ministry.[2] If by ' foreign reformers ' our author meant, as most readers would suppose him to mean, the first authors and most illustrious champions

---

[1] See Epiphanius adv. Hær., lxxv. sect. 4, vol. i. p. 908, and St. Chrysostom on 1 Tim. iv. 14, vol. xi. p. 672. Even St. Jerome restricts the right of ordination to bishops. See above, p. 176. Blondel (p. 311 sq.) supposes that he is speaking there only with reference to his own time ; but this is unreasonable. For if he had known that presbyters, even in the most ancient times, had been allowed to ordain, it is certain he would have said so in an argument where his purpose was to represent presbyters as equal to bishops.

[2] See 'Const. Hist.,' vol. i. p. 137.

of the foreign Reformation, in other words, of original
Protestantism, I am sorry to say, he has stated what is not
correct. What their 'means' may have been is one thing;

Wish of the
original
Protestants
to retain
Ordination
by bishops.
what their 'wishes' were is another. And if their own words
are to be trusted, it is certain that their 'wishes' were the
very reverse of that which the words I have quoted would
lead us to suppose. In the 'Apology for the Confession of
Augsburg,' drawn up by Melancthon in 1531 (eleven years
after the excommunication of Luther by the Pope), and
adopted by the whole Protestant body, we read as follows :—

'With respect to canonical (i.e. episcopal) ordination, we
have often professed before the Diet, that it is our most
earnest wish and desire (nos summâ voluntate cupere) to preserve the ecclesiastical polity and orders in the Church. . .
But the bishops,' that is, the unreformed papal bishops,
'either compel our clergy to renounce and anathematise the
doctrine which we have set forth in our confession, or they
put them to death with the utmost cruelty and injustice.
This is the reason which prevents our clergy from ac-
knowledging these bishops. This is the cause why the
canonical Church government, which we for our part *most
anxiously wished* to preserve (nos magnopere cupiebamus
conservare), has in some places ceased to exist.'[1] I admit
there is evidence (especially in the 'Smalcald Articles,' and
in the treatise 'de Primatu Papæ,' both drawn up in 1537)
that the Lutheran party, smarting under continued provoca-

---

[1] Cap. vii. Hase, p. 204. The few lines further on in the same
s me 'wish' is again expressed a chapter.

tion, began to waver in their recognition of the abstract right of an episcopal ministry ; but I am also prepared to show that to the very close of Luther's life their prevailing sentiment was such as that which I have just exhibited. It is sufficient to refer to their *ultimatum*, presented to the elector of Wittenberg on January 14, 1545, and to the correspondence which took place at that time, when the struggle had been carried on between them and their opponents for nearly thirty years. They then wrote, *inter alia* : ' Nothing seems more likely to promote harmony, than *restoring to the bishops ordination*, which has always been accounted their chief, or single, function.' [1] And in the manifesto itself which bears the subscription of Luther, Melancthon, and five others, these words occur : ' We are as little disposed as any men to dissolve or weaken the constitution and government of the Church ; and it is our *anxious wish* (valdè optamus) that the bishops and their colleagues in that government would truly discharge the duties of their calling, in which case we offer them our obedience. . . In short, *there is no other way* to a holy concord than this, that the bishops should embrace the true doctrine of the Gospel, and the right use of the sacraments, and *that we should obey them as the governors of the Church, to which we pledge ourselves.* [2] Luther died in the year after he had set his name to this remarkable document.

It is evident from these extracts that the greatest of the

[1] Seckendorf, 'Hist. Luth.,' ii. p. 538.

[2] Ibid., p. 531. See also the testimony of the prince of Anhalt, quoted in ' Irenicum,' p. 409.

foreign reformers not only 'wished' (contrary to Hallam's misrepresentation) to retain an episcopal ministry; but that they would not have considered themselves justified in ordaining as presbyters, if they could have obtained ordination for their adherents from a reformed episcopate. And for my own part, I have no doubt they would have regarded ordination, practised under the circumstances in which presbyterian ordination is now practised in this country, to be no less a usurpation than the papal usurpation against which they strove.

Contrary determination of the Westminster Assembly.
The difficulties which beset the members—especially the presbyterian members—of the Westminster Assembly in the following century were of another kind. Our presbyterian brethren at the present day are wont to boast of their zealous *Protestantism*; and they are apt to think that we 'episcopalians' fall short of them in this respect. But it is certain that their forefathers' still accepted guides, the Westminster divines, departed much further than we have ever done from the principles maintained by the first and true *Protestants*—by Luther, by Melancthon, and even by Calvin [1]

---

[1] See his treatise 'De Necess. Reform. Eccles.,' 1544, quoted above, p. 139, and his 'Letter to the King of Poland,' 1554, Epist., p. 191. See also the narrative of the proposals made by him and Bullinger to King Edward VI. in 1549, in Strype's 'Life of Parker,' i. p. 140; 'Life of Cranmer,' i. p. 296; and Bramhall's Works, iii. p. 483. I am quite aware that views of a different character (such as his own irregular office and position rendered necessary) are to be found in other parts of Calvin's works, especially those of an early date. See Cook's 'History of Reform.,' ii. p. 380, note.

—on the question of the right constitution of the Christian ministry. In their **zeal and impatience to** destroy prelacy root and branch—as they solemnly pledged themselves to do, before they had begun to examine the Scriptural authority upon which it rests [1]—**they made apostles to be** wholly **extraordinary** ministers; they made Timothy and Titus to **be wholly extraordinary** ministers; they made ' prophets' to **be** wholly extraordinary ministers. Thus they deprived themselves of every text, of every Scriptural example, upon which they could found the continuance of ordination. The divines of **the Assembly,** who were champions of Independency, were not slow to observe this, and they secretly rejoiced over the confusion which it caused among their presbyterian opponents, while it gave the utmost advantage to their own system, their own theory of ordination, which they proposed to derive not from above, but from **below;** **not** from the institution of Christ, through His apostles, but from the will and choice of the congregation—a revolution **of all** previous principle and **practice in the Church, for which the** presbyterian divines, hostile as they were to all **apostolical** succession except **in their own** order, were not **prepared.** Nothing can, I had almost said, be more melancholy—nothing certainly can **be more** unsatisfactory to a Christian mind—than to see the manner in which **the two** parties of disputants **quarrelled over the prey—the sacred** privilege of **ordination—of which they** had combined to

---

[1] **See above,** Lecture i. p. 78.

despoil the rightful possessors. 'After a keen and even stormy debate of fourteen days' duration, the subject was laid aside, in compliance with the request of Lord Say, who favoured the Independents.' This is the account of Dr. Hetherington,[1] a stanch Presbyterian, as derived from the journal of Lightfoot,[2] who, being a member of the Assembly, was present at the discussion.

Promise now required in presbyterian ordination.

It appears, then, that by presbyterian ordination, *except under circumstances of extreme necessity* [3] *which may be thought to justify it,* bishops are deprived of their undoubted right —of their special prerogative in the Christian ministry— given to them not for their own pride or pleasure, but for the benefit of the Church upon the grounds which I explained in my first lecture. But what are the circumstances under which presbyterian ordination is now administered in this country? Only under a pledge upon the part of the recipient that he will do nothing 'directly or indirectly' to the prejudice or subversion of presbyterianism; and under a profession of his belief that it is 'founded upon the Word

---

[1] 'Hist. of the Westminster Assembly,' 3rd edit., 1856, p. 175.

[2] First published in 1824. See pp. 114-131.

[3] This plea has generally been admitted in favour of foreign Protestants by the great Anglican divines down to the time of the Savoy Conference, 1661-62; e.g. by Hooker, 'E. P.,' vii. 15; Field, book iii. p. 157; Mason, 'Def. of Protest.,' Ordin., p. 139; Bishop Hall, vol. x. pp. 149-54, vol. xi. p. 21. And see the references in 'Irenicum,' p. 413. Since 1662 the Church of England, both by her own law and by the teaching of her best divines, has declined to be a party to a plea which has in fact ceased to be a real or sufficient one. Compare above, p. 213, note 1, and Bunsen's 'Church of Future,' p. 23.

of God and agreeable thereto.'[1]   Now consider what this
profession implies. To say that presbyterianism is 'founded
upon the Word of God and agreeable thereto,' is to say that
for fifteen centuries the universal Church misunderstood the
Word of God, or did not care to follow it. Is there no
responsibility incurred in making such an assertion, and in
requiring others to make it? It may be made in ignorance;
but can it be made with a due knowledge of the facts? and
is not a due knowledge of the facts incumbent upon all
who are to presume to make it, and still more upon all who
require it to be made? It is certain that every Church of
which we read in the New Testament was prelatical, and
that no Church was presbyterian, unless we are to separate
the apostles from the Churches which they founded, contrary
to the universally accepted principle of the primitive
Christians, and to the express teaching of the New Testament itself. It is equally certain that from the apostolic
times to the sixteenth century every Church whose history
is known to us is seen to have been prelatical; and that no
Church throughout the world, whose history is known to us,
is seen to have been presbyterian : and it is inconceivable
that this should have been the case if presbyterianism were
really founded upon the Word of God, or agreeable thereto ;
however the authors and promoters of it, provoked by papal
corruptions or actuated by political discontent, may have
persuaded themselves into this conviction ; and some of

---

[1] See above, Lect. ii. p. 195 sq.

them, by degrees, into the conviction, still more monstrous, which condemned and sought to extirpate prelacy as contrary to God's Word. It is also certain, as I have shown See pp. 218-220. above, that the first and ablest of the reformers, such as Luther, Melancthon, and even Calvin, *drifted into presbyterianism from a supposed necessity, and not from choice*—a necessity which they openly avowed and regretted ; but is it to be conceived that they would have expressed such regret had they believed that system to be 'founded upon the Word of God, and to be agreeable thereto'? Once more, if presbyterian ordination had been 'founded upon the Word of God, and agreeable thereto,' can we conceive that it would have been disallowed, not only by the Church of Rome, and all the Churches of the East, but by the Church of England and its affiliated branches throughout the world?[1] Must we not ask, then, under such circumstances : Is it right, is it just, to require of young men entering upon the Christian ministry not only to accept a position which has no distinct Scriptural or historical basis, but *to bind themselves for ever to maintain a system which places them in virtual and irretrievable antagonism to an array of testimony and of authority, so vastly great and so nearly, if not absolutely, unanimous?* For what is there to be set on the other side ? Are we to be referred to the condition of continental presbyterianism—of Protestant Germany, or Holland, or Switzerland, or France — as giving either evidence of the past, or promise for the future,

---

[1] See above, **Lect.** ii. pp. 137-140.

sufficient to justify the course in question? If so, let us hear the testimony of one of the ablest German Protestants of modern times, who, while he was a devoted patriot, was also a most competent witness in all other respects. 'Long has it been clear to me,' wrote the late Baron Bunsen, 'that in Protestant Germany *no Church exists.* Pious individuals there are, standing singly. But *the Church itself is fallen and is destroyed.* How many a one is silently longing after a better order of things, or, may be, asking how should the Church be built up again? *Many a one in despair has become Romanist.'* Again, in another place, 'Our Church *has yet to be built.'* [1] Such, by the confession of this unexceptionable witness, is the result of three centuries of non-episcopal Protestantism in the land which gave it birth. On the other hand, when Bunsen had to speak of episcopal England, he called it 'the bulwark of religion and of civil liberty.' And again, 'One cannot cease to cling with heart and mind to that country, with which the freedom and the glory of the Reformation would perish.' [2]

I have dwelt long, and spoken strongly—not, I would hope, too strongly—upon this grave question ; and, before I quit it, let me say, in regard to individuals now living, how earnestly I desire to be understood as condemning no man, as accusing no man. If there be a wrong committed, it is committed, I am sure, without any evil purpose or design—

---

[1] 'Memoirs of Baron Bunsen,' vol. i. p. 181 and p. 418. Similar testimonies might be given respecting the state of Protestantism in the other countries named.

[2] Ibid., p. 464 and p. 354.

inadvertently, unconsciously. And all I would plead for is, that we should endeavour to bring about amendment in that for which no man living is directly responsible, and of which —having now the option of what is better—no wise or competently learned judge, as I venture to think, can thoroughly approve. I would even admit that though *fieri non debuit, factum valet* ; and accepting *the present,* as God Himself has manifestly accepted it, in its many fruits of love and of a lively faith, I would ask of God and man, *for the future,* in the words and in the spirit of the direction of St. Paul for the Church of Crete, and of the prayer of Bishop Andrewes for the Church of England [1]—ἐπιδιορθῶσαι τὰ λείποντα, ' to set in order *the things that are wanting.*' (Tit. i. 5.)

Third evil conse-
quence :—
Disuse of.
Confirma-
tion.

3. It has been frequently observed, that acts of aggression seldom stand alone, and that one false step commonly leads to another. This will be illustrated by the matter of which we have next to speak, viz. Confirmation. We read among the acts of the famous Glasgow Assembly of 1638, ' Concerning confirmation, ... seeing episcopacy is condemned, imposition of hands by bishops falleth to the ground.' [2] And

A Scriptural
ordinance.

yet, as we have shown that episcopacy is plainly Scriptural and apostolical, so we are prepared to show that the ordinance of confirmation rests upon the authority of Scripture, being mentioned in due order, after baptism, as among the fundamental 'principles of the doctrine of Christ' in Heb. vi. 1 ; and upon the practice of the apostles, as re-

[1] See Bishop Andrewes' ' Preces Privatæ,' p. 68 ; also pp. 96, 260.

[2] 'Acts of General Assembly,' p. 20.

corded concerning St. Peter and St. John in Acts viii. 14-17, and in Acts xix. 5, 6, concerning St. Paul. It is also attested by abundant evidence of ancient authors. I shall content myself with one quotation from St. Jerome, not only because it affords all-sufficient proof that, when he lived, confirmation was sanctioned and observed *universally* in the Church, but because it refutes what the same author has told us elsewhere respecting ordination, as if it were the single peculiar function of the episcopal office. The testimony appears in the course of a supposed dialogue between a Luciferian dissenter and an orthodox churchman; but this only brings out the fact which is stated on the one side, and admitted on the other, more strongly.

Universal in the Church. Testimony of St. Jerome.

' *Lucif.*—Know you not it is the practice of the Churches that to persons who have been baptized, the laying on of hands should be administered, and so the Holy Ghost invoked upon them? Do you ask *where* this is written? I answer, in the Acts of the Apostles. But even if it did not rest, as it does, upon the authority of Scripture, *the consentient practice of the whole Church to this effect would have the weight of a command.*

' *Orthod.*—Such, I grant, is the custom of the Churches, that to those who have been baptized by presbyters and deacons at a distance from the larger cities, the bishop goes out for the purpose of administering the laying on of hands, and of invoking the gift of the Holy Ghost.' [1]

---

[1] 'Adv. Lucifer,' c. viii. vol. ii. p. 164. A similar interpretation of that same passage of the Acts, above referred to, is given by St.

No one who is competent to judge can doubt that con-firmation is a very important ordinance, and would be calculated to do much good were it only of human Observed by Lutherans. Testimony of Bunsen. institution.[1]   Accordingly it is observed among Lutherans in many parts of Germany, even without a bishop. This ap-pears, for instance, from a work which I just now quoted, the lately published ' Memoirs of Baron Bunsen,' who, though as far removed as any man from the least tincture of super-stition, regarded the administration of this rite to the several members of his family, as they grew up, with the liveliest interest.[2] At the same time, that the practice among German Protestants is less general than it ought to be, or that not being episcopal it is not satisfactory at least to some, appears, from the complaint of the learned Lutheran Delitzsch in his Commentary upon the Epistle to the Hebrews vi. 2, where he asks, ' Can we suppose that the apostolic writer of this Epistle would represent *the laying on*

Cyprian, Ep. lxxiii. c. ix. ; and he adds, 'The same is now practised also among us.' See also St. Augus-tin, ' De Trin.,' xv. 26. ' In Epist. Joann.,' Tract., vi. 10. ' De Bapt. adv. Don.,' iii. 21.

[1] On the rite of confirmation, as *symbolising unity*, being adminis-tered by bishops only, see the author's Oxford Ramsden Sermon, for 1857, pp. 9-12 : ' It follows from what has been said, that if confirmation be neglected, it cannot

be otherwise but that schism will prevail. It cannot be otherwise but that *the nets will be broken*, and broken the more irreparably in proportion to the *neglect.*' The prevalence of dissent in England, and of sectarianism in America, is there traced to that neglect as it existed in former years.

[2] See ' Bunsen's Memoirs,' vol. i. pp. 315, 559 sq., 630, vol. ii. p. 17, note, 216, 352.

of hands, following after baptism, as among *the fundamentals of Christianity,* if it were not a holy ordinance and had not a divine promise annexed to it?' And then he adds: 'Unhappily, the Church of the present lacks many things in comparison with the Church of the first century; but that deficiency will only become greater, if it (i.e. the Church of the present) forms thereon mere theories, not to say empty dreams.' [1]

I hope I may be allowed to express a wish that our Presbyterian friends would lay these words to heart. I cannot but think that their ministers incur a very serious responsibility in withholding confirmation from the young. We strongly condemn in the Church of Rome the denying of the cup to the laity. I have no desire to press the two cases into a close comparison; but while I admit that the latter cannot be censured too severely, I am utterly at a loss to excuse the former. If the testimony which a clergyman of North America, who was once a Presbyterian minister, has published respecting one of his own children, be verified only in a single case out of many hundreds, the result would suffice to justify the ordinance, irrespective of our obligation to observe it on other accounts. The narrative is a touching one, and I give it you simply as I find it in the father's own words :—

Confirmation ought not to be withheld from the young.

'One of those little ones—the first that was given me, and the first that I gave the Church—is now among them that sleep in Jesus. In the glow of childhood, in her fifteenth

[1] Quoted by the Bishop of Lincoln, *in loc.*

year, she expressed the usual desire to be confirmed at the next visitation of the bishop. As her father was beyond the seas, her friends advised her to await his return. But with the grace already given her, she urged her request very importunately. . . . She was accordingly confirmed, under the most gratifying appearances of sincerity and earnestness. A new measure of the Spirit evidently rested upon her from that hour; she spoke in a sweeter tongue; she led a more heavenly life; not noisy but still, not ostentatious but retiring; not even conscious was she of the impression made upon her heart and life, nor of that impression so sweetly reflected upon those around her. . . . And such a life of gentleness and holiness, and self-denial and prayer and humble usefulness, it has never been my lot to know in one so young. And God has rewarded it. Within a year from the time that she knelt under the bishop's hands, she entered joyfully into the rest for which she had been unconsciously maturing, and was "so blessed, she blessed the hand of death." ' [1]

Fourth evil consequence: — Disuse of other catholic ordinances.

4. To proceed with my argument. Closely allied, as consequences flowing, more or less directly, from the abandonment of the threefold ministry, are :

a. The discontinuance of daily public worship.

b. The renunciation of the catholic observance of the great fasts and festivals of the Church, such as Advent, Christmas, Lent, Passiontide, Easter, Ascension, Whitsuntide.

---

[1] 'A Presbyterian Clergyman looking for the Church,' p. 95.

c. The infrequency of administration of Holy Communion.

d. The disallowal of Communion to the sick and dying.

I trace all these to abandonment of what I venture to call the legitimate ministry, because, wherever that abandonment has taken place, such results will be found to have ensued in a greater or less degree. There may appear at first sight to be no connexion between the threefold ministry and (for example) liturgical worship. But in truth the connexion is not far to seek. A system which claims to be more or less directly of divine institution, as compared with one which is of human origin, will naturally inspire greater reverence in all our dealing with divine things ; and consequently will lead us to shrink from approaching the Majesty of God, in His solemn worship, through the extemporaneous effusions of each individual minister. Again: a system of graduated authority, as compared with parity among ministers (as we see in a monarchy compared with a republic) will no less naturally lead to the same result : and in the minister himself, there can scarcely fail to be less respect for an office which he has received from his equals, and a lower estimate of the value of its functions, except so far as they depend upon the exercise of his own personal gifts. Now either of these principles, and still more both combined, may suffice to account for each of those four results, which I just now specified as effects of the abandonment of the threefold ministry.

It was far from being the intention of our reformers in this country that the daily public worship, which had been celebrated in the churches before the Reformation, should alto-

Daily public worship ordered by Scotch reformers.

gether cease. In the first Book of Discipline (1560), though they did not attempt to enforce any general rule upon the subject, yet they expressly contemplate that 'some kirks might convene *every day*; some *twice*, some *thrice* in the week' (c. xi.). And in 'the short Sum' of the same book, 'for the Instruction of Ministers and Readers in their Office,' they go further : 'In towns we require (they say) *every day* either sermon or public prayers, with some reading of Scriptures.' And again: 'In every notable town we require that at the least once in the week *beside the* Sunday, the

Origin of its disuse.

whole people convene to the preaching' (c. x.). But when liturgical worship came to be superseded, as it did very soon under the new system, by prayer more or less extempo-raneous, the greater effort and the necessity for at least some preparation, which this latter practice would in almost all cases impose upon the minister—together with di-minished regard for public prayer itself simply as such [1]—produced the neglect which now, I believe, everywhere pre-vails of all stated provision for week-day services. The same causes—that is, on the one hand, lack of reverence, cloaking itself under the dread of superstition, in regard to the use of all things sacred and of the ministry itself ; and, on the other hand, the greater difficulty in meeting the require-

---

[1] Dr. R. Lee testified, not long since, that the sermon had come to be regarded as 'the grand centre' of the whole service, 'the other acts being considered as mere *garnish-ing.*'—*Reform of the Church of Scot-land,* p. 11.

ments of all special occasions in the absence of prescribed
liturgical forms—these causes, I say, have brought about Other defects traced
to the same
cause.
also the other consequences to which I just now referred,
viz. the non-observance of the great fasts and festivals;[1] the
sad infrequency[2] 'of the breaking of bread,' so unlike the
practice of the primitive Christians, as recorded in the New
Testament; and the disallowal of it altogether except to
those who can attend the public Communion on the rare
occasions when it is administered. Far be it from us to
boast as if the threefold ministry, wheresoever it is exercised,
either among ourselves or elsewhere, could be acquitted of
all deficiency in these respects. But this at least may be
said with truth. Breathing as we do in this country an
atmosphere which unhappily is most unfavourable to all
such usages; still there is, I believe, no diocese in which the
prediction of the Psalmist is not publicly fulfilled, that in
the days of the Messiah 'prayer should be made for Him
continually, and daily should He be praised' (Ps. lxxii. 15);

---

[1] They were repudiated in the first 'Book of Discipline' (c. i.), which things, among other observances there condemned as 'inventions of the Papists, because in God's Scriptures they neither have commandment nor assurance, we judge them utterly to be abolished from this realm; affirming further that the obstinate maintainers and teachers of *such abominations* ought not to escape the punishment of the civil magistrate' (!). The observance of the great holidays is based upon Scriptural principles, as well as upon the authority of the Church. See above, p. 12.

[2] 'I should hail with thankfulness . . . . a more frequent dispensation of the Holy Communion (in not a few parishes there is yet, shamelessly, but the single annual celebration)—say, quarterly, or at least three times a-year.'—Dr. John Wylie's *Pastoral Reminiscences*, 1868, p. 324.

no diocese in which there is not at least one church wherein the lamp of God is trimmed, and the spiritual incense ascends from day to day, according to the practice of the Church, Jewish and Christian, from the beginning; and where intercession is made for all the rest, and for the whole of Christ's body militant throughout the world.

London and Edinburgh compared.

And if we compare episcopalian London with presbyterian Edinburgh in this respect, what is the result? In and around London (as appears from a statistical record for the present year, 1869) there are 588 churches, and of these there is *daily service* in more than one-fifth—that is, considerably more than 100; and *weekly administration of the Holy Communion* at nearly one-fourth of the same churches.[1] Who can tell how much the safety of the British Empire throughout the world may depend upon these acts of public worship in its great metropolis? In Edinburgh, and even in Glasgow with its venerable Cathedral, among all the Presbyterian denominations, including the Established Church, there is not, I believe, a single place of worship which is opened daily; or, as a rule, on any day but Sunday for public prayer.

Furthermore, with respect to the rarity of Holy Communion, I am tempted to observe that this is one of the many instances, in which there is practically a meeting of

[1] See 'Mackeson's Guide to the Churches of London and its Suburbs.' The same 'Guide' for 1872 represents a considerable increase both in daily services and weekly Communions. See also the testimony of 'Pietas Londinensis,' 1712, in regard even to the last century.

extremes between popery and presbyterianism. In the present case I attribute the coincidence to the exaggeration of
the true form and character of the Christian ministry and
of its divinely ordered functions on the one hand ; and to
their equally undue diminution and depreciation on the other.
It is well known that the infrequency of lay communicating
—rendered only more glaring by the constant private Masses
of the priests—came, as a general practice, into the Church of
Rome when the clergy had assumed ultra-sacerdotal powers ;
and when all that was said or read in public worship was in a
tongue not commonly understood. The same infrequency
as regards not the people only but the ministers also came
into Protestant communities when the sacred ministry had,
in a great measure, denied itself, by sharing its sacred
functions with lay presbyters ; and, as if secretly conscious
of its inherent defects, it shrunk from the assertion of the
true doctrine and practice of the Sacramental Ordinances of
the Gospel ; till at length the public recital of the Lord's
Prayer, and of the Catholic Creeds, and even the reading of
the inspired volume itself, had been commonly discontinued.[1]

The failures and deficiencies which I have been led to
notice, not (God knows) as desiring to seek occasion for
censure, but simply in order to carry out and complete the
argument upon which we are engaged, are such as men would

---

[1] See Dr. Lee's 'Reform, &c.,' p. 11, 31, 80. It is but just to say, in regard to the first and last of the three particulars, mentioned above, that great improvement has taken place of late years ; and perhaps the statement quoted, made as it was with reference to the earlier part of the present century, may have been somewhat exaggerated.

not readily acquiesce in, if they related to the comforts and accommodations of this present life. As it is, they relate to things of infinitely more importance. The question then occurs—Shall no effort be made to remedy or amend them, when their continuance cannot be otherwise than a cause to many of just dissatisfaction—it may be also to some of grave disaster? Again, be it remembered that we have been speaking only of a system, and its seen results, as testified by those who were themselves adherents of it.

Fifth evil conse-
quence :—
Alienation
of endow-
ments from
purposes
intended
by the
donors.
5. There is, proceeding from the same cause, another consequence by which wrong—though doubtless, it must be said, legalised wrong—is committed, and that, in regard not only to things moral and spiritual, but material also. I will not refer to the building of churches by Episcopalians formerly, which are now held by Presbyterians; nor to the founding of exhibitions at the Universities for our advantage which are now applied to the benefit of Presbyterians; but I will ask what is the history of the foundation of some portion at least of those professorships—I mean the theological—which alone are now reserved to the Established Church, and from which, therefore, we are excluded? For example, of the four professorships in the faculty of divinity at the University of Aberdeen, three were founded under episcopacy, viz. in 1616, 1620, and 1674; and, we may reasonably infer, for episcopalian purposes. Is it fair—is it right—that the chairs of these professorships [1] should be now used to instil into the minds

---

[1] Even the lay professors are still required (by the Act of 1853) to declare solemnly, that in the discharge of their office they will never,

of young candidates for the sacred ministry principles and sentiments more or less hostile to episcopacy, and consequently not only to us and to our system, but also *to the system of the Church of England*? Must it not be admitted that if we are wrong, and are in consequence deprived of the inheritance which our forefathers provided for us, then the Church of England is also wrong; and if the Church of England is right, then are we also right; or at least not so far wrong, that we deserve to be trampled on and despoiled? Neither will it suffice to compare with spoliation such as that under which we suffer the case of the ante-Reformation endowments taken from the Church of Rome. The nation, as a body, had waked up to the conviction—a sound and just conviction—that the Church of Rome, whatever it might be and do in Italy, in this country was, and was exercising, not only a usurped but an anti-national authority; which authority, therefore, and the instruments that upheld it, might and ought to be taken away. I need not say that nothing of the kind ever has been or could be alleged against ourselves.

6. I pass on to notice a sixth evil consequence which must always ensue more or less wherever separation abounds; and which, as is only too obvious, prevails in this country to a lamentable extent—I allude to the evident waste of power and of the means of doing good, of all kinds, when in

directly or indirectly, teach anything opposed to . . . . the Westminster Confession of Faith.

a case where a single ministry would have sufficed, especially in country districts, four or five ministers are to be found, drawing the perplexed and bewildered people so many different ways;[1] while they themselves (a further unhappy consequence) are reduced in many instances to a state bordering upon penury,[2] without the possibility of making fit provision for their families ; so that their positions have come to be spoken of jestingly as 'not *livings* but *starvings.*' And to say the truth—though it may sound as if spoken with undue bitterness—it is only well that we should all be starved, like discordant jurymen on a trial for life and death, until we can bring ourselves to agree better than we now do upon the momentous verdict which, in a general sense, it is our office to deliver. Yes; if our mutual charity be *starved*, if we be *straitened*, as St. Paul speaks, *in our own bowels*, it is no more than just that we should be straitened also in the nourishment which they crave. We meet indeed with but little commiseration, and—must it not be said?—we deserve less.[3]

---

[1] 'While there is in some places an enormous waste of Christian energy, owing to several sects overlapping and embarrassing each other, in others fields white unto the harvest are not touched by a single sickle.' — *Report of Committee of Church of Scotland on Christian Life and Work*, presented at General Assembly, May 20, 1870.

[2] On the necessity of a due provision for the ministers of religion, see Barrow's 'Consecration Sermon,' vol. i. p. 318.

[3] Let the reader weigh well the statements made in the following testimony :—

'While our country is overchurched at so great an expense, *the spiritual destitution of the land is year by year increasing.* As steadily as the churches grow in

7. To these considerations connected with a ministerial supply, which **is excessive** because beyond the requirements of the population, **it may** be added that the levelling of ranks among the clergy, consequent upon the discontinuance of the three orders, has involved the lowering of their social position, and the withdrawal of all those dignities and distinctions which, sometimes combining leisure **(more or less) with** emolument, were wont to be spoken of as 'prizes' in **the** Church. In other words, the system of presbyterian parity has a tendency to destroy, and has actually destroyed, not only the inducements, but also the opportunities of high clerical cultivation.[1] **This at a time when** learning, in at

number, the wave of ignorance, and poverty, and irreligion rises higher and higher. In five-and-twenty years the churches have nearly doubled; and as one of the most natural functions of a church is the care of the poor, we might argue that poverty must have diminished in a corresponding ratio. Yet what is the fact? *The cost of maintaining the poor has increased from* 300,000*l.* *to* 900,000*l.* ; and though it would be rash to assert that they were long ago adequately maintained, *they were yet in a better state than to-day.* More than a thousand schools have been added during that period, yet the unwelcome assertion stares us in the face that 90,000 children are growing up without school instruction. Glasgow, with 196 churches, has a population outside all these churches of 130,000. Edinburgh, with 20 churches too many, has made public confession that its poor are unrelieved, and that 40,000 or 50,000 are living without any ordinances of religion. *These are awful facts to ponder—especially for Presbyterians.* For we do not hesitate to lay the blame of them very much at their door. Ask anyone for the explanation of this state of matters, and the answer is immediately given—THE DISSENSIONS OF THE CHURCHES.'—*The Glasgow Herald*, April 1870.

[1] The want of a high-class indigenous theological literature in Scot-

least some portion of the clergy, is more than ever required, is a serious loss. And the same cause has led to a further evil, scarcely less to be deplored. I allude to the fact that the office of the ministry has come to be filled almost exclusively out of one, viz. the middle class, and not always by the most talented and most enterprising of that class, because to such at the present day openings more promising and more remunerative are presented in other lines of life. This is a result which operates in various ways most injuriously upon the whole body of society. It has commonly sent the younger sons of the Scottish gentry and aristocracy to seek their fortunes in India;[1] whereas, had they remained at home and become clergymen (as is the case very generally with persons of a corresponding condition in England), they might have done incalculable good by assisting to draw together all classes of the population throughout the country, and in some instances, at least, would doubtless have exhibited (as is seen in England among clergy of that class)

land has often been lamented by Presbyterians themselves. Much has been done to supply the defect by translations from German divines. And it must not be forgotten that the valuable 'Ante-Nicene Library' is due not only to the enterprise of Scottish publishers, but to the learning and scholarship of Scottish editors, though one of them till recently was located in England.

[1] Mr. Bright, in his speech at Edinburgh, November 3, 1868, observed that 'nearly all Scotchmen know something about India, especially what are called the more comfortable and wealthier classes: for there is hardly one of their families which has not sent some members out to make their fortune in that distant country.' The cause of this will be found mainly, I believe, in the presbyterianism of this country, which has thus benefited India at the expense of the fatherland.

the best examples of clerical efficiency, combined with clerical self-denial. Upon this and other accounts it is not too much to say that presbyterianism could never have produced that humblest, holiest specimen of an English parish priest, the high-born author of ' The Country Parson.' [1] On the other hand, it would be desirable, perhaps, for the Church of England that a larger proportion of her clergy should be drawn from the middle class. The truth is that the Church, in order to do her work effectually, requires for her ministers men from all classes. She requires men of gentle blood, of refined taste, who will be able to speak at once with acceptance and with authority to the rich and powerful; but she also requires men who, from their own experience, will know how to enter into the wants and sympathise with the feelings of those whose lot is cast in different and even opposite circumstances. Happily, in this country there is no lack of admirable examples of the latter description; but for the former, it must be confessed, we have to look almost in vain. And yet, in a state of society in which the aristocratical element prevails so largely as it does amongst ourselves, it cannot be otherwise than a serious disadvantage when the ministers of religion have little or no direct personal connexion with that element.[2]

8. A further evil consequence, not yet fully developed,

[1] See Barnabas Oley's Preface, c. v.

[2] See the valuable remarks in Burke's ' Reflections on the French Revolution.' Works, vol. v. pp.

194 sq., 295. And upon the subject of this section generally, comp. Hooker, ' E. P.,' book vii. cc. xvi.-xxiv.

Eighth
evil conse-
quence :—
Difficulty
in dealing
with the
great ques-
tion of
national
education.

but threatening to become so more and more, the longer we
remain in our present state, is the supposed necessity of
dealing with education in such a way, that in order to render
it national or general, we must make it *irreligious*, or at least
must *separate it from religion.* That this is no idle fear has
been made only too apparent by the bill upon that subject
recently[1] introduced into the House of Lords. The distinguished member of the Government who brought forward
that measure openly avowed its object in these words :—' It
is proposed,' he said, ' to cut off the connexion between
the education in Scotland and the tenets of any religion
taught there ;' and he proceeded to 'appeal to the various
religious bodies in this country to lay aside their differences
and dissensions,' in order to co-operate with the promoters
of the bill in effecting such a result. I too have appealed—
and I now appeal again—to our various religious bodies to
lay aside their differences and dissensions, but with a very
different aim. Doubtless it is better—and so far I agree
with the resolutions of the Glasgow Committee of the 24th
April last—doubtless it is better that our schools should continue denominational, than that they should become merely
secular. But we in Scotland are fond of demanding the
express authority of Scripture for what we do in all such
matters. And where, I would ask, is the Scriptural authority for 'denominationalism'? Is not the very term itself

---

[1] The reader will bear in mind
that these lectures were written in
the earlier part of 1869. The remarks above remain unchanged, as
being equally applicable at the
present moment, February 1872.

no better than a piece of hypocrisy; used only because we are unwilling to call our various self-styled 'Churches' what St. Paul would have called them—so many schisms? Be this, however, as it may, it is certain that the legislative proposal which we now deprecate would never have been entertained if statesmen had not grown impatient, only too naturally, of our 'divisive courses;' and regarding them as a hopeless impediment in the way both of the necessary extension and improvement of education, they have resolved, after giving us full and repeated warning, to take the matter into their own hands.

It is now fifteen years ago since the first announcement of a bill, similar in its irreligious tendency to that which I just now alluded to, induced me to come forward and to found upon it an appeal similar to the appeal which I am making now; and the circumstances for the most part being still the same, I may be allowed perhaps to repeat a small portion of the public address which I then delivered.[1] The author's sentiments as expressed in the year 1854.

'I am quite unable'—I then said—'to express the forebodings I entertain respecting the momentous issues which are at stake in that measure'—the bill which was then before Parliament for the extension and amendment of our national education. 'Only let me say, if it pass into a law, Satan, our great enemy, will have gained an advantage over

---

[1] In the City Hall, Perth, May 4, 1854. What appears to the author the best solution of the religious difficulty in national education for Scotland under existing circumstances was stated by him in his Charge for last year, 1871, pp. 12–14.

us, such as I dread to contemplate. He it is, I believe, who has been foremost in raising the cry of the neglect of education, and in persuading us to appeal to our civil rulers for the remedy of the evil; not that he desires to see it remedied, but because he knows that any legislation which may be adopted, in deference to that discordant cry, will turn to his advantage; will tend to weaken still further the foundations of religious faith; to form a focus of still more bitter and unchristian animosity in every town and village throughout the land; to poison the well-spring of truth and godliness, by separating the young from the superintendence of their pastor; and, above all, to withdraw the keystone from the parochial system—that triumphal arch, against which his most fiendish spite will always be directed, because it records and contributes to maintain the victory of the Gospel over this and other Christian nations which he had formerly held in his own darkness and in the shadow of death.

'It is, I would humbly trust, in no other spirit than that of a Scottish patriot, of one who could weep over his adopted country when he sees that she is driving fast upon quicksands from which there can be no escape except with the wreck of her religious faith; it is in no other spirit than this that I venture to raise my voice, and entreat that legislation may be suspended, or carried no further than is absolutely necessary in the meantime for the maintenance and efficiency of the present system, until some greater measure of unanimity can be obtained, upon sound and settled principles, agreeable to the Word of God, which will warrant our legislation to be sound also. And where can we find these principles in our present divisions?[1]   O my brethren ! let us think whether, while we have been disputing in mistaken zeal about the royalty of Christ, we have not rather plaited a crown of thorns, and put it upon His head ! And now, if under the malignant influence of these dissensions, we shall go on to take from Him His little ones, to take from Him those concerning whom He has said, " Of such is the kingdom of Heaven ; " take them from the bosom of His Church, and give them over to the charge of that cruel stepmother, the starveling world ; give them to be educated by a master of any religion, or of no religion ; if, I say, we shall do this, what punishment, think you, will suffice to expiate our guilt?   Will war, will famine, will

---

[1] I desire to submit to the reader's earnest attention the following propositions :—

(*a*) It may be doubted whether separation from a true branch of the Church is justifiable *under any circumstances* :—1. Because it is contrary to the plain teaching of Scripture ; and, 2. Because the evil which it inflicts is sure to be greater, *in the long run*, than any good which it can hope to do.

(*b*) All the separations of which we have experience appear to have arisen from causes quite insufficient.

(*c*) They have all proceeded upon the false assumption (in dependence upon which the precepts of Scripture against separation have been set aside), that if the Church to which we belong does, or suffers to be done, what *we think in our consciences* to be evil, we become responsible for the evil, unless we separate ; whereas all we are responsible for is, to endeavour, by every lawful means, to withstand and correct it.

(*d*) The Reformation in the sixteenth century was not a separation on the part of the Reformers, but a rejection of usurped authority.

It is believed that a conscientious examination of these propositions would go far, by God's help, to enable us to see our way out of our divisions.

pestilence, will any or all of these [1] be a sufficient chastisement for a nation which has been so signally blessed, and which, notwithstanding, shall be so heartless, so ungrateful, as to adopt a system of education of which the very heathen would be ashamed?

The real character of Christian education.

'There was a time when the people of this country would not have endured that even a Scottish parliament should presume to legislate in regard to things spiritual. But now, it would seem, the Church has no alternative but to abdicate her office in favour of whatever law it may please Parliament to impose:—so short-sighted has been the wisdom, and so calamitous the zeal, with which we have taken on us to support the throne and royalty of Christ by ways that are none of His. For is not the education of Christians a spiritual thing? Is it not of all things the most spiritual? Is not the Holy Spirit Himself the Author of it? Is it not He who alone can order the unruly wills and affections of sinful men, or of weak, wayward children, so as to make either the one or the other to become dutiful, humble, chaste, temperate, truthful, pious, loyal—and so to fulfil the end of all true education? Yes; though *one* has declared recently, on a public occasion, that he can find no authority in the Word of God for assigning to the clergy the superintendence of education, as if the same divine voice which

---

[1] The address was delivered at the time of the appointment of a day for national humiliation, in consequence of the recent visitation of cholera, and of the Crimean War, in which we were then engaged.

commanded, "Feed my sheep," had not also commanded, "Feed my lambs;" and though *another* has jeeringly remarked that he sees no mention of schools in the New Testament, but "the school of one Tyrannus;" let us, my brethren, be persuaded that education is a *spiritual* thing. Yes; and let us not go further than we have already gone in breaking up the foundations of our faith as a Christian people; let us not require of our rulers in the State to do for us what our own divisions have rendered impossible to be done, except in a manner of which we shall soon find reason bitterly to repent; let us be assured that all the difficulties of the educational question have arisen out of these divisions, and that the more we attempt to extricate ourselves, while we persist in this sinful course, the deeper we shall sink into false principles, the more surely shall we bring down upon our heads the divine displeasure. How many questions have these dissensions already opened, which heretofore we should have been ashamed to entertain! How perplexing, and how melancholy, would be the report of all the arguments which have been urged upon the ministry of the day by the various deputations which have gone up from this country, each in turn endeavouring to impress upon them its own peculiar views! What might not our own children say of us when they see us so much confused, or, what is worse, so violently opposed to each other, in regard to the system by which they are to be educated! Would it not seem as if, while we are all so eager to promote their improvement, we ourselves have need that one teach us again which be the first principles of our duty both in Church and State?'[1]

Inserted
February
1872.

[Eighteen years have elapsed since the foregoing words were spoken, and still we find ourselves in the same or even greater perplexities; and our governors can suggest to us nothing wiser, nothing more worthy of our dignity and responsibilities, as a Christian people, than that religion should be cast out as a **bone** to the dogs, to become an occasion **of** so many sectarian conflicts and dissensions as **there** are to be so-called boards of education throughout the land.]

Such, then, are some of the evil consequences which have obviously arisen out of our abandonment of the principle of religious unity. There are others still remaining to **be** specified which extend even more widely, and will require us to take **a yet broader view.**

Ninth
evil conse-
quence :—
Practical
denial of the
character
of the
Church as
a corporate
institution.

9. Is it not then, I would venture to ask, a result deeply to be deplored by all its **true** members that the system of Christianity, **in its** practical aspects, is no longer seen in the character which its Divine Author intended it to bear—that

---

[1] 'A Parochial Schoolmaster' lately wrote to the 'Edinburgh Courant' (May 17, 1869): 'The facts of Scripture are very imperfectly learnt in the Sunday school, for there is in general such a *keen competition* to secure attendance that the children speedily come to think that they *confer an obligation on their teachers* by attending, and consequently consult their own inclinations in the matter of work.' I have reason to know that instances are not uncommon of children attending the Sunday schools of *two or three different denominations* on the same day with the view to some *material* advantage at the year's end.

is, a corporate character? Not only has the 'one Body' of
Christ become a monster of many bodies, but the corporation, which He designed to institute, is, in a manner, indi-
vidualised ; the 'members in particular' have come to be
everything, and the Body nothing. The 'communion of
saints' is still an article of the belief we profess, but is it an
article of the life we lead? And what is the result? A
large portion of the duty which the Scripture enjoins upon
us as Christians is not only not performed by us, but the
performance of it is rendered impossible. For example, the
Scripture lays down as a first principle of our membership
in Christ's mystical Body—which it also teaches is *one* and
undivided [1]—that if one member suffer, all the members
should suffer with it, or if one member be honoured, all the
members should rejoice with it (1 Cor. xii. 26). But is this
possible in our present state? Can the Established Churchman rejoice, when we Episcopalians prosper, or when the
Free Church prospers, or when the United Presbyterians
prosper? No! in reason and in conscience, we must
mutually desire not the prosperity, but the overthrow of
each other.[2] It is true, as individuals loving and esteeming
each other in many instances, we desire to escape from this
miserably false and unchristian conclusion, to which we are

Neglect of
relative
duties
unavoidable.

---

[1] 1 Cor. i. 13, xii. 12, 13, 27 ; Eph.
i. 23, iv. 4, 5, 12, 13, v. 23, 30 ; Col.
i. 24 ; Rom. xii. 5.

[2] I do not forget that St. Paul
had grace to 'rejoice' that Christ
was preached, though 'of envy and
strife' (Phil. i. 15-18) ; but there is
no reason to suppose that the *strife*
had led to formal separation, or
that it involved more than want of
due consideration and respect to St.
Paul personally.

practically shut up by our respective circumstances ; and, conscience-smitten at the sight of the deformity of the con- dition to which we are reduced, and desiring to throw the best veil over it that we can, we are fain to have recourse to various devices—such as the **Evangelical** Alliance, and miscellaneous prayer meetings, and interchange of *pulpits* between ministers who never meet at the *same table* for Holy Communion—in order to soothe, as we would hope, the yearnings of our hearts, and to allay the thirstings of our spirit, as in a dry land where no water is. But the experi- ence now of many years, utterly barren of all substantial fruit, may have sufficed to teach us that God will never suffer the devices of man to supply the place of His own ordinances ; while the inconsistency of our well-meant endeavours must have forced upon us the conviction at every turn that we were only throwing dust in each other's eyes : and some of us, it may be, in the consciousness of a participation in a self-imposed delusion, can scarcely refrain from smiling at each other; as **Cicero** supposes of the Roman augurs, when they chanced to meet. Again, there are duties—religious duties—which masters of a household owe to their servants, superiors to their dependents ; duties of example ; duties of teaching, of admonition, of warning ; duties of superintendence, of encouragement in their Chris- tian course : but how can any of these be fully and ade- quately discharged, when the Christian course, in which they respectively walk, in regard to the public profession and practice of religion, is not the same ; when the course in which the master walks is, perhaps, opposed to that in which the servant walks, and when the latter will be not unlikely to resent any interference upon the part of the former on that account? The disorganisation of domestic life, in too many instances, and especially of the wholesome relations between the upper and lower classes of society, consequent upon the prevalence of our religious divisions, is indeed one of the most bitter fruits of those divisions;[1] and akin to this is the diminished influence which, on the same account, and through fear of the mutual jealousies among us, ministers of the Gospel, as such, are, for the most part, allowed to exercise over all proceedings of a public character. Even in good works of a semi-sacred kind, such as the management of our infirmaries, the laity would seem to be unwilling, in some instances, to share with us the grave responsibility which they impose upon themselves; doubtless because they have seen reason to apprehend that greater embarrassment might arise out of our several differences than advantage from our common help. In this respect, at least, the disunion in England being comparatively less, the clergy there are still in a position to confer far greater benefits upon the whole community.

---

[1] See the conclusion of the Earl of Rosebery's inaugural address at the Philosophical Institution, November 4, 1871, in which he characterised class-separations as the crying evil of Scotland. 'A great page records the bloodless and prosperous history of the Scottish union (with England); a greater page *lies vacant before us* on which to inscribe *a fairer union still*;' i.e. of the classes of our population among themselves.

I must not quit this section of our present argument without alluding to the position which our sovereigns themselves are obliged to occupy in consequence of the disagreement between their Scotch and English subjects upon the matter which we are now considering. The ' Confession of Faith' would teach them, as a main part of their duty, 'to take order that *unity* and peace be preserved in the Church.'[1] But what is one of the first acts which we impose upon them, as a condition of their being allowed to ascend the throne? We require them to take two different oaths, by which they promise equally to uphold two ecclesiastical systems which, as they now exist, are confessedly irreconcileable. Thus they find themselves yoked to two professions which have proved their discordancy by their historical antagonism. They are placed in circumstances which *tempt*—nay, to a certain extent, *compel*—them to 'halt between two opinions.' Such a predicament can scarcely fail to be injurious both to those who are placed in it, and to the mass of the people who are liable to be influenced by the example of their rulers.[2] It obviously tends to impair their confidence in the unity and consistency of divine truth ; to foster the growth of indifferentism upon religious questions of other and, it may be, still more important, kinds ; to weaken the principles of the unstable ; to offend the consciences of the earnest-minded ; and, at the

[1] See Westminster Confession, c. xxiii. 3.

[2] 'What manner of man the ruler of the city is, such are all they that dwell therein.'—*Eccles.* x. 2. Comp. Cic. 'de Leg.,' iii. 24.

same time, to undermine the loyalty of all by diminishing the sentiments of esteem and veneration in which the monarchy itself is held. The evil had been comparatively dormant till these latter years ; but the frequent visits to this country of our gracious Sovereign who now reigns, and her own considerate desire to adapt herself, as far as possible, to the feelings of all her subjects, and the supposed demands of her position, have combined to force it upon public notice, and to compel us to regard it as a stumbling-block which (for her sake and for our own), we should desire to remove. For we cannot escape out of this dilemma. If it be indeed a matter of indifference, then unquestionably we do wrong to make it a subject of such solemn obligation ; if it be not indifferent, then we do wrong to constrain our rulers virtually to regard it as if it were, by obliging them to become equal supporters of both systems.

And the same evil operates in a greater or less degree upon a large proportion of our population ; more especially of the upper classes, who have ties and associations which bind and often draw them to England. Take the case of a landed proprietor who possesses large estates in both countries. He finds one form of religion established in the one country, and a different form established in the other. What is he to do? If he is an earnest and conscientious man, it is impossible that his sympathies should be with both those forms ; and not being bound, as the holder of the crown is, to be a *monstrum biforme* in religion—a Protestant of two denominations—it is not unlikely that he may choose to

Alienation of classes from each other.

belong to neither ; as we have recently seen in the case of a
young and promising nobleman, who being placed under such
circumstances, preferred to go over to the Church of Rome.

Tenth
evil conse-
quence :—
Greater
prevalence
of unsound
doctrine.
10. I shall touch but slightly upon the evil effect which,
as akin to the foregoing, I have next to specify ; not because
it is less deplorable than others—for there is none which, in
itself, is more injurious—but because among ourselves the
experience of it has been less manifest than elsewhere ; I
mean the more general prevalence of unsound and heretical
opinion (together with exaggeration of some portions of the
Truth and neglect or disparagement of others), which are
wont to take place when the true framework of the ministry
has been mutilated or renounced. No one who is acquainted with the history of continental Protestantism,
especially at Geneva, in Holland, and in parts of Germany,
can doubt that, following upon the disorganisation of the
Church's ministry, and upon the concurrent disuse (partial or
entire) of liturgical worship, there has arisen a laxity of doctrine which has wellnigh divested Christianity of all its distinctive truth.[1] That the same effect has not followed in this
country, or followed in a far less degree, I must be allowed
to think is due (through God's blessing) to the fact, that the
operation of the same causes has been kept in check, if not

---

[1] A correspondent of the 'Times,'
writing from Berlin, in August
1869, used these words : ' Three-
fourths of all educated men in
Germany are estranged from the
dogmatic teaching of the Christian
creed. . . . Only a small fraction of
the nation attends divine service.
. . . . Who that knows modern
Germany would call it *a Christian
land?* ' Compare the testimony of
Bunsen, as given above, p. 225.

by the presence among us, at least to some extent, of a reformed episcopal ministry, yet unquestionably by the powerful influence of the writings of the great English divines, and
of the English Prayer Book ; which have never ceased to act,
however secretly, yet with a most sure and salutary effect.
In Germany, the same spirit of a learned and ingenious
scepticism, which denied the personality of the poet Homer,
has occupied itself in seeking to explain away the facts and
testimonies upon which episcopacy rests, and in substituting
for them theoretical fancies of its own invention. But it did
not stop there. It has proceeded, in a not unnatural course,
to undermine the authority of revelation, by attempting to
disprove the genuineness and authenticity of large portions
of Holy Scripture, including the life of our blessed Lord
Himself. In this country, a community of situation and of
interest has induced our presbyterian fellow-countrymen to
avail themselves of the labours of that sceptical erudition in
justifying their repudiation of the threefold ministry ; but it is
matter for earnest congratulation that they have shrunk, for
the most part, from the use of the more deeply poisoned
weapons which the same armoury would have supplied ;
and—be it spoken to our shame—it has been left to some,
who have possessed every advantage, and are, or were, in
communion with ourselves, to borrow and apply those
weapons in the attacks which they have made upon the
inspiration and veracity of the Word of God.

11. The next evil consequence which I have to name
is, the disadvantage under which separation places every

Eleventh
evil conse-
quence :—

Christian community in its endeavours to uphold and extend the Gospel. It is obvious that, if the uniformity of the Christian ministry which once existed could be restored, at least among the people of this island, the great work of Christian evangelisation might then be carried on by us, both at home and abroad, with far greater success than we can expect to meet with, disorganised and divided as we now are ; and consequently disentitled to receive, so largely as we might otherwise hope to do in such a cause, the divine blessing, without which our best efforts can be of no avail. At home, for example, the report issued in the early part of last year (February 1868) concerning the miserable condition of the poor in Edinburgh, while it confessed inability to discover ' which is the first link in the chain of causation,' yet did, in fact, suggest this as the one great obstacle that stood in the way of effectually grappling with the mass of evil which had been found to exist. And accordingly, in an able article which appeared in the 'Scotsman' newspaper upon that report, it was observed that 'the remedial agencies proposed, though more or less in practice at present, do not answer their purpose, because they exist in operation *without co-operation.* They do not *work together* for good. The supreme and central remedial measure aimed at in the present instance is the concentration of our isolated forces of beneficence, which are now in so monstrous and mischievous a degree clashing with, and counteracting or neutralising each other—where indeed they do not *augment* the evils they were meant to mitigate—in a chaos of ill-directed,

Impediments in the way of converting the heathen, and of recovering our own lapsed population.

and therefore often fruitless, endeavour. Order is Heaven's first law, and economy is like unto it. Our charities being confessedly *disorderly* and wasteful, how **can** we expect them to be *blessed*? . . . It is one of the **chief** curses of our **present** *no system* that, by the distrust which **attends it, the springs** of charitable giving and doing **are dried up at their very sources.' Such is a** specimen of our condition **at home,** according to a testimony which is all **the more valuable** because it is given not from any religious **or ecclesiastical** point of view. **I may add, that the** before-named valuable **and** trustworthy report represents what **it calls ' the lapsed** classes in Edinburgh ' as constituting **more** than one-fourth of the entire population. **It is thus that** the broken law of unity still continues **to avenge itself by introducing a Babel**like confusion, which, even when **we would be** doing good, baffles and defeats **our aims !** [1]

Abroad, the interesting address, delivered shortly **afterwards** in the General Assembly by Dr. Norman McLeod, upon his return from India, afforded only another **evidence, in addi**tion to countless testimonies before given to the same effect ; [2]

Dr. N. McLeod on India.

[1] ' The multiplication of sects among us has multiplied the appliances for developing the activity of professing Christians, but has *not only not diminished* the proportion of practical heathen to the members of Churches among us, but *is at the present moment one of the chief barriers to the proper application of Christian power to the work of reclaiming such* heathen.'—*Report of Committee on Christian Life and Work,* presented to the General Assembly of the Church of Scotland, May 20, **1870.** Compare above, p. 239 sq., note 3.

[2] See the author's ' Discourse on Scottish Reformation,' Append., c. vi. And add Speech of Bishop of Bombay, 'Colonial Church Chronicle,' March **1872,** p. 101.

S

viz. that nothing acts as a greater hindrance in missionary enterprise than conflicting systems among the missionaries. Accordingly, he denounced denominationalism. He would have us teach the people of India that what they want— what they must have—is a Church of India. But with what face can we, Scotch and English, presume—and upon what principles can we attempt—to teach them this, so long as we ourselves have a Church of England, and a Church of Scotland, which are not at one, which are dissenters—denominationalists—to each other?

Bishop Piers
Claughton of
Colombo.

I have said that Dr. N. McLeod's testimony is only one of many to the same effect. A sermon upon 'The Christian Ministry and the Controversies concerning it,' preached (1867) in the Cathedral of Colombo, by the bishop of that see, now Archdeacon of London, contains the following passage, which, from the allusion in the first words, though addressed to others so many thousand miles away, would seem to speak in an especial manner to ourselves :—

' Happily, the question between our Scottish brethren and ourselves is daily becoming more simple and plain, cleared from the difficulties which beset it in the days of our fathers. One by one causes of difference have melted away, or are being canvassed in an impartial spirit with a view to their just settlement.' And then apparently addressing Presbyterians and others who were not of his own flock—for the occasion being a Christmas ordination had probably attracted many such, and, as it would seem, some of the heathen also—the bishop proceeds :—' What we wish is

that you should **understand** the stress laid in Scripture **on**
the unity of God's people—**that you should not accept a**
mere consent to meet amicably **now and then** for actual
communion **in Christ.** And here, in the **face of the un-**
converted heathen, I tell you plainly, **as one put in** charge
with the Gospel, and I do not say it for the **first time**—*you*
Christians must get rid of your manifold and needless divisions,
before you have so much as a reason to look for success in your
endeavours to convince those heathen of the truth of your own
religion' [1] (p. 6).

Such is a sample of the **testimonies which** have come to us
from the far-distant East. **Let us compare with** them **the**
evidence which **we have also received from the far-distant**
West, and among **a** population whose condition, though
nominally Christian, would appear to be almost more **alien**
from genuine Christianity than heathenism itself. **The**
friends of Dr. Stephen Elliot, who was bishop of Georgia, a
southern State of North America, for **more than** twenty-five
years, and who died in December 1866, have since published
a volume of his admirable sermons, one of which, written in
the last year of his life, and therefore with all the benefit of
his ripe experience, is upon the text of Hosea viii. 11 :—
'Because **Ephraim hath** made many altars to sin, altars

---

[1] This last statement has received a remarkable **confirmation from the** leader of the Indian **Theists—Baboo Keshub** Chunder Sen—who, in a most interesting address which he delivered at a public **meeting in** London, April 1870, **complained** that ' so many *different doctrines and rituals* were presented to the Hindoo by the **missionaries of** *differing Churches,* that he was quite bewildered and confounded by them '

shall be unto him to sin.' The solemn warnings which that
sermon contains would make it very valuable if it were
reprinted and circulated in this country. After remarking
that 'the tendency of the times is to strike at everything
positive and distinctive—to put all systems, all institutions,
nay, all men, upon an ignoble level' (p. 166) ; and after
tracing the consequences of Jeroboam's politic (as it seemed)
and plausible disobedience to God's express command in
separating himself and his people from the one appointed
temple and altar and priesthood at Jerusalem—consequences
which appeared first in a multiplicity of altars throughout
the land of Israel, until at length, under Ahab and Jezebel
and Joram, idolatry, the foulest and most degrading, usurped
the place of the worship of Jehovah—it thus proceeds :—

'And are we not in this country passing through precisely this experience ? . . . Are we not dividing and subdi-
viding into innumerable sects, each one setting up its own
altar, and each altar further and still further removed from
the doctrine and discipline of Christ? . . . Has not the
progress been rapidly downward, striking in turn at everything distinctive in doctrine, and bringing in arrangements
of religious worship more and more radical? Is not God mani-
festing the law of His government by permitting these altars
to multiply, and, as they multiply, to be more and more irregular and profane ? . . . Look at the rapid deterioration of
religion in many parts of the United States, once the most
rigid and devout ! Look at the doctrines which are now
publicly proclaimed throughout the land, which are gathering

disciples, which are forming sects ; doctrines of devils, fit only for execration and condemnation ! . . . " Ephraim is making many altars to sin ;" . . . and true to the principle of its action, his law is being fast made the banner under which idols of every hue and shape—idols of imagination, of sentiment, of will, of pride, of lust—are to take the place of Christ and His Church. And what is worse, Christians seem blinded to the condition of things, and are comforting themselves with the idea that religion is advancing through the land, when it is really fast running into the foulest corruption ' (p. 169 sq.).

12. One more evil consequence, requiring us to take a large and comprehensive view, if we would pay due regard not only to our spiritual and religious, but also to our secular and political interests, consists in the advantage which our establishment of two different and discordant forms of Protestantism affords to the Church of Rome. I am sorry that it should be necessary to speak of any Church as if we were justified in regarding it with suspicion and distrust, and still more, as if it were an adversary, whom it is our duty to withstand. But such, unhappily, is our case towards the Church of Rome ; and not ours only, but the case of every other Church that refuses to submit to her despotic sway. She must be resolutely withstood, because she considers it her duty to press forward that šway wherever she can do so with the least prospect of success. And what have we to oppose to that aggressive spirit ? Not long since I saw it stated in a public journal that, whereas half a century ago,

[margin note:] Twelfth evil consequence:— Advantage given to popery and voluntaryism.

the number of Roman Catholic clergy in Great Britain did
not amount to 300, it now exceeds 1,500; being considerably more than the number of ministers of the Established
Church in Scotland.   And all that force of Romanist clergy
have been trained, be it remembered, *upon one and the same
system*.   But how have we been trained?   To fight against
each other.   Look at the Catechism, sanctioned and put
forth by the General Assembly of the Free Church in 1847.
It has, it is true, its ' anti-papal testimony;' but it has also
what it calls its ' anti-prelatical testimony.'   Or if not trained
to fight against each other, we learn, I had almost said, to
do worse—to dissemble and slur over differences which,
nevertheless, so long as they exist, must be sufficient to keep
us from all effectual co-operation.   It is not my avowal, but
the avowal of the late Dr. Robert Lee, that the two Established Churches of this island ' as now existing, are rather
antagonists than allies.' [1]   Nor could this well be otherwise,
when the establishment of one has been founded upon the
disestablishment of that which was, and is, in communion
with the other.   How, then, are they to cease to be antagonists and to become allies?   ONLY BY THE DISCOVERY AND
ACCEPTANCE OF THE TRUTH.   I have done my best—not
hastily, not superficially, but after full and patient enquiry—
to ascertain the truth in regard to the main point of difference which now separates the two Church establishments ;
and, until it shall be shown by a more laborious and more
competent enquirer that I have fallen into error, I shall

[1] ' Reform of the Church of Scotland,' p. 41.

venture to think that I have demonstrated to the satisfaction of every fair and candid mind what the truth in question really is. I am equally prepared to prove that the true system of Christianity, as revealed to us for our guidance in the Word of God is, what—in opposition to *popery* from one point of view, and to *voluntaryism* from another—may best be called *the national system*; that is, the system by which each nation orders and establishes its own Church, as in the sight of God (who has given to each its own language, its own character, its own bounds of habitation), not in a spirit of innovation, or of self-sufficiency, but in accordance with the Scriptures, the faith, and ministry, everywhere received among Christians, when the Church was one, and before the universal Roman Empire, providentially formed with the view to the extension of Christianity, had been, with the view to its consolidation, no less providentially broken up. By a process of argument similar to that which has been used in demonstration of the threefold ministry, it may be shown that this national system, as it had been foretold by God's ancient prophets long before,[1] so in the fulness of time it was actually accomplished. It may be shown that the command for the evangelisation of the world was 'to baptize'—not individuals merely, but 'all the nations' as such,[2]—and that what Christ 'commanded,' has been 'observed.' *Wherever Christianity was received, there it*

National Christianit: the true system.

Proved from history and Scripture.

---

[1] See Isaiah xlix. 22, 23 ; lii. 15 ; lx. 10-12, 16. Ps. ii. 8-12 ; lxxii. 11.
[2] Matt. xxviii. 19.

became national ; just as, wherever it became national, there it had previously become episcopal. It may be shown that, confessing our belief (as the Scripture teaches) in the session of Christ 'at the right hand of God,' we thereby intend that 'all power has been given to Him in heaven and in earth ;' [1] we virtually confess no less than this, that ' by Him ' and for Him ' kings reign and princes decree justice ; ' [2] in other words, we virtually confess not only *the headship of Christ over His Church*, but *His acquired right to all national and political power*, to be administered in His name by the secular magistrate, as all ecclesiastical power is, or ought to be, administered in His name by the spiritual magistrate. [3]

Nor is there in these solemn truths anything at variance with the word of Christ Himself (if only it be not, as too often it is, misinterpreted), when He declared to Pilate, ' My kingdom is not of this world.' That is, not received, or derived ' *from* [4] this world ;' no, not ' *from* hence,' as He presently repeats, thus explaining His meaning in the end of the same verse (John xviii. 36) ; but ' *here, in* this world,' as St. Augustin declares (and so ' of this world,' in a most

St. John xviii. 36, as explained by St. Augustin in loc.

---

[1] Ps. cx. 1.   Mark xvi. 19. Eph. i. 20. Col. iii. 1. Heb. i. 3 ; x. 12. Matt. xxviii. 18. See also Dan. vii. 13, 14. Rev. i. 5 ; xvii. 14 ; xi. 15.

[2] Prov. viii. 15.

[3] That is, in Scriptural language, the two powers, of the sword and of the keys. See Rom. xiii. 1–6.

[1] Pet. ii. 13, 14. Eph. i. 19–22. Heb. xiii. 7, 8, 17. 1 Thess. v. 12. Phil. ii. 29, 30.

[4] The preposition in the Greek indicates this. To express what we commonly understand by ' of this world,' the genitive case would have been used without a preposition.

real and true sense), 'is His kingdom, and all the powers of the world, by divine right, are subject to it.'[1]

And yet, while all this can be shown, as I believe, to be the very true teaching of the Word of God, I am far from maintaining that circumstances can never arise in which fidelity to her Divine Bridegroom may not *provoke*, nay, *compel* the Church to sue for a divorce from her earthly bridegroom.

But this I do say, and would most steadfastly maintain—being taught to do so by the sure voice of prophecy—Woe to the State which so treats its Church as to force her to such a course! Woe to the nation, that having been once baptized, tears, as it were, the Cross from off its forehead and repudiates its acceptance of Christ as its King ![2]

With these convictions, I confess, I am not much disposed to listen to calculations as to what the voluntary system may, or may not, be able to effect. I consider that God Himself has spoken upon the point, and that the national system alone is in accordance with His will; as shown, not only by the teaching of His Word, but also *by the working of His providence, which has once wrought for Christianity its establishment throughout the civilised world.* But if nations

Success of voluntary system delusory.

---

[1] This is also the interpretation of St. Chrysostom and of Theophylact. See the author's Perth Lecture, 1854, p. 28.

[2] 'The nation and kingdom that will not serve *thee* (the Church) shall perish ; yea, those nations shall be utterly wasted.'—Isaiah lx. 12. 'Be wise now therefore, O ye kings. . . . Kiss the Son, lest he be angry, and so ye perish from the way, when his wrath is kindled but a little.'—Ps. ii. 10-12.

take a retrograde course; if they so far fall away as to prove themselves unworthy of this better condition designed for them by God; then by all means let them make the best of the alternative that remains to them—the alternative of voluntaryism. Only let them not vaunt themselves in so doing; let them not boast as if they had chosen the better part when they have fallen back upon the worse; and let them not expect that the divine blessing will still rest upon them no less than if they had dutifully adhered to the divine will. No!—and meanwhile, as members of the Church, let us feel assured that the present successes, which we are called upon to admire[1] in the working of the voluntary system, whether in this country or elsewhere, are by no means a conclusive proof, either of the sufficiency of the system itself, or of the goodness of the cause in behalf of which it is exerted. Such successes will be often due in a great degree to local or occasional circumstances; and, so soon as the established system is set aside, one great incentive to the activity of voluntaryism, which arises out of a spirit of opposition to the power and prerogatives bestowed upon its rival, will be withdrawn. But if we are to be told that a cause must necessarily be a good one which is attended with such appearances of success, then, I would ask, what effects have ever been produced more extraordinary, or

---

[1] On the other hand, we have received warning from several of the American bishops when they visited this country, not to be led away by the promises of a system which their own experience had found to be delusive.

more admirable, than those glorious specimens of ecclesiastical architecture—our abbeys and cathedral churches—erected under the influence of the papal system, when the corruptions of that system were at their greatest height? Or, again, what success was apparently ever greater than that of the sword, when drawn in behalf of the cause of the false prophet, Mahomet? Nor is the result in such cases difficult to account for. Error can appeal to motives more powerful, at least for a time, than those which the truth appeals to. Error will not scruple to make use of instruments which the truth would be unwilling or ashamed to employ.

The system, then, of a national established Church, or, in other words, of a union between the Church and the State of every nation professing to be Christian—this I believe to be the true, the only true and divinely intended system ; and *this*, as regards ourselves, and the highly favoured nation to which it is our privilege to belong, popery and voluntaryism are now combining to destroy. And if our opposing front is to continue still divided, and at variance, between prelacy and presbyterianism, is there not too much reason to fear that, eventually, they will succeed? And when the national system has given way, it is idle to expect that the system of voluntaryism, with *no bond of union in itself*, will long be able to withstand the spurious but attractive *unity of the Church of Rome.* The secularisation of a State which has once been Christian can never be regarded without regret by a Christian mind. I say nothing of the circumstances which may be thought to justify it in a country situated as

Union of Church and State, why endangered.

See above, p. 4 and p. 225.

Ireland is (1869) at the present time.   But believing as **I do**
that the measures which we are now witnessing would never
have been proposed if there had been no such difference as
unhappily exists between the **two chief** bodies of Protestants
—Episcopalians and Presbyterians—in that country, I cannot
but see in the threatened legislation a solemn warning which
we ourselves, whether Englishmen or Scotchmen, should lay
to heart.

Opinion of
Macaulay—
in what
sense to be
received.
  I do not forget the expressed opinion of Lord Macaulay,
that the union accomplished in 1707 between England and
Scotland has been a great blessing to both countries,
'*because*, in constituting **one State, it left two Churches.'**[1]
And I grant that there is a sense in which that **sentiment is**
true.   Assuming that the religious profession of a majority
of the people was fairly represented in 1690 by the **dises-**
tablishment of episcopacy and establishment **of presby-**
terianism in its room—an assumption, however, which a
strict investigation of the facts of the case will scarcely
justify[2]—but supposing this, **which is the** popular belief, it
certainly would have been most undesirable that any attempt
should have been made to force upon Scotland the **reac-**
ceptance of episcopacy as a condition of the union between
the two **countries.   But that the circumstances were such as**
to require **the establishment of ' two Churches,' unlike each**
other, in the **same State—this, so far from having** proved a

---

[1] ' Hist. of England,' vol. iv. p.   202 sq. ; and comp. Sage's ' Pres-
268.   bytery Examined,' pp. 312–333.
[2] See Burton's ' Hist.,' vol. ii. p.

great blessing, must be acknowledged to have been the very reverse by all who have at heart the interests of true religion, and who also desire the continuance of the union between Church and State. For what—after little more than a century and a half—has been the result, as we now see it sufficiently developed, of this *ecclesiastical biformity* within the same kingdom? It started with the anomaly that Scotch Presbyterians were thenceforth to be admitted[1] to legislate for the Episcopal Church of England, and English Episcopalians to legislate for the Presbyterian Church of Scotland. Hence churchmen and dissenters—both being capable of either description, according to the point of view from which they were regarded—would be equally at a loss to maintain their true character; and the barrier was broken down which had hitherto fenced ecclesiastical legislation, in respect to the Church establishments of both countries, from illegitimate intrusion. It is easy to see that by such a policy something more than *the thin end of the wedge* was inserted; whereby all the subsequent breaches into the constitution, upon its ecclesiastical side, have followed logically.

Such, then, and so many are the evil consequences which flow more or less directly from the abandonment of the one constitution which was once universal in the ministry of the

Forenamed evil consequences traced to their origin.

---

[1] During the operation of the penal laws against Scottish episcopacy in the last century, none but Presbyterians or members of the *qualified* episcopal congregations, who were virtually Independents, could be elected from Scotland to serve in Parliament.

Church, and which (as we have seen reason to conclude) was designed by Christ to be maintained in all countries and

Satanical
principle and
devices.

at all times. Can we doubt that results so injurious to the interests of religion have been caused through the agency of that evil spirit who is represented in Scripture as the great enemy of God and man? 'Divide et impera'—Divide and govern !—such has ever been his master principle, his most successful policy. Divide man from his Maker; divide fellow-Christians, Church against Church, altar against altar; divide class from class, rich and poor. Finally, divide Church and State. Yes; in opposition to the first great principle [1] of Christ, our Friend and Saviour, 'Unite and conquer'—such has been from the beginning the principle and the policy of our enemy and destroyer. St. Paul could say, and say truly, 'We are not ignorant of his devices.' Can the same be said now? What other explanation can be given of the many popular apologies which we hear for continuance in our present state, but that they are devices of Satan, and that they who use them, use them in ignorance of their true character? Is it not, for instance, a melancholy proof of such ignorance when a man fancies that he can be *more edified* in breaking the intended order, and oftentimes, the express command of Christ, than in keeping it? When he flatters himself that because the Gospel is *spiritual,* therefore he may dispense with its *forms,* its *laws* and *ordinances* ; because *the Scriptures* are above all to be read and searched, therefore *the Church* is not to be

[1] See Bishop Andrewes' sixth serm. on 'Resurrection,' vol. ii. p. 279 sq.

heard or known ; because all Christians are in a certain
sense *priests*, as in a certain sense also they are all kings,
therefore a duly ordained *ministry* has no proper claim to
his submission and regard; because religion is a matter
between *God and every man's conscience*, therefore it is not a
matter as between *man and his fellow-men* ; because every
man is to obey his own *conscience*, therefore the guidance or
supposed guidance of conscience, however ignorant and
ill-informed, is to suffice to bar *all other guidance*, however
legitimate and however wise and enlightened ; because
offences must needs come, and the offence of schism among the
rest, therefore there is *no such sin as schism*, or if there be, it
is needless or impossible to ascertain *in what it consists, or
how it is to be avoided.* What sophistry ! What delusion !
What half-truth—always better for the purposes of Satan than
entire falsehood ! What ignorance of his devices is there
in all this ! What appeal to the natural pride of man's
heart ! What pandering to his envy, jealousy, distrust of
others—to his own self-confidence, self-sufficiency, self-love !
What renunciation of all meekness and humility ! Or again,
when pleading, as I am pleading in these lectures, for one
uniform constitution in the ministry of the Church, we are
met with the taunt, instead of argument, that our position is
a narrow and an antiquated one—as if the prescribed way
that leadeth unto life were not also narrow !—and that presbyterianism is valuable and must be maintained, if on no
other account yet on this—because it serves as a standing
protest against a position so illiberal ;—can there be

conceived a device of Satan more similar to that with which he tempted our first parents, when, under a promise of extended knowledge, he induced them to disobey God's plain command?

Summing up of the whole argument. For, to sum up now the argument upon which we have been engaged, it will stand thus :—

First head. I. We find, in the first place, that a definite and orderly organisation of the Christian ministry was to have been expected *à priori*, from various considerations :—

1. From the corporate idea and delineation of the Church as revealed in Scripture.

2. From the analogy of order in the external world.

3. From the correspondence between the Christian Church and the Jewish, in which the system of a threefold ministry was prescribed by God.

4. From the mystical analogy between such a ministry and the divine object of Christian worship.

5. From the analogy of the form of government which is acknowledged to be the best for civil society.

6. From the sacred character and high importance of the functions to be performed by the said ministry.

Second head. II. We find, in the second place, concerning the three-fold or episcopal ministry :—

1. That it is plainly Scriptural and apostolical.

2. That it was universal in the Church from the earliest period at which it could be reasonably expected to be fully organised, down to the Reformation in the sixteenth century.

3. That it is still universal in the East, and, for the most part, also in the West, either in a reformed or unreformed condition.

4. That in either case, both before and since the Reformation, it has ever been regarded as essential to the complete constitution of a Christian Church.

III. We find, in the third place, that, wherever the said form of ministry has been discontinued, there sundry evil consequences have ensued more or less directly ; for instance :— Third head.

1. A breach of unity, which such discontinuance has involved, contrary to the express command of God, and a gradually increasing indifference to the sin of schism.

2. A usurpation of the rights and powers of the episcopal ministry, especially of the power of Ordination, by other bodies, whose credentials are at best open to question.

3. A withholding of the ordinance of Confirmation from the young.

4. A discontinuance of other catholic ordinances, such as daily public worship, frequent Communion, observance of the great Christian fasts and festivals, administration of Communion to the sick and dying.

5. An appropriation of ecclesiastical and especially professorial endowments to purposes at variance with those for which they were bestowed.

6. A waste of ministerial power and of charitable resources of all kinds consequent upon separation.

T

7. A lowering of the social position of the clergy, and a loss of means and opportunities for theological study.

8. A temptation to have recourse to systems of education which, in order to be general or national, must be, more or less, irreligious.

But besides these we find other consequences of a still wider and more disastrous scope; viz. :—

9. A practical denial of the true character of the Church as a corporate institution; and, arising therefrom, a neglect of relative duties, and an interference with the beneficial action of the several classes of society one towards another.

10. A greater and more unrestrained prevalence of false or unsound doctrine.

11. An increase of difficulty thrown in the way of evangelising the heathen, and of converting the lapsed masses of our own population both at home and abroad.

12. Advantage given to the papal system and to the principle of voluntaryism, in opposition to the true system of national Christianity, and to the principle of the union of Church and State.

Scotch 'Episcopalians'— their fidelity to principle: This, then, is what we *find*, upon the question before us; and this, I verily believe, is the *finding* of the truth itself. It is for reasons such as these, and not from any foolish and bigoted adherence to a weak and indefensible position, that a large, and not the least intelligent or least influential portion of the community in Scotland, notwithstanding many great and calamitous vicissitudes, have still adhered to the original constitution of their Church; have still desired to retain a ministry such as in England has never ceased to be retained—not by individuals only, but by the nation itself—except during the interval of the great Rebellion. That when they were in the ascendant, our forefathers used their authority meekly and moderately—in times when meekness or moderation were not to be found on any side—is not maintained : on the contrary, that they too often did the very reverse, is freely confessed and penitently deplored. But it is maintained that, whatever may have been their faults or excesses in that respect, these were no necessary consequence, no proper fruit, of the system itself which they so misused. Nor when we speak of adherence to a prelatical Church, is it to be understood that we desire to weaken—still less to exclude—either government by synods, or the just influence of the laity; both of which it has been the wisdom of the presbyterian system to vindicate and uphold, and which we believe to be no less Scriptural and apostolical than prelacy itself. Neither do we desire to see the ecclesiastical element in the State unduly subjected to the civil element ; any more than we desire to see the civil power oppressed and overridden by the ecclesiastical ; and any advantage which Scotland may possess, more especially in the former of these respects, we should wish not only to be maintained in this country, but to be extended to England also. On the other hand, we have no wish to see repeated in this country sundry inconveniences which still attach to the Southern Church ; such as the monstrous, unmanageable size of the larger

attended by failings in the past which are now deplored.

What kind of prelacy is desired.

T 2

dioceses [1]—an evil deplored by none more than by many of the bishops themselves ; the virtual abeyance of synodical action, and consequently of an important portion of the rights, both of the lower orders of the clergy and also of the laity ; and the substitution of multitudinous and often jarring societies for the action of the Church itself.

Prelatical abuses no necessary part of the system itself.

Yes ; let it be repeated, again and again, that while we advocate, upon the grounds which have been stated and for the good of all, the due recognition of a prelatical ministry, we would yield to no one in condemning prelatical abuses of all kinds—prelatical exorbitances, prelatical despotism. And yet, though this avowal be frankly made, let it be borne in mind that neither personal delinquencies, however great, nor general corruption, however dominant, would seem (so far as we can learn from Scripture) to justify a departure from the system itself, the administration of which is so dishonoured. *Even a Judas must have a successor.* The ancient prophets, severely as they denounced the degeneracy of the Jewish priesthood, never counselled separation from them.[2] Our Blessed Lord Himself gave command to

---

[1] It was wisely urged by John Knox, more than three centuries ago, in his 'Brief Exhortation to England,' A.D, 1559 : 'Let no man be charged in preaching of Christ Jesus above that which one man may do ; I mean *that your bishopricks be so divided,* that of every one, as they be now for the most part, be made ten.' A sufficient evidence that

he at least did not wish to see episcopacy abolished but well reformed. See Works, vol. v. p. 515 ; comp. 'Irenicum,' p. 415 ; and Bingham, vol. ix. p. 412 sq.

[2] See St. Augustin, Ep. xciii.: 'Toleraverunt Prophetæ contra quos tanta dicebant, nec communionem sacramentorum illius populi relinquebant.'—Vol. ii. p. 354.

His disciples that even the scribes and Pharisees, abomina-
ble hypocrites and false teachers as they were, should be
still obeyed and respected in the exercise of their authority,
because they sat in Moses' seat.[1]   It will be admitted that
these remarks belong naturally to the argument upon which
we have been engaged.   In point of fact, however, it cannot, I believe, be truly said that prelacy has ever been
rejected in this country simply for its own demerits.[2]   In
1560 it was rejected because it had been allied with popery.
In 1638 it was rejected in consequence of the unconstitu-
tional means by which Charles I. attempted to force upon
the people the acceptance of a liturgy.   In 1690 it was
rejected because the bishops, who were then its representatives, refused to acknowledge King William III. as the
legitimate sovereign of these realms.

May it not, then, be allowed to us to hope that nearly
two centuries of exclusion from its just position may have
sufficed to atone not only for the mistake—the loyal and
not ignoble mistake—which it then made, but also for the
other misdeeds and shortcomings of which it is acknowledged to have been guilty in its days of power?   May it
not be allowed to us to hope that this Christian appeal in
its behalf will meet with some consideration from the Christian conscience of the people of this land?   The appeal to
them—to them as Christians—is not uncalled for, because

Appeal to
the people
of Scotland.

---

[1] Matt. xxiii. 1-3. See St.
Chrysostom on 1 Thess., Hom. x.
1 ; and on Coloss., Hom. iii. 4.

[2] See Bishop Sage, 'Presbytery
Examined,' p. 306, and compare
his pathetic appeal (1695), p. 399.

we have been assured by no mean authority that the General Assembly, whatever else it may be induced to alter or relax, must never be expected to move a hand towards opening the doors by which—I will not say *we*—but *the Catholic and apostolic ministry* is now excluded from all entrance into the National Church, as by law established. The appeal *itself* is not uncalled for; because the consummation of the union with England has given to the discussion which it raises an augmented interest, which cannot but find an echo in the breast of every true Christian, and which no true patriot will be slow to recognise. It will be felt by such that the advantages of that union must be incomplete so long as united action in religious matters is rendered impossible by the discordancy which exists between the two Church establishments as they now stand. It is true they are both Protestant. But so is Independency, so is Anabaptism, so is Socinianism, so is Unitarianism, so is Quakerism. And is it not true that in the past they have protested against each other, almost as vehemently as either of them has protested against Rome? Is it not the fact that each country harbours in its bosom allies of the other's Church which are, not from choice, but from necessity, the foes of its own? What power upon earth can reconcile this melancholy, this disastrous state of things? Again I say, THE POWER OF TRUTH. Only ascertain the truth as (I am sure) it can be ascertained, and act upon it as (I am sure) it can be acted on, and harmony will ensue. Otherwise, we must be prepared not only for the continuance of the same evil consequences which

Advantages of the union between the two countries incomplete.

have been pointed out, and for their propagation (if they remain unchecked) in an aggravated form; but for the addition of others still more calamitous, when the punishments which will be due to national apostacy are to fall upon us.

At least, then, let us hear no more that the matter is a small or unimportant one, when the results involved in it are such that it would be impossible to conceive any greater or more momentous. Neither let us be told that certainty in respect to it, sufficient for all practical purposes, is not to be obtained, when, if we take in the evidence as a whole, inspired and uninspired, what is there which has been more plainly manifested? What is there in regard to which we are placed under stronger obligations to obey the guidance which reason, Scripture, and experience combine to offer? Nor, once more, let us be told—as Edward Stillingfleet, when a youth of twenty-four, told the readers of his 'Irenicum,' but afterwards, when his knowledge had been enlarged, and his judgment matured, confessed that he had yielded more than the truth allowed [1]—let us not be told that because good and learned men have been ranged on either side as disputants on this question, therefore the question is one which may and ought to be looked upon as indifferent. For what is the real truth in regard to the premiss upon which this conclusion rests? The truth is, the dispute has *not* been simply between opponents equally

Importance of results involved in this appeal.

[1] See 'Irenicum,' p. 2 sq.; and comp. Life prefixed to the folio edition of his works, vol. i. p. 4. See also above, p. 38, note 1.

good and learned, but between the judgment and practice of the universal Church on the one hand, and, on the other hand, the private opinion of individuals, influenced in great measure by considerations external to the merits of the case itself.

Condition of the Church of England not really a discouraging one.

Meanwhile I am aware that there are some who would call off our thoughts from the state of our own country, and even from the crisis now arisen in Ireland, in order to ask, with little feeling of good-will, whether the Church of England itself be not tottering to its fall. For my own part, I entertain no such opinion. On the contrary, I am persuaded that, if left to itself, if saved from the disturbing effects caused, through Parliament or otherwise, by the operation of Scotch or of Irish influences, its security, in its established position, in the present and for the future, would be as great or greater than it has ever been. I am sure there never was a time when its bishops and clergy, taken upon the whole, have been more devoted to their sacred calling. That in a body of men amounting to upwards of 20,000 some are to be found who, in a stirring and unsettled age like this, are, from motives of various kinds, bad and good, unable to resist the temptation of extreme opinions, or extreme practices—this can occasion no surprise. But, for the most part, the symptom which the body itself exhibits is the healthiest of all symptoms; viz. a desire for its own self-improvement, with a view to its greater and more effective usefulness. And the consequence is, that the influence of the clergy in England—notwithstanding the unhappy draw-

backs to which I have referred—was never at a greater
height. I will not ask you to accept this statement upon
my authority, but upon authority which will, I believe, be
thought sufficient. A liberal journal of high repute, averse
to any but the broadest sentiments upon matters of religion,
gave expression to the following strong and distinct testimony in December last (1868) :—

Testimony
of a Liberal
journal.

'This is, we think, the fair and legitimate inference to
be drawn from the (late) elections :—that the Church of
England is not tottering, nor likely to totter; that it is
planted deep in the affections of the English people.'—
Spectator.

The speech of Mr. Gladstone at Greenwich, upon his
re-election in the same month, contained a declaration of
opinion precisely similar but in fuller terms ; when his own
feelings or interests might have tempted him rather to
question or suppress the truth. He is reported to have
said :—

Of the Prime
Minister.

'The elections have undoubtedly shown a strong attachment, on the part of the great body of the people in England, to the Church of England. And I am glad of that
attachment, and of the great influence of the clergy; though
I venture to think they have used their influence improperly.
I am glad, however, that it has been gained in the main by
the conviction that the clergy do their duty. They may
differ—there may be wise men and foolish men among
them ; but, speaking generally, they are men in earnest ;
they are men who attract the respect of the people by

working hard in their vocation. The Church of England, it may be truly said, ministers to the people; less so, perhaps, in these great centres of the population, where it is relatively weakest, but, taking the country as a whole, *the Church of England ministers to the people.* (Cheers.) Doing so, it is appreciated.'

It is important to bear in mind that these words not only proceeded from a speaker who had far more reason to flatter the dissenting interest, but were addressed to one of those overgrown suburban populations in which the Church labours under greatest disadvantage; and that their truth appears to have been acknowledged by those who heard them.

Adjustment of ministry would lead to greater harmony of doctrine and worship.

I said at the beginning that if this question, which affects the constitution of the ministry, could be first adjusted, I should anticipate comparatively little difficulty in the solution of others, the importance of which, though they have been merely touched upon in subordination to this, it must not be supposed that I am either capable of forgetting or willing to underrate. I am led to entertain the hope which I have expressed from various considerations. In the history of the past, since the Reformation, I find a general concurrence between Episcopalians and Presbyterians in the use of the same doctrinal standards to a great extent, even at the periods when their antagonism upon the question of Church government was at its height. On the one hand, it is certain that John Knox must have signed the Articles of the Church of England;[1] and in the following century it appears from what occurred in the Westminster Assembly that the same Articles were not unacceptable even to the Independents;[2] while, at the present time, it is not uncommon, I believe, among Presbyterians, to require the standard work of Bishop Pearson on the Creed to be studied as the principal text-book by candidates for the ministry. On the other hand, the old Scotch Confession of 1560, the work of Knox and his fellow-reformers, was allowed by Episcopalians during the period both of their first and second establishment.[3] In regard to questions of worship, the experience of the present leaves no room to doubt that a gradual approximation of sentiment is setting in, before which it may be hoped that existing barriers, which exclude even the partial use of a liturgy, will eventually disappear. To these considerations it is to be added that the promoters of the change at the Revolution in 1690, so far as they were actuated by religious motives, professed to take account of no other differences between their own party and the party of the Church which they disestablished, but such only as concerned the constitution of the ministry; and even these,

---

[1] See the author's 'Discourse on Scottish Reformation,' p. 36 sq.

[2] 'The Independents professed to agree with the Church of England in its Articles.'—Hetherington's *History of the Westminster Assembly*, p. 137. The Assembly spent ten weeks in debating upon the first fifteen Articles, but 'that part of their proceedings led to no practical result.' Ibid., p. 122.

[3] See Bishop Russell's 'Appendix to Keith,' p. 492.

by their own avowal, they regarded in the light of popular feeling—not to say of popular prejudice—as it existed at the time, rather than of any judgment professing to be formed upon conviction of the truth.

But whatever may be the weight which is due to these last remarks, for myself I shall feel that I have ample cause to be more than satisfied if **I may succeed** in recommending what I believe to be the first great instrument of unity; if I may assist, **however feebly or** remotely, in obtaining a triumph for the truth **upon** the single point which has formed the main subject of this **appeal.** God is witness **that I have not** argued, and pressed the matter upon your attention, for the sake of victory, or of self-interest, **nor from any** other motive, but such as may **become a lover of his** country and a minister of the Gospel of the Prince of Peace. In every discussion, in **every controversy** in which I have engaged with **the same object in view, it has never been my** aim to detract from the **esteem in which some who** have differed from **me are deservedly held; and I** have often declined an encounter, or desisted from **it at** an apparent **disadvantage, when I saw that nothing was to** be gained but **the paltry satisfaction of exposing the errors or the** weakness of an opponent, with **no prospect of** benefit to the **cause** itself. That cause, if it be of **man, will** come to **nought**; but if it **be of God—as I humbly but** confidently trust it is—of His **Spirit, and of His Truth,** then, though **I myself** may not live to see **any ripened fruit of my own labours, yet,** when the time of harvest shall arrive, others will enter into those labours; and God grant, of His infinite mercy, that both sower and reaper may rejoice together in a better— a peaceful and united—world! Meanwhile, you will not, I am sure, grudge to me the indulgence of feelings which a descendant, however unworthy, of an ancient and honourable lineage may be allowed to entertain, if in any way I have contributed to remove the thick cloud of misapprehension and mistrust under which episcopacy in this country has been doomed to lie. It is sometimes seen in the generations of this world, that while succession to the title has been retained by the rightful heir, the property has gone to another and less legitimate branch of the same family. I think I have shown that something like this has happened in the present case. At the same time, without seeking to extenuate the failings of our ancestors, I venture to claim for them the remembrance of services which shed lustre upon many a page of our country's history (witness the names of Turgot and of Kennedy, of Elphinstone and of Forbes, of Gawin Douglas and of Leighton); and which reach upward to the time when our first forefathers were converted from the worship of idols to serve, in the faith of Christ, the One living and true God. It only remains for me to add that as Luther, when excommunicated, appealed to the pope, 'melius informando'—that is, in the hope that the time would come when he would be accessible to a fuller and purer knowledge of the Gospel—so we, being

Bishops who have deserved well of their Church and country.

excluded from the pale of the National Church establishment in this country (though not in England), appeal to the enlightened consciences of our fellow-countrymen and fellow-Christians to do us justice, and at the same time to do justice to themselves and to the sacred cause of ' TRUTH, UNITY, AND CONCORD.'

PRAYER FOR UNITY.

O GOD, the Father of our LORD JESUS CHRIST, our only Saviour, the Prince of Peace, give grace to us and to all Thy people in this land, seriously to lay to heart the great dangers we are in by our unhappy divisions. Take away all hatred and prejudice, and whatsoever else may hinder us from godly Union and Concord: that, as there is but one Body, and one Spirit, and one hope of our Calling, one Lord, one Faith, one Baptism, one God and Father of us all, so we may seek henceforth to be all of one heart and of one soul, united in one holy bond of Truth and Peace, of Faith and Charity, and may with one mind and one mouth glorify Thee, through Jesus Christ our Lord. *Amen.*

GENERAL INDEX.

INDEX OF TEXTS OF SCRIPTURE.

LONDON: PRINTED BY
SPOTTISWOODE AND CO., NEW-STREET SQUARE
AND PARLIAMENT STREET

GENERAL LIST OF WORKS

PUBLISHED BY

Messrs. LONGMANS, GREEN, and CO.

PATERNOSTER ROW, LONDON.

History, Politics, Historical Memoirs, &c.

JOURNAL of the REIGNS of KING GEORGE IV. and KING WILLIAM IV. By the late CHARLES C. F. GREVILLE, Esq. Edited by HENRY REEVE, Esq. Fifth Edition. 3 vols. 8vo. 36s.

RECOLLECTIONS and SUGGESTIONS, 1813-1873. By JOHN Earl RUSSELL, K.G. New Edition, revised and enlarged. 8vo. 16s.

The HISTORY of ENGLAND from the Fall of Wolsey to the Defeat of the Spanish Armada. By JAMES ANTHONY FROUDE, M.A. late Fellow of Exeter College, Oxford.

> LIBRARY EDITION, Twelve Volumes, 8vo. price £8. 18s.
> CABINET EDITION, Twelve Volumes, crown 8vo. price 72s.

The ENGLISH in IRELAND in the EIGHTEENTH CENTURY. By JAMES ANTHONY FROUDE, M.A. late Fellow of Exeter College, Oxford. 3 vols. 8vo. price 48s.

The HISTORY of ENGLAND from the Accession of James the   ond. By Lord MACAULAY.

> STUDENT'S EDITION, 2 vols. crown 8vo. 12s.
> PEOPLE'S EDITION, 4 vols. crown 8vo. 16s.
> CABINET EDITION, 8 vols. post 8vo. 48s.
> LIBRARY EDITION, 5 vols. 8vo. £4.

LORD MACAULAY'S WORKS. Complete and Uniform Library Edition. Edited by his Sister, Lady TREVELYAN. 8 vols. 8vo. with Portrait price £5. 5s. cloth, or £8. 8s. bound in tree-calf by Rivière.

On PARLIAMENTARY GOVERNMENT in ENGLAND; its Origin, Development, and Practical Operation. By ALPHEUS TODD, Librarian of the Legislative Assembly of Canada. 2 vols. 8vo. price £1. 17s.

The CONSTITUTIONAL HISTORY of ENGLAND, since the Accession of George III. 1760—1860. By Sir THOMAS ERSKINE MAY, C.B. The Fourth Edition, thoroughly revised. 3 vols. crown 8vo. price 18s.

DEMOCRACY in EUROPE; a History. By Sir THOMAS ERSKINE MAY, K.C.B. 2 vols. 8vo.   [*In the press.*

The NEW REFORMATION, a Narrative of the Old Catholic Movement, from 1870 to the Present Time; with an Historical Introduction. By THEODORUS. 8vo. price 12s.

A

The OXFORD REFORMERS — John Colet, Erasmus, and Thomas More; being a History of their Fellow-work. By FREDERIC SEEBOHM. Second Edition, enlarged. 8vo. 14s.

LECTURES on the HISTORY of ENGLAND, from the Earliest Times to the Death of King Edward II. By WILLIAM LONGMAN, F.S.A. With Maps and Illustrations. 8vo. 15s.

The HISTORY of the LIFE and TIMES of EDWARD the THIRD. By WILLIAM LONGMAN, F.S.A. With 9 Maps, 8 Plates, and 16 Woodcuts. 2 vols. 8vo. 28s.

INTRODUCTORY LECTURES on MODERN HISTORY. Delivered in Lent Term, 1842; with the Inaugural Lecture delivered in December 1841. By the Rev. THOMAS ARNOLD, D.D. 8vo. price 7s. 6d.

WATERLOO LECTURES; a Study of the Campaign of 1815. By Colonel CHARLES C. CHESNEY, R.E. Third Edition. 8vo. with Map, 10s. 6d.

HISTORY of ENGLAND under the DUKE of BUCKINGHAM and CHARLES the FIRST, 1624–1628. By SAMUEL RAWSON GARDINER, late Student of Ch. Ch. 2 vols. 8vo. with two Maps, price 24s.

The SIXTH ORIENTAL MONARCHY; or, the Geography, History, and Antiquities of Parthia. By GEORGE RAWLINSON, M.A. Professor of Ancient History in the University of Oxford. Maps and Illustrations. 8vo. 16s.

The SEVENTH GREAT ORIENTAL MONARCHY; or, a History of the Sassanians: with Notices, Geographical and Antiquarian. By G. RAWLINSON, M.A. Professor of Ancient History in the University of Oxford. 8vo. with Maps and Illustrations.   [In the press.

A HISTORY of GREECE. By the Rev. GEORGE W. COX, M.A. late Scholar of Trinity College, Oxford. VOLS. I. & II. (to the Close of the Peloponnesian War). 8vo. with Maps and Plans, 36s.

GENERAL HISTORY of GREECE to the Death of Alexander the Great. By the Rev. GEORGE W. COX, M.A. late Scholar of Trinity College, Oxford; Author of 'The Aryan Mythology' &c. Crown 8vo. [In the press.

GREEK HISTORY from Themistocles to Alexander, in a Series of Lives from Plutarch. Revised and arranged by A. H. CLOUGH. New Edition. Fcp. with 44 Woodcuts, 6s.

The TALE of the GREAT PERSIAN WAR, from the Histories of Herodotus. By GEORGE W. COX, M.A. New Edition. Fcp. 3s. 6d.

The HISTORY of ROME. By WILLIAM IHNE. VOLS. I. and II. 8vo. price 30s. The Third Volume is in the press.

GENERAL HISTORY OF ROME from the Foundation of the City to the Fall of Augustulus, B.C. 753—A.D. 476. By the Very Rev. C. MERIVALE, D.D. Dean of Ely. With Five Maps. Crown 8vo. 7s. 6d.

HISTORY of the ROMANS under the EMPIRE. By the Very Rev. C. MERIVALE, D.D. Dean of Ely. 8 vols. post 8vo. 48s.

The FALL of the ROMAN REPUBLIC; a Short History of the Last Century of the Commonwealth. By the same Author. 12mo. 7s. 6d.

The STUDENT'S MANUAL of the HISTORY of INDIA, from the Earliest Period to the Present. By Colonel MEADOWS TAYLOR, M.R.A.S. M.R.I.A. Second Thousand. Crown 8vo. with Maps, 7s. 6d.

The HISTORY of INDIA, from the Earliest Period to the close of Lord Dalhousie's Administration. By J. C. MARSHMAN. 3 vols. crown 8vo. 22s. 6d.

The **NATIVE STATES** of **INDIA** in **SUBSIDIARY ALLIANCE**
with the BRITISH GOVERNMENT; an Historical Sketch. With a Notice of
the Mediatized and Minor States. By Colonel G. B. MALLESON, C.S.I. Guardian
to His Highness the Maharájá of Mysore. With 6 Coloured Maps. 8vo. 15s.

INDIAN POLITY; a View of the System of Administration in India.
By Lieutenant-Colonel GEORGE CHESNEY, Fellow of the University of Calcutta.
New Edition, revised; with Map. 8vo. price 21s.

The **IMPERIAL** and **COLONIAL CONSTITUTIONS** of the **BRI-**
TANNIC EMPIRE, including INDIAN INSTITUTIONS. By Sir EDWARD
CREASY, M.A. With 6 Maps. 8vo. price 15s.

HISTORY of the **REPUBLIC** of **FLORENCE**. Translated from the
Italian of the Marchese GINO CAPPONI by SARAH FRANCES ALLEYNE. 2 vols.
8vo.   [In the press.

STUDIES from **GENOESE HISTORY**. By Colonel G. B. MALLESON,
C.S.I. Guardian to His Highness the Maharájá of Mysore. Crown 8vo. 10s. 6d.

CRITICAL and **HISTORICAL ESSAYS** contributed to the *Edinburgh
Review*. By the Right Hon. LORD MACAULAY.
CHEAP EDITION, authorised and complete. Crown 8vo. 3s. 6d.

CABINET EDITION, 4 vols. post 8vo. 24s.	LIBRARY EDITION, 3 vols. 8vo. 36s.
PEOPLE'S EDITION, 2 vols. crown 8vo. 8s.	STUDENT'S EDITION, 1 vol. cr. 8vo. 6s.

HISTORY of **EUROPEAN MORALS**, from Augustus to Charlemagne
By W. E. H. LECKY, M.A. Second Edition. 2 vols. 8vo. price 28s.

HISTORY of the **RISE** and **INFLUENCE** of the **SPIRIT** of
RATIONALISM in EUROPE. By W. E. H. LECKY, M.A. Cabinet Edition,
being the Fourth. 2 vols. crown 8vo, price 16s.

The **HISTORY** of **PHILOSOPHY**, from **Thales** to **Comte**. By
GEORGE HENRY LEWES. Fourth Edition. 2 vols. 8vo. 32s.

The **HISTORY** of the **PELOPONNESIAN WAR**. By THUCYDIDES.
Translated by R. CRAWLEY, Fellow of Worcester College, Oxford. 8vo. 21s.

The **MYTHOLOGY** of the **ARYAN NATIONS**. By GEORGE W.
Cox, M.A. late Scholar of Trinity College, Oxford. 2 vols. 8vo. 28s.

TALES of **ANCIENT GREECE**. By GEORGE W. Cox, M.A. late
Scholar of Trin. Coll. Oxon. Crown 8vo. price 6s. 6d.

HISTORY of **CIVILISATION** in England and France, Spain and Scotland. By HENRY THOMAS BUCKLE. New Edition of the entire Work, with
a complete INDEX. 3 vols. crown 8vo. 24s.

SKETCH of the **HISTORY** of the **CHURCH** of **ENGLAND** to the
Revolution of 1688. By the Right Rev. T. V. SHORT, D.D. Lord Bishop of
St. Asaph. Eighth Edition. Crown 8vo. 7s. 6d.

MAUNDER'S HISTORICAL TREASURY; General Introductory Outlines of Universal History, and a series of Separate Histories. Latest Edition,
revised by the Rev. G. W. Cox, M.A. Fcp. 8vo. 6s. cloth, or 10s. calf.

CATES' and **WOODWARD'S ENCYCLOPÆDIA** of **CHRONOLOGY**,
HISTORICAL and BIOGRAPHICAL; comprising the Dates of all the Great
Events of History, including Treaties, Alliances, Wars, Battles, &c.; Incident-
in the Lives of Eminent Men and their Works, Scientific and Geographical Discoveries, Mechanical Inventions, and Social Improvements. 8vo. price 42s.

The **HISTORICAL GEOGRAPHY** of **EUROPE**. By E. A. FREEMAN,
D.C.L. late Fellow of Trinity College, Oxford. 8vo. Maps.   [In the press.

The **ERA** of the **PROTESTANT REVOLUTION**. By F. SEEBOHM.
With 4 Coloured Maps and 12 Diagrams on Wood. Fcp. 8vo. 2s. 6d.

A 2

The CRUSADES. By the Rev. G. W. Cox, M.A. late Scholar of Trinity College, Oxford. With Coloured Map. Fcp. 8vo. 2s. 6d.

The THIRTY YEARS' WAR, 1618-1648. By Samuel Rawson Gardiner, late Student of Christ Church. With Coloured Map. Fcp. 8vo. 2s. 6d.

The HOUSES of LANCASTER and YORK; with the Conquest and Loss of France. By James Gairdner, of the Public Record Office. With Five Coloured Maps. Fcp. 8vo. 2s. 6d.

EDWARD the THIRD. By the Rev. W. Warburton, M.A. late Fellow of All Souls College, Oxford. With 3 Coloured Maps and 8 Genealogical Tables. Fcp. 8vo. 2s. 6d.

REALITIES of IRISH LIFE. By W. Steuart Trench, late Land Agent in Ireland to the Marquess of Lansdowne. the Marquess of Bath, and Lord Digby. Cheaper Edition. Crown 8vo. price 2s. 6d.

Biographical Works.

AUTOBIOGRAPHY. By John Stuart Mill. 8vo. price 7s. 6d.

The LIFE and LETTERS of LORD MACAULAY. By his Nephew, G. Otto Trevelyan, M.P. 2 vols. 8vo. [In the press.

ADMIRAL SIR EDWARD CODRINGTON, a Memoir of his Life; with Selections from his Private and Official Correspondence. Abridged from the larger work, and edited by his Daughter, Lady Bourchier. With Portrait, Maps, &c. Crown 8vo. 7s. 6d.

The LIFE of NAPOLEON III. derived from State Records, Unpublished Family Correspondence, and Personal Testimony. By Blanchard Jerrold. 4 vols. 8vo. with numerous Portraits and Facsimiles. Vols. I. and II. price 18s. each. The Third Volume is in the press.

LIFE and LETTERS of Sir GILBERT ELLIOT, First EARL of MINTO. Edited by the Countess of Minto. 3 vols. 8vo. 31s. 6d.

ESSAYS in MODERN MILITARY BIOGRAPHY. By Charles Cornwallis Chesney, Lieutenant-Colonel in the Royal Engineers. 8vo. 12s. 6d.

The MEMOIRS of SIR JOHN RERESBY, of Thrybergh, Bart. M.P. for York, &c. 1634—1689. Written by Himself. Edited from the Original Manuscript by James J. Cartwright, M.A. 8vo. price 21s.

ISAAC CASAUBON, 1559-1614. By Mark Pattison, Rector of Lincoln College, Oxford. 8vo. 18s.

BIOGRAPHICAL and CRITICAL ESSAYS, reprinted from Reviews, with Additions and Corrections. Second Edition of the Second Series. By A Hayward, Q.C. 2 vols. 8vo. price 28s. Third Series, in 1 vol. 8vo. price 14s.

LORD GEORGE BENTINCK; a Political Biography. By the Right Hon. Benjamin Disraeli, M.P. Crown 8vo. price 6s.

The LIFE OF ISAMBARD KINGDOM BRUNEL, Civil Engineer. By Isambard Brunel, B.C.L. With Portrait, Plates, and Woodcuts. 8vo. 21s.

RECOLLECTIONS of PAST LIFE. By Sir Henry Holland, Bart. M.D. F.R.S. late Physician-in-Ordinary to the Queen. Third Edition. Post 8vo. price 10s. 6d.

The LIFE and LETTERS of the Rev. SYDNEY SMITH. Edited by his Daughter, Lady Holland, and Mrs. Austin. Crown 8vo. price 2s. 6d.

LEADERS of PUBLIC OPINION in IRELAND; Swift, Flood, Grattan, and O'Connell. By W. E. H. LECKY, M.A. New Edition, revised and enlarged. **Crown 8vo.** price 7s. 6d.

DICTIONARY of GENERAL BIOGRAPHY; containing Concise Memoirs and Notices of the most Eminent Persons of all Countries, from the Earliest Ages. By W. L. R. CATES. New Edition, extended in a Supplement to the Year 1875. Medium 8vo. price 25s. The SUPPLEMENT (comprising 502 additional Notices and Memoirs) separately, price 4s. 6d.

The OFFICIAL BARONAGE of ENGLAND, Shewing the Offices and Honours held by every Peer from 1065 to 1875; also the Personal Characteristics of each, their Armorial Bearings, Family Colours, Badges, and Mottoes. With more than 1,200 Illustrations (Portraits, Effigies, Shields of Arms, and Autographs). By JAMES E. DOYLE. Fcp. 4to. [In the press.

LIFE of the DUKE of WELLINGTON. By the Rev. G. R. GLEIG, M.A. Popular Edition, carefully revised; with copious Additions. **Crown 8vo.** with Portrait, 5s.

FELIX MENDELSSOHN'S LETTERS from *Italy and Switzerland*, and *Letters from 1833 to 1847*, translated by Lady WALLACE. New Edition, with Portrait. 2 vols. crown 8vo. 5s. each.

MEMOIRS of SIR HENRY HAVELOCK, K.C.B. By JOHN CLARK MARSHMAN. Cabinet Edition, with Portrait. Crown 8vo. price 3s. 6d.

VICISSITUDES of FAMILIES. By Sir J. BERNARD BURKE, C.B. Ulster King of Arms. New Edition, remodelled and enlarged. 2 vols. crown 8vo. 21s.

The RISE of GREAT FAMILIES, other Essays and Stories. By Sir J. BERNARD BURKE, C.B. Ulster King of Arms. Crown 8vo. price 12s. 6d.

ESSAYS in ECCLESIASTICAL BIOGRAPHY. By the Right Hon. Sir J. STEPHEN, LL.D. Cabinet Edition. Crown 8vo. 7s. 6d.

MAUNDER'S BIOGRAPHICAL TREASURY. Latest Edition, reconstructed, thoroughly revised, and in great part rewritten; with 1,000 additional Memoirs and Notices, by W. L. R. CATES. Fcp. 8vo. 6s. cloth; 10s. calf.

LETTERS and LIFE of FRANCIS BACON, including all his Occasional Works. Collected and edited, with a Commentary, by J. SPEDDING, Trin. Coll. Cantab. Complete in 7 vols. 8vo. £4. 4s.

The LIFE, WORKS, and OPINIONS of HEINRICH HEINE. By WILLIAM STIGAND. 2 vols. 8vo. with Portrait of Heine, price 28s.

Criticism, Philosophy, Polity, &c.

The LAW of NATIONS considered as INDEPENDENT POLITICAL COMMUNITIES; the Rights and Duties of Nations in Time of War. By Sir TRAVERS TWISS, D.C.L., F.R.S. New Edition, revised; with an Introductory Juridical Review of the Results of Recent Wars, and an Appendix of Treaties and other Documents. 8vo. 21s.

CHURCH and STATE: their relations Historically Developed. By T. HEINRICH GEFFCKEN, Professor of International Law at the University of Strasburg. Translated from the German by E. FAIRFAX TAYLOR. [In the press.

A SYSTEMATIC VIEW of the SCIENCE of JURISPRUDENCE. By SHELDON AMOS, M.A. Professor of Jurisprudence to the Inns of Court, London. 8vo. price 18s.

A PRIMER of the ENGLISH CONSTITUTION and GOVERNMENT. By Sheldon Amos, M.A. Professor of Jurisprudence to the Inns of Court. Second Edition, revised. Crown 8vo. 6s.

The INSTITUTES of JUSTINIAN; with English Introduction, Translation and Notes. By T. C. Sandars, M.A. Sixth Edition. 8vo. 18s.

SOCRATES and the SOCRATIC SCHOOLS. Translated from the German of Dr. E. Zeller, with the Author's approval, by the Rev. Oswald J. Reichel, M.A. Crown 8vo. 8s. 6d.

The STOICS, EPICUREANS, and SCEPTICS. Translated from the German of Dr. E. Zeller, with the Author's approval, by Oswald J. Reichel, M.A. Crown 8vo. price 14s.

The ETHICS of ARISTOTLE, with Essays and Notes. By Sir A. Grant, Bart. M.A. LL.D. Third Edition. 2 vols. 8vo. 32s.

The POLITICS of ARISTOTLE; Greek Text, with English Notes. By Richard Congreve, M.A. New Edition, revised. 8vo. 18s.

The NICOMACHEAN ETHICS of ARISTOTLE newly translated into English. By R. Williams, B.A. Fellow and late Lecturer of Merton College, and sometime Student of Christ Church, Oxford. 8vo. 12s.

PICTURE LOGIC; an Attempt to Popularise the Science of Reasoning by the combination of Humorous Pictures with Examples of Reasoning taken from Daily Life. By A. Swinbourne, B.A. With Woodcut Illustrations from Drawings by the Author. Second Edition. Fcp. 8vo. price 5s.

ELEMENTS of LOGIC. By R. Whately, D.D. late Archbishop of Dublin. New Edition. 8vo. 10s. 6d. crown 8vo. 4s. 6d.

Elements of Rhetoric. By the same Author. New Edition. 8vo. 10s. 6d. crown 8vo. 4s. 6d.

English Synonymes. By E. Jane Whately. Edited by Archbishop Whately. Fifth Edition. Fcp. 8vo. price 3s.

On the INFLUENCE of AUTHORITY in MATTERS of OPINION. By the late Sir George Cornewall Lewis, Bart. New Edition. [Nearly ready.

DEMOCRACY in AMERICA. By Alexis de Tocqueville. Translated by Henry Reeve, Esq. New Edition. 2 vols. crown 8vo. 16s.

ORDER and PROGRESS: Part I. Thoughts on Government; Part II. Studies of Political Crises. By Frederic Harrison, M.A. of Lincoln's Inn. 8vo. price 14s.

COMTE'S SYSTEM of POSITIVE POLITY, or TREATISE upon SOCIOLOGY. Translated from the Paris Edition of 1851-1854, and furnished with Analytical Tables of Contents. In Four Volumes, 8vo. each forming in some degree an independent Treatise :—

Vol. I. General View of Positivism and its Introductory Principles. Translated by J. H. Bridges, M.B. Price 21s.

Vol. II. Social Statics, or the Abstract Laws of Human Order. Translated by F. Harrison, M.A. Price 14s.

Vol. III. Social Dynamics, or the General Laws of Human Progress (the Philosophy of History). Translated by E. S. Beesly, M.A. [In the press.

Vol. IV. Synthesis of the Future of Mankind. Translated by R. Congreve, M.D.; and an Appendix, containing the Author's Minor Treatises, translated by H. D. Hutton, M.A. [In preparation.

BACON'S ESSAYS with **ANNOTATIONS**. By R. WHATELY, D.D.
late Archbishop of Dublin. New Edition, 8vo. price 10s. 6d.

LORD BACON'S WORKS, collected and edited by J. SPEDDING, M.A.
R. L. ELLIS, M.A. and D. D. HEATH. 7 vols. 8vo. price £3. 13s. 6d.

The **SUBJECTION of WOMEN**. By JOHN STUART MILL. New
Edition. Post 8vo. 5s.

On **REPRESENTATIVE GOVERNMENT**. By JOHN STUART MILL.
Crown 8vo. price 2s.

On **LIBERTY**. By JOHN STUART MILL. **New Edition**. Post
8vo. 7s. 6d. Crown 8vo. price 1s. 4d.

PRINCIPLES of POLITICAL ECONOMY. By JOHN STUART MILL.
Seventh Edition. 2 vols. 8vo. 30s. Or in 1 vol. crown 8vo. price 5s.

ESSAYS on SOME UNSETTLED QUESTIONS of POLITICAL
ECONOMY. By JOHN STUART MILL. Second Edition. 8vo. 6s. 6d.

UTILITARIANISM. By JOHN STUART MILL. **New** Edition. **8vo. 5s**

DISSERTATIONS and DISCUSSIONS: Political, Philosophical, and
Historical. By JOHN STUART MILL. New Editions. 4 vols. 8vo. price £2. 7s.

EXAMINATION of Sir. **W. HAMILTON'S PHILOSOPHY**, and of the
Principal Philosophical Questions discussed in his Writings. By JOHN STUART
MILL. Fourth Edition. 8vo. 16s.

An **OUTLINE of the NECESSARY LAWS of THOUGHT**; a Treatise
on Pure and Applied Logic. By the Most Rev. W. THOMSON, Lord Archbishop
of York, D.D. F.R.S. New Edition. Crown 8vo. price 6s.

PRINCIPLES of ECONOMICAL PHILOSOPHY. By HENRY DUNNING
MACLEOD, M.A. Barrister-at-Law. Second Edition. In Two Volumes. VOL. I.
8vo. price 15s. VOL. II. PART I. price 12s.

A **SYSTEM of LOGIC, RATIOCINATIVE and INDUCTIVE**. By JOHN
STUART MILL. Ninth Edition. Two vols. 8vo. 25s.

SPEECHES of the RIGHT HON. LORD MACAULAY, corrected
Himself. People's Edition, crown 8vo. 3s. 6d.

The **ORATION of DEMOSTHENES on the CROWN**. Translated by
the Right Hon. Sir R. P. COLLIER. Crown 8vo. price 5s.

FAMILIES of SPEECH: Four Lectures delivered before the Royal
Institution of Great Britain. By the Rev. F. W. FARRAR, D.D. F.R.S. New
Edition. Crown 8vo. 3s. 6d.

CHAPTERS on LANGUAGE. By the Rev. F. W. FARRAR, D.D. F.R.S.
New Edition. Crown 8vo. 5s.

HANDBOOK of the ENGLISH LANGUAGE. For the use of Students
of the Universities and the Higher Classes in Schools. By R. G. LATHAM, M.A.
M.D. &c. late Fellow of King's College, Cambridge; late Professor of English in
Univ. Coll. Lond. The Ninth Edition. Crown 8vo. price 6s.

A **DICTIONARY of the ENGLISH LANGUAGE**. By R. G. LATHAM,
M.A. M.D. Founded on the Dictionary of Dr. SAMUEL JOHNSON, as
edited by the Rev. H. J. TODD, with numerous Emendations and Additions.
In Four Volumes, 4to. price £7.

A **PRACTICAL ENGLISH DICTIONARY**, on the Plan of White's
English-Latin and Latin-English Dictionaries. By JOHN T. WHITE, D.D. Oxon.
and T. C. DONKIN, M.A. Assistant-Master, King Edward's Grammar School,
Birmingham. Post 8vo. [In the press.

THESAURUS of ENGLISH WORDS and PHRASES, classified and arranged so as to facilitate the Expression of Ideas, and assist in Literary Composition. By P. M. ROGET, M.D. New Edition. Crown 8vo. 10s. 6d.

LECTURES on the SCIENCE of LANGUAGE. By F. MAX MÜLLER, M.A. &c. The Eighth Edition. 2 vols. crown 8vo. 16s.

MANUAL of ENGLISH LITERATURE, Historical and Critical. By THOMAS ARNOLD, M.A. New Edition. Crown 8vo, 7s. 6d.

SOUTHEY'S DOCTOR, complete in One Volume. Edited by the Rev. J. W. WARTER, B.D. Square crown 8vo. 12s. 6d.

HISTORICAL and CRITICAL COMMENTARY on the OLD TESTA-MENT; with a New Translation. By M. M. KALISCH, Ph.D. VOL. I. *Genesis*, 8vo. 18s. or adapted for the General Reader, 12s. VOL. II. *Exodus*, 15s. or adapted for the General Reader, 12s. VOL. III. *Leviticus*, PART I. 15s. or adapted for the General Reader, 8s. VOL. IV. *Leviticus*, PART II. 15s. or adapted for the General Reader, 8s.

A DICTIONARY of ROMAN and GREEK ANTIQUITIES, with about Two Thousand Engravings on Wood from Ancient Originals, illustrative of the Industrial Arts and Social Life of the Greeks and Romans. By A. RICH, B.A. Third Edition, revised and improved. Crown 8vo. price 7s. 6d.

A LATIN-ENGLISH DICTIONARY. By JOHN T. WHITE, D.D. Oxon. and J. E. RIDDLE, M.A. Oxon. Revised Edition. 2 vols. 4to. 42s.

WHITE'S COLLEGE LATIN-ENGLISH DICTIONARY (Intermediate Size), abridged for the use of University Students from the Parent Work (as above). Medium 8vo. 18s.

WHITE'S JUNIOR STUDENT'S COMPLETE LATIN-ENGLISH and ENGLISH-LATIN DICTIONARY. New Edition. Square 12mo. price 12s.

   Separately { The ENGLISH-LATIN DICTIONARY, price 5s. 6d.
        The LATIN-ENGLISH DICTIONARY, price 7s. 6d.

A LATIN-ENGLISH DICTIONARY, adapted for the Use of Middle-Class Schools. By JOHN T. WHITE, D.D. Oxon. Square fcp. 8vo. price 3s.

An ENGLISH-GREEK LEXICON, containing all the Greek Words used by Writers of good authority. By C. D. YONGE, B.A. New Edition. 4to. price 21s.

Mr. YONGE'S NEW LEXICON, English and Greek, abridged from his larger work (as above). Revised Edition. Square 12mo. price 8s. 6d.

A GREEK-ENGLISH LEXICON. Compiled by H. G. LIDDELL, D.D. Dean of Christ Church, and R. SCOTT, D.D. Dean of Rochester. Sixth Edition. Crown 4to. price 36s.

A LEXICON, GREEK and ENGLISH, abridged from LIDDELL and SCOTT's *Greek-English Lexicon*. Fourteenth Edition. Square 12mo. 7s. 6d.

A PRACTICAL DICTIONARY of the FRENCH and ENGLISH LAN-GUAGES. By L. CONTANSEAU. Revised Edition. Post 8vo. 10s. 6d.

CONTANSEAU'S POCKET DICTIONARY, French and English, abridged from the above by the Author. New Edition. Square 18mo. 3s. 6d.

NEW PRACTICAL DICTIONARY of the GERMAN LANGUAGE; German-English and English-German. By the Rev. W. L. BLACKLEY, M.A and Dr. CARL MARTIN FRIEDLÄNDER. Post 8vo. 7s. 6d.

The MASTERY of LANGUAGES; or, the Art of Speaking Foreign Tongues Idiomatically. By THOMAS PRENDERGAST. 8vo. 6s.

Miscellaneous Works and Popular Metaphysics.

LECTURES delivered in AMERICA in 1874. By CHARLES KINGSLEY, F.L.S. F.G.S. late Rector of Eversley. Crown 8vo. price 5s.

THE MISCELLANEOUS WORKS of THOMAS ARNOLD, D.D. Late Head Master of Rugby School and Regius Professor of Modern History in the University of Oxford, collected and republished. 8vo. 7s. 6d.

MISCELLANEOUS and POSTHUMOUS WORKS of the Late HENRY THOMAS BUCKLE. Edited, with a Biographical Notice, by HELEN TAYLOR. 3 vols. 8vo. price 52s. 6d.

MISCELLANEOUS WRITINGS of JOHN CONINGTON, M.A. late Corpus Professor of Latin in the University of Oxford. Edited by J. A. SYMONDS, M.A. With a Memoir by H. J. S. SMITH, M.A. 2 vols. 8vo. 28s.

ESSAYS, CRITICAL and BIOGRAPHICAL. Contributed to the *Edinburgh Review.* By HENRY ROGERS. New Edition, with Additions. 2 vols. crown 8vo. price 12s.

ESSAYS on some THEOLOGICAL CONTROVERSIES of the TIME. Contributed chiefly to the *Edinburgh Review.* By HENRY ROGERS. New Edition, with Additions. Crown 8vo. price 6s.

RECREATIONS of a COUNTRY PARSON. By A. K. H. B. FIRST and SECOND SERIES, crown 8vo. 3s. 6d. each.

The Common-place Philosopher in Town and Country. By A. K. H. B. Crown 8vo. price 3s. 6d.

Leisure Hours in Town; Essays Consolatory, Æsthetical, Moral, Social, and Domestic. By A. K. H. B. Crown 8vo. 3s. 6d.

The Autumn Holidays of a Country Parson; Essays contributed to *Fraser's Magazine,* &c. By A. K. H. B. Crown 8vo. 3s. 6d.

Seaside Musings on Sundays and Week-Days. By A. K. H. B. Crown 8vo. price 3s. 6d.

The Graver Thoughts of a Country Parson. By A. K. H. B. FIRST, SECOND, and THIRD SERIES, crown 8vo. 3s. 6d. each.

Critical Essays of a Country Parson, selected from Essays contributed to *Fraser's Magazine.* By A. K. H. B. Crown 8vo. 3s. 6d.

Sunday Afternoons at the Parish Church of a Scottish University City. By A. K. H. B. Crown 8vo. 3s. 6d.

Lessons of Middle Age; with some Account of various Cities and Men. By A. K. H. B. Crown 8vo. 3s. 6d.

Counsel and Comfort spoken from a City Pulpit. By A. K. H. B. Crown 8vo. price 3s. 6d.

Changed Aspects of Unchanged Truths; Memorials of St. Andrews Sundays. By A. K. H. B. Crown 8vo. 3s. 6d.

Present-day Thoughts; Memorials of St. Andrews Sundays. By A. K. H. B. Crown 8vo. 3s. 6d.

Landscapes, Churches, and Moralities. By A. K. H. B. Crown 8vo. price 3s. 6d.

SHORT STUDIES on GREAT SUBJECTS. By James Anthony Froude, M.A. late Fellow of Exeter Coll. Oxford. 2 vols. crown 8vo. price 12s.

LORD MACAULAY'S MISCELLANEOUS WRITINGS:—
Library Edition. 2 vols. 8vo. Portrait, 21s.
People's Edition. 1 vol. crown 8vo. 4s. 6d.

LORD MACAULAY'S MISCELLANEOUS WRITINGS and SPEECHES.
Student's Edition, in crown 8vo. price 6s.

The Rev. SYDNEY SMITH'S ESSAYS contributed to the Edinburgh Review. Authorised Edition, complete in 1 vol. Crown 8vo. price 2s. 6d.

The Rev. SYDNEY SMITH'S MISCELLANEOUS WORKS; including his Contributions to the *Edinburgh Review.* Crown 8vo. 6s.

The WIT and WISDOM of the Rev. SYDNEY SMITH; a Selection of the most memorable Passages in his Writings and Conversation. 16mo. 3s. 6d.

The ECLIPSE of FAITH; or, a Visit to a Religious Sceptic. By Henry Rogers. Latest Edition. Fcp. 8vo. price 5s.

Defence of the Eclipse of Faith, by its Author; a rejoinder to Dr. Newman's *Reply.* Latest Edition. Fcp 8vo. price 3s. 6d.

CHIPS from a GERMAN WORKSHOP; Essays on the Science of Religion, on Mythology, Traditions, and Customs, and on the Science of Language. By F. Max Müller, M.A. &c. 4 vols. 8vo. £2. 18s.

ANALYSIS of the PHENOMENA of the HUMAN MIND. By James Mill. A New Edition, with Notes, Illustrative and Critical, by Alexander Bain, Andrew Findlater, and George Grote. Edited, with additional Notes, by John Stuart Mill. 2 vols. 8vo. price 28s.

An INTRODUCTION to MENTAL PHILOSOPHY, on the Inductive Method. By J. D. Morell, M.A. LL.D. 8vo. 12s.

ELEMENTS of PSYCHOLOGY, containing the Analysis of the Intellectual Powers. By J. D. Morell, M.A. LL.D. Post 8vo. 7s. 6d.

The SECRET of HEGEL; being the Hegelian System in Origin, Principle, Form, and Matter. By J. H. Stirling, LL.D. 2 vols. 8vo. 28s.

SIR WILLIAM HAMILTON; being the Philosophy of Perception: an Analysis. By J. H. Stirling, LL.D. 8vo. 5s.

The SENSES and the INTELLECT. By Alexander Bain, M.D. Professor of Logic in the University of Aberdeen. Third Edition. 8vo. 15s.

The EMOTIONS and the WILL. By Alexander Bain, LL.D. Professor of Logic in the University of Aberdeen. Third Edition, thoroughly revised, and in great part re-written. 8vo. price 15s.

MENTAL and MORAL SCIENCE: a Compendium of Psychology and Ethics. By the same Author. Third Edition. Crown 8vo. 10s. 6d. Or separately: Part I. *Mental Science,* 6s. 6d. Part II. *Moral Science,* 4s. 6d.

LOGIC, DEDUCTIVE and INDUCTIVE. By the same Author. In Two Parts, crown 8vo. 10s. 6d. Each Part may be had separately:—
Part I. *Deduction,* 4s. Part II. *Induction,* 6s. 6d.

A BUDGET of PARADOXES. By Augustus De Morgan, F.R.A.S. and C.P.S. 8vo. 15s.

APPARITIONS; a Narrative of Facts. By the Rev. B. W. Saville, M.A. Author of 'The Truth of the Bible' &c. Crown 8vo. price 4s. 6d.

A TREATISE of HUMAN NATURE, being an Attempt to Introduce the Experimental Method of Reasoning into Moral Subjects; followed by Dialogues concerning Natural Religion. By DAVID HUME. Edited, with Notes, &c. by T. H. GREEN, Fellow and Tutor, Ball. Coll. and T. H. GROSE, Fellow and Tutor, Queen's Coll. Oxford. 2 vols. 8vo. 28s.

ESSAYS MORAL, POLITICAL, and LITERARY. By DAVID HUME. By the same Editors. 2 vols. 8vo. price 28s.

The PHILOSOPHY of NECESSITY; or, Natural Law as applicable to Mental, Moral, and Social Science. By CHARLES BRAY. 8vo. 9s.

UEBERWEG'S SYSTEM of LOGIC and HISTORY of LOGICAL DOCTRINES. Translated, with Notes and Appendices, by T. M. LINDSAY, M.A. F.R.S.E. 8vo. price 16s.

FRAGMENTARY PAPERS on SCIENCE and other Subjects. By the late Sir H. HOLLAND, Bart. Edited by his Son, the Rev. F. HOLLAND. 8vo. price 14s.

Astronomy, Meteorology, Popular Geography, &c.

BRINKLEY'S ASTRONOMY. Revised and partly re-written, with Additional Chapters, and an Appendix of Questions for Examination. By J. W. STUBBS, D.D. Fellow and Tutor of Trinity College, Dublin, and F. BRUNNOW, Ph.D. Astronomer Royal of Ireland. Crown 8vo. price 6s.

OUTLINES of ASTRONOMY. By Sir J. F. W. HERSCHEL, Bart. M.A. Latest Edition, with Plates and Diagrams. Square crown 8vo. 12s.

ESSAYS on ASTRONOMY, a Series of Papers on Planets and Meteors, the Sun and Sun-surrounding Space, Stars and Star-Cloudlets; with a Dissertation on the approaching Transit of Venus. By RICHARD A. PROCTOR, B.A. With 10 Plates and 24 Woodcuts. 8vo. 12s.

THE TRANSITS of VENUS; a Popular Account of Past and Coming Transits, from the first observed by Horrocks A.D. 1639 to the Transit of A.D. 2012. By R. A. PROCTOR, B.A. Second Edition, with 20 Plates (12 coloured) and 38 Woodcuts. Crown 8vo. 8s. 6d.

The UNIVERSE and the COMING TRANSITS : Presenting Researches into and New Views respecting the Constitution of the Heavens; together with an Investigation of the Conditions of the Coming Transits of Venus. By R. A. PROCTOR, B.A. With 22 Charts and 22 Woodcuts. 8vo. 16s.

The MOON ; her Motions, Aspect, Scenery, and Physical Condition. By R. A. PROCTOR, B.A. With Plates, Charts, Woodcuts, and Three Lunar Photographs. Crown 8vo. 15s.

The SUN; RULER, LIGHT, FIRE, and LIFE of the PLANETARY SYSTEM. By R. A. PROCTOR, B.A. Second Edition, with 10 Plates (7 coloured) and 107 Figures on Wood. Crown 8vo. 14s.

OTHER WORLDS THAN OURS; the Plurality of Worlds Studied under the Light of Recent Scientific Researches. By R. A. PROCTOR, B.A. Third Edition, with 14 Illustrations. Crown 8vo. 10s. 6d.

The ORBS AROUND US; Familiar Essays on the Moon and Planets, Meteors and Comets, the Sun and Coloured Pairs of Stars. By R. A. PROCTOR, B.A. Second Edition, with Charts and 4 Diagrams. Crown 8vo. price 7s. 6d.

SATURN and its SYSTEM. By R. A. Proctor, B.A. 8vo. with 14
Plates, 14s.

A NEW STAR ATLAS, for the Library, the School, and the Observatory,
in Twelve Circular Maps (with Two Index Plates). Intended as a Companion
to 'Webb's Celestial Objects for Common Telescopes.' With a Letterpress
Introduction on the Study of the Stars, illustrated by 9 Diagrams. By R. A.
Proctor, B.A.   Crown 8vo. 5s.

SCHELLEN'S SPECTRUM ANALYSIS, in its application to Terrestrial Substances and the Physical Constitution of the Heavenly Bodies. Translated by Jane and C. Lassell; edited, with Notes, by W. Huggins, LL.D.
F.R.S. With 13 Plates (6 coloured) and 223 Woodcuts. 8vo. price 28s.

CELESTIAL OBJECTS for COMMON TELESCOPES. By the Rev.
T. W. Webb, M.A. F.R.A.S. Third Edition, revised and enlarged; with Maps,
Plate, and Woodcuts. Crown 8vo. price 7s. 6d.

AIR and RAIN; the Beginnings of a Chemical Climatology. By
Robert Angus Smith, Ph.D. F.R.S. F.C.S. With 8 Illustrations. 8vo. 24s.

AIR and its RELATIONS to LIFE; being, with some Additions,
the Substance of a Course of Lectures delivered at the Royal Institution of
Great Britain in 1874. By Walter Noel Hartley, F.C.S. Demonstrator of
Chemistry at King's College, London. With 66 Woodcuts. Small 8vo. 6s.

NAUTICAL SURVEYING, an INTRODUCTION to the PRACTICAL
and THEORETICAL STUDY of. By J. K. Laughton, M.A. Small 8vo. 6s.

MAGNETISM and DEVIATION of the COMPASS. For the Use of
Students in Navigation and Science Schools. By J. Merrifield, LL.D.
18mo. 1s. 6d.

DOVE'S LAW of STORMS, considered in connexion with the Ordinary
Movements of the Atmosphere. Translated by R. H. Scott, M.A. 8vo. 10s. 6d.

KEITH JOHNSTON'S GENERAL DICTIONARY of GEOGRAPHY,
Descriptive, Physical, Statistical, and Historical; forming a complete Gazetteer
of the World. New Edition, revised and corrected. 1 vol. 8vo. [Nearly ready.

The PUBLIC SCHOOLS ATLAS of MODERN GEOGRAPHY. In 31
Coloured Maps, exhibiting clearly the more important Physical Features of the
Countries delineated, and Noting all the Chief Places of Historical, Commercial,
or Social Interest. Edited, with an Introduction, by the Rev. G. Butler, M.A.
Imperial 8vo. bound, price 5s. or imperial 4to. 5s. cloth.

The PUBLIC SCHOOLS MANUAL of MODERN GEOGRAPHY. By
the Rev. George Butler, M.A. Principal of Liverpool College; Editor of 'The
Public Schools Atlas of Modern Geography.'   [In preparation.

The PUBLIC SCHOOLS ATLAS of ANCIENT GEOGRAPHY Edited,
with an Introduction on the Study of Ancient Geography, by the Rev. George
Butler, M.A. Principal of Liverpool College.   [In preparation.

MAUNDER'S TREASURY of GEOGRAPHY, Physical, Historical,
Descriptive, and Political. Edited by W. Hughes, F.R.G.S. Revised Edition,
with 7 Maps and 16 Plates. Fcp. 6s. cloth, or 10s. bound in calf.

Natural History and *Popular Science.*

TEXT-BOOKS of SCIENCE, MECHANICAL and PHYSICAL, adapted for the use of Artisans and of Students in Public and Science Schools. Edited by T. M. GOODEVE, M.A. and C. W. MERRIFIELD, F.R.S.

Edited by T. M. GOODEVE, M.A.

ANDERSON'S Strength of Materials, small 8vo. **3s. 6d.**
BLOXAM'S Metals, 3s. 6d.
GOODEVE'S Elements of Mechanism, 3s. 6d.
————— Principles of Mechanics, 3s. 6d.
GRIFFIN'S Algebra and Trigonometry, 3s. 6d. Notes, 3s. 6d.
JENKIN'S Electricity and Magnetism, 3s. 6d.
MAXWELL'S Theory of Heat, 3s. 6d.
MERRIFIELD'S Technical Arithmetic and Mensuration, **3s. 6d. Key, 3s. 6d.**
MILLER'S Inorganic Chemistry, 3s. 6d.
SHELLEY'S Workshop Appliances, 3s. 6d.
WATSON'S Plane and Solid Geometry, 3s. 6d.

Edited by C. W. MERRIFIELD, F.R.S.

ARMSTRONG'S Organic Chemistry, **3s. 6d.**
THORPE'S Quantitative Chemical Analysis, 4s. 6d.
THORPE & MUIR'S Qualitative Analysis, 3s. 6d.

ELEMENTARY TREATISE on PHYSICS, Experimental and Applied. Translated and edited from GANOT'S *Éléments de Physique* by E. ATKINSON, Ph.D. F.C.S. **Seventh Edition,** revised and enlarged; with 4 Coloured Plates and 758 Woodcuts. **Post 8vo. 15s.**

NATURAL PHILOSOPHY for GENERAL READERS and YOUNG PERSONS; being a Course of Physics divested of Mathematical Formulæ expressed in the language of daily life. Translated from GANOT'S *Cours de Physique* and by E. ATKINSON, Ph.D. F.C.S. Second Edition, with 2 Plates and 429 Woodcuts. Crown 8vo. price 7s. 6d.

HELMHOLTZ'S POPULAR LECTURES on SCIENTIFIC SUBJECTS. Translated by E. ATKINSON, Ph.D. F.C.S. Professor of Experimental Science, Staff College. With an Introduction by Professor TYNDALL. 8vo. with numerous Woodcuts, price 12s. 6d.

On the SENSATIONS of TONE as a Physiological Basis for the Theory of Music. By HERMANN L. F. HELMHOLTZ, M.D. Professor of Physics in the University of Berlin. Translated, with the Author's sanction, from the Third German Edition, with Additional Notes and an Additional Appendix, by ALEXANDER J. ELLIS, F.R.S. &c. 8vo. price 36s.

The HISTORY of MODERN MUSIC, a Course of Lectures delivered at the Royal Institution of Great Britain. By JOHN HULLAH, Professor of Vocal Music in Queen's College and Bedford College, and Organist of Charterhouse. New Edition, 1 vol. post 8vo. [*In the press*

SOUND. By JOHN TYNDALL, LL.D. D.C.L. F.R.S. Third Edition, including Recent Researches on Fog-Signalling; Portrait and Woodcuts. Crown 8vo. 10s. 6d.

HEAT a MODE of MOTION. By JOHN TYNDALL, LL.D. D.C.L. F.R.S. Fifth Edition. Plate and Woodcuts. Crown 8vo. 10s. 6d.

CONTRIBUTIONS to MOLECULAR PHYSICS in the DOMAIN of RADIANT HEAT. By J. TYNDALL, LL.D. D.C.L. F.R.S. With 2 Plates and 31 Woodcuts. 8vo. 16s.

RESEARCHES on **DIAMAGNETISM** and **MAGNE-CRYSTALLIC** ACTION; including the Question of Diamagnetic Polarity. By J. TYNDALL, M.D. D.C.L. F.R.S. With 6 **plates** and many Woodcuts. 8vo. 14s.

NOTES of a **COURSE** of **SEVEN LECTURES** on **ELECTRICAL** PHENOMENA and THEORIES, delivered at the Royal Institution, A.D. 1870. By JOHN TYNDALL, LL.D., D.C.L., F.R.S. Crown 8vo. 1s. sewed; 1s. 6d. cloth.

SIX LECTURES on **LIGHT** delivered in America in **1872** and 1873. By JOHN TYNDALL, LL.D. D.C.L. F.R.S. Second Edition, with Portrait, Plate, and 59 **Diagrams.** Crown 8vo. 7s. 6d.

NOTES of a **COURSE** of NINE LECTURES on **LIGHT** delivered at the Royal Institution, A.D. 1869. By JOHN TYNDALL, LL.D. **D.C.L.** F.R.S. Crown 8vo. price 1s. sewed, or 1s. 6d. cloth.

ADDRESS delivered before the British Association **assembled** at Belfast. By JOHN TYNDALL, F.R.S. President. 8th Thousand, with New Preface and the Manchester Address. 8vo. 4s. 6d.

FRAGMENTS of SCIENCE. By JOHN TYNDALL, LL.D. D.C.L. F.R.S. New Edition. *[In the press.*

LIGHT SCIENCE for **LEISURE HOURS**; a Series of Familiar Essays on Scientific Subjects, Natural Phenomena, &c. By R. A. PROCTOR, B.A. First and Second Series. Crown 8vo. 7s. 6d. each.

A **TREATISE** on **MAGNETISM**, General and Terrestrial. **By** HUMPHREY LLOYD, D.D. D.C.L., Provost of Trinity College, Dublin. 8vo. 10s. 6d.

ELEMENTARY TREATISE on the **WAVE-THEORY** of **LIGHT**. By HUMPHREY LLOYD, D.D. D.C.L. Provost of Trinity College, Dublin. Third Edition, revised and enlarged. 8vo. price 10s. 6d.

The **CORRELATION** of **PHYSICAL FORCES.** By the Hon. Sir W. R. GROVE, M.A. F.R.S. one of the Judges of the Court of Common Pleas. Sixth Edition, with other Contributions to Science. 8vo. price 15s.

An **ELEMENTARY EXPOSITION** of the **DOCTRINE** of **ENERGY**. By D. D. HEATH, formerly Fellow of Trinity College, Cambridge. Post 8vo price 4s. 6d.

The **COMPARATIVE ANATOMY** and **PHYSIOLOGY** of the **VERTE-** BRATE ANIMALS. By RICHARD OWEN, F.R.S. D.C.L. With 1,472 Woodcuts. 3 vols. 8vo. £3. 13s. 6d.

PRINCIPLES of ANIMAL MECHANICS. By the Rev. S. HAUGHTON, F.R.S. Fellow of Trin. Coll. Dubl. M.D. Dubl. and D.C.L. Oxon. Second Edition, with 111 Figures on Wood. 8vo. 21s.

ROCKS CLASSIFIED and **DESCRIBED.** By BERNHARD VON COTTA. English Edition, by P. H. LAWRENCE; with English, German, and French Synonymes. Post 8vo. 14s.

The **ANCIENT STONE IMPLEMENTS, WEAPONS, and ORNA-** MENTS of **GREAT BRITAIN.** By JOHN EVANS, F.R.S. F.S.A. With 2 Plates and 476 Woodcuts. 8vo. price 28s.

The **NATIVE RACES** of the **PACIFIC STATES** of **NORTH AMERICA.** By HUBERT HOWE BANCROFT. Vol. I. Wild Tribes, their Manners and Customs, with 6 Maps. 8vo. 25s. Vol. II. Native Races of the Pacific, 25s. Vol. III. Myths and Languages, 25s. To be completed early in the year 1876, in Two more Volumes: Vol. IV. Antiquities and Architectural Remains. Vol. V. Aboriginal History and Migrations; Index to the Entire Work.

PRIMÆVAL WORLD of SWITZERLAND. By Professor Oswald Heer, of the University of Zurich. Translated by W. S. Dallas. F.L.S., and edited by James Heywood, M.A., F.R.S. 2 vols. 8vo. with numerous Illustrations. [*In the press.*

The ORIGIN of CIVILISATION and the PRIMITIVE CONDITION of Man; Mental and Social Condition of Savages. By Sir John Lubbock, Bart. M.P. F.R.S. Third Edition, with 25 Woodcuts. 8vo. 18s.

BIBLE ANIMALS; being a Description of every Living Creature mentioned in the Scriptures, from the Ape to the Coral. By the Rev. J. G. Wood, M.A. F.L.S. With about 100 Vignettes on Wood. 8vo. 21s.

HOMES WITHOUT HANDS; a Description of the Habitations of Animals, classed according to their Principle of Construction. By the Rev. J. G. Wood, M.A. F.L.S. With about 140 Vignettes on Wood. 8vo. 14s.

INSECTS AT HOME; a Popular Account of British Insects, their Structure, Habits, and Transformations. By the Rev. J. G. Wood, M.A. F.L.S. With upwards of 700 Illustrations. 8vo. price 21s.

INSECTS ABROAD; a Popular Account of Foreign Insects, their Structure, Habits, and Transformations. By J. G. Wood, M.A. F.L.S. Printed and illustrated uniformly with 'Insects at Home.' 8vo. price 21s.

STRANGE DWELLINGS; a description of the Habitations of Animals, abridged from 'Homes without Hands.' By the Rev. J. G. Wood, M.A. F.L.S. With about 60 Woodcut Illustrations. Crown 8vo. price 7s. 6d.

OUT of DOORS; a Selection of original Articles on Practical Natural History. By the Rev. J. G. Wood, M.A. F.L.S. With Eleven Illustrations from Original Designs engraved on Wood by G. Pearson. Crown 8vo. price 7s. 6d.

GAME PRESERVERS and BIRD PRESERVERS, or 'Which are our Friends?' By George Francis Morant, late Captain 12th Royal Lancers & Major Cape Mounted Riflemen. Crown 8vo. price 5s.

A FAMILIAR HISTORY of BIRDS. By E. Stanley, D.D. F.R.S. late Lord Bishop of Norwich. Seventh Edition, with Woodcuts. Fcp. 3s. 6d.

The SEA and its LIVING WONDERS. By Dr. George Hartwig. Latest revised Edition. 8vo. with many Illustrations, 10s. 6d.

The TROPICAL WORLD. By Dr. George Hartwig. With above 160 Illustrations. Latest revised Edition. 8vo. price 10s. 6d.

The SUBTERRANEAN WORLD. By Dr. George Hartwig. With 3 Maps and about 80 Woodcuts, including 8 full size of page. 8vo. price 10s. 6d.

The POLAR WORLD, a Popular Description of Man and Nature in the Arctic and Antarctic Regions of the Globe. By Dr. George Hartwig. With 8 Chromoxylographs, 3 Maps, and 85 Woodcuts. 8vo. 10s. 6d.

THE AERIAL WORLD. By Dr. G. Hartwig. New Edition, with 8 Chromoxylographs and 60 Woodcut Illustrations. 8vo. price 21s.

KIRBY and SPENCE'S INTRODUCTION to ENTOMOLOGY, or Elements of the Natural History of Insects. 7th Edition. Crown 8vo. 5s.

MAUNDER'S TREASURY of NATURAL HISTORY, or Popular Dictionary of Birds, Beasts, Fishes, Reptiles, Insects, and Creeping Things. With above 900 Woodcuts. Fcp. 8vo. price 6s. cloth, or 10s. bound in calf.

MAUNDER'S SCIENTIFIC and LITERARY TREASURY. New Edition, thoroughly revised and in great part rewritten, with above 1,000 new Articles, by J. Y. Johnson. Fcp. 8vo. 6s. cloth, or 10s. calf.

HANDBOOK of HARDY TREES, SHRUBS, and HERBACEOUS
PLANTS, containing Descriptions, Native Countries, &c. of a Selection of the
Best Species in Cultivation ; together with Cultural Details, Comparative
Hardiness, Suitability for Particular Positions, &c. By W. B. HEMSLEY. Based on
DECAISNE and NAUDIN'S *Manuel de l'Amateur des Jardins*, and including the 264
Original Woodcuts. Medium 8vo. 21s.

A GENERAL SYSTEM of BOTANY DESCRIPTIVE and ANALYTICAL.
I. Outlines of Organography, Anatomy, and Physiology ; II. Descriptions and
Illustrations of the Orders. By E. LE MAOUT, and J. DECAISNE, Members of
the Institute of France. Translated by Mrs. HOOKER. The Orders arranged
after the Method followed in the Universities and Schools of Great Britain, its
Colonies, America, and India ; with an Appendix on the Natural Method, and
other Additions, by J. D. HOOKER, F.R.S. &c. Director of the Royal Botanical
Gardens, Kew. With 5,500 Woodcuts. Imperial 8vo. price 52s. 6d.

The TREASURY of BOTANY, or Popular Dictionary of the Vegetable
Kingdom ; including a Glossary of Botanical Terms. Edited by J. LINDLEY,
F.R.S. and T. MOORE, F.L.S. assisted by eminent Contributors. With 274
Woodcuts and 20 Steel Plates. Two Parts, fcp. 8vo. 12s. cloth, or 20s. calf.

The ELEMENTS of BOTANY for FAMILIES and SCHOOLS.
Tenth Edition, revised by THOMAS MOORE, F.L.S. Fcp. 8vo. with 154 Woodcuts, 2s. 6d.

The ROSE AMATEUR'S GUIDE. By THOMAS RIVERS. Fourteenth
Edition. Fcp. 8vo. 4s.

LOUDON'S ENCYCLOPÆDIA of PLANTS ; comprising the Specific
Character, Description, Culture, History, &c. of all the Plants found in
Great Britain. With upwards of 12,000 Woodcuts. 8vo. 42s.

BRANDE'S DICTIONARY of SCIENCE, LITERATURE, and ART.
Re-edited by the Rev. GEORGE W. COX, M.A. late Scholar of Trinity College,
Oxford ; assisted by Contributors of eminent Scientific and Literary Acquire-
ments. New Edition, revised. 3 vols. medium 8vo. 63s.

Chemistry and *Physiology.*

A DICTIONARY of CHEMISTRY and the Allied Branches of other
Sciences. By HENRY WATTS, F.R.S. assisted by eminent Contributors.
Seven Volumes, medium 8vo. price £10, 16s. 6d.

ELEMENTS of CHEMISTRY, Theoretical and Practical. By W. ALLEN
MILLER, M.D. late Prof. of Chemistry, King's Coll. London. New
Edition. 3 vols. 8vo. £3. PART I. CHEMICAL PHYSICS, 15s. PART II.
INORGANIC CHEMISTRY, 21s. PART III. ORGANIC CHEMISTRY, New Edition
in the press.

SELECT METHODS in CHEMICAL ANALYSIS, chiefly INOR-
GANIC. By WILLIAM CROOKES, F.R.S. With 22 Woodcuts. Crown 8vo.
price 12s. 6d.

A PRACTICAL HANDBOOK of DYEING and CALICO PRINTING.
By WILLIAM CROOKES, F.R.S. With 11 Page Plates, 49 Specimens of Dyed and
Printed Fabrics, and 36 Woodcuts. 8vo. 42s.

OUTLINES of PHYSIOLOGY, Human and **Comparative. By JOHN** MARSHALL, F.R.C.S. Surgeon to the University College Hospital. 2 vols. crown 8vo. with 122 Woodcuts, 32s.

PHYSIOLOGICAL ANATOMY and PHYSIOLOGY of MAN. By the late R. B. TODD, M.D. F.R.S. and W. BOWMAN, F.R.S. of King's College. With numerous Illustrations. Vol. II. 8vo. 25s.

VOL. I. New Edition by Dr. LIONEL S. BEALE, F.R.S. in course of publication, with many Illustrations. PARTS I. and II. price 7s. 6d. each.

HEALTH in the HOUSE; a Series of Lectures on Elementary Physiology in its application to the Daily Wants of Man and Animals, delivered to the Wives and Children of Working Men in Leeds and Saltaire. By CATHERINE M. BUCKTON. Third Edition, revised. Small 8vo. Woodcuts, 5s.

The Fine Arts, and *Illustrated Editions.*

A DICTIONARY of ARTISTS of the ENGLISH SCHOOL : Painters, Sculptors, Architects, Engravers, and Ornamentists ; with Notices of their Lives and Works. By S. REDGRAVE. 8vo. 16s.

POEMS. By WILLIAM B. SCOTT. I. Ballads and Tales. II. Studies from Nature. III. Sonnets &c. Illustrated by 17 Etchings by W. B. SCOTT (the Author) and L. ALMA TADEMA. Crown 8vo. price 15s.

HALF-HOUR LECTURES on the HISTORY and PRACTICE of the FINE and ORNAMENTAL ARTS. By W. B. SCOTT, Assistant Inspector in Art, Department of Science and Art. Third Edition, with 50 Woodcuts. Crown 8vo. 8s. 6d.

The THREE CATHEDRALS DEDICATED to ST. PAUL, in LONDON ; their History from the Foundation of the First Building in the Sixth Century to the Proposals for the Adornment of the Present Cathedral. By WILLIAM LONGMAN, F.A.S. With numerous Illustrations. Square crown 8vo. 21s.

IN FAIRYLAND ; Pictures from the Elf-World. By RICHARD DOYLE. With a Poem by W. ALLINGHAM. With Sixteen Plates, containing Thirty-six Designs printed in Colours. Second Edition. Folio, price 15s.

The NEW TESTAMENT, illustrated with Wood Engravings after the Early Masters, chiefly of the Italian School. Crown 4to. 63s. cloth, gilt top; or £5 5s. elegantly bound in morocco.

SACRED and LEGENDARY ART. By MRS. JAMESON.

Legends of the Saints and Martyrs. New Edition, with 19 Etchings and 187 Woodcuts. 2 vols. square crown 8vo. 31s. 6d.

Legends of the Monastic Orders. New Edition, with 11 Etchings and 88 Woodcuts. 1 vol. square crown 8vo. 21s.

Legends of the Madonna. New Edition, with 27 Etchings and 165 Woodcuts. 1 vol. square crown 8vo. 21s.

The History of Our Lord, with that of his Types and Precursors. Completed by Lady EASTLAKE. Revised Edition, with 31 Etchings and 281 Woodcuts. 2 vols. square crown 8vo. 42s.

B

The Useful Arts, Manufactures, &c.

GWILT'S ENCYCLOPÆDIA of ARCHITECTURE, with above 1,600
Engravings on Wood. New Edition, revised and enlarged by WYATT
PAPWORTH. 8vo. 52s. 6d.

HINTS on HOUSEHOLD TASTE in FURNITURE, UPHOLSTERY,
and other Details. By CHARLES L. EASTLAKE, Architect. New Edition,
with about 90 Illustrations. Square crown 8vo. 14s.

PRINCIPLES of MECHANISM, designed for the Use of Students in
the Universities, and **for Engineering Students** generally. **By** R.
WILLIS, M.A. F.R.S. &c. Jacksonian Professor in the University of Cambridge. Second Edition, enlarged; with 374 Woodcuts. 8vo. 18s.

LATHES and TURNING, Simple, Mechanical, and Ornamental.
By W. HENRY NORTHCOTT. With about 240 Illustrations. 8vo. 18s.

PERSPECTIVE ; or, the Art of Drawing what One Sees. Explained
and adapted to **the use** of those Sketching **from Nature.** By Lieut. W. H.
COLLINS, R.E. F.R.A.S. With 37 Woodcuts. **Crown 8vo. price 5s.**

INDUSTRIAL CHEMISTRY; a Manual for Manufacturers and **for**
use in Colleges or Technical Schools. Being a Translation of Professors Stohmann
and Engler's German Edition of PAYEN'S *Précis de Chimie Industrielle*, by Dr.
J. D. BARRY. Edited and supplemented by B. H. PAUL, Ph.D. 8vo. with Plates
and Woodcuts. 　　　　　　　　　　　　　　　　　　　　　　[*In the press.*

URE'S DICTIONARY of ARTS, MANUFACTURES, and MINES.
Seventh Edition, rewritten and enlarged by ROBERT HUNT, F.R.S. assisted by
numerous Contributors eminent in Science and the Arts, and familiar with
Manufactures. With above 2,100 Woodcuts. 3 vols. medium 8vo. £5 5s.

HANDBOOK of PRACTICAL TELEGRAPHY. By R. S. CULLEY
Memb. Inst. C.E. Engineer-in-Chief of Telegraphs to **the Post Office.** Sixth
Edition, with 144 Woodcuts and 5 Plates. 8vo. price 16s.

The ENGINEER'S HANDBOOK; explaining the Principles which
should guide the Young Engineer in the Construction of Machinery, with the
necessary Rules, Proportions, and Tables By C. S. LOWNDES. Post 8vo. 5s.

ENCYCLOPÆDIA of CIVIL ENGINEERING, Historical, Theoretical,
and **Practical.** By E. CRESY, C.E. With above 3,000 Woodcuts. 8vo. 42s.

OCCASIONAL PAPERS on SUBJECTS connected with CIVIL EN-
GINEERING, **GUNNERY,** and Naval Architecture. By MICHAEL SCOTT,
Memb. Inst. C.E. & of Inst. N.A. 2 vols. 8vo. with Plates, 42s.

TREATISE on MILLS and MILLWORK. By Sir W. FAIRBAIRN,
Bart. F.R.S. **New Edition,** with 18 Plates and 322 Woodcuts. 2 vols. 8vo. 32s.

USEFUL INFORMATION for ENGINEERS. By Sir W. FAIRBAIRN,
Bart. F.R.S. Revised Edition, with Illustrations. 3 vols. crown 8vo. price 31s. 6d.

The APPLICATION of CAST and WROUGHT IRON to Building
Purposes. **By** Sir W. FAIRBAIRN, Bart. F.R.S. Fourth Edition, enlarged ; with
6 Plates and 118 Woodcuts. 8vo. price 16s.

A TREATISE on the STEAM ENGINE, in its various Applications to Mines, Mills, Steam Navigation, Railways, and Agriculture. By J. BOURNE, C.E. Eighth Edition; with Portrait, 37 Plates, and 546 Woodcuts. 4to. 42s.

CATECHISM of the STEAM ENGINE, in its various Applications to Mines, Mills, Steam Navigation, Railways, and Agriculture. By the same Author. With 89 Woodcuts. Fcp. 8vo. 6s.

HANDBOOK of the STEAM ENGINE. By the same Author, forming a KEY to the Catechism of the Steam Engine, with 67 Woodcuts. Fcp. 9s.

BOURNE'S RECENT IMPROVEMENTS in the STEAM ENGINE in its various applications to Mines, Mills, Steam Navigation, Railways, and Agriculture. By JOHN BOURNE, C.E. New Edition, with 124 Woodcuts. Fcp. 8vo. 6s.

PRACTICAL TREATISE on METALLURGY, adapted from the last German Edition of Professor KERL'S *Metallurgy* by W. CROOKES, F.R.S. &c. and E. BÖHRIG, Ph.D. M.E. With 625 Woodcuts. 3 vols. 8vo. price £4 19s.

MITCHELL'S MANUAL of PRACTICAL ASSAYING. Fourth Edition, for the most part rewritten, with all the recent Discoveries incorporated, by W. CROOKES, F.R.S. With 199 Woodcuts. 8vo. 31s. 6d.

LOUDON'S ENCYCLOPÆDIA of AGRICULTURE: comprising the Laying-out, Improvement, and Management of Landed Property, and the Cultivation and Economy of Agricultural Produce. With 1,100 Woodcuts. 8vo. 21s.

London's Encyclopædia of Gardening: comprising the Theory and Practice of Horticulture, Floriculture, Arboriculture, and Landscape Gardening. With 1,000 Woodcuts. 8vo. 21s.

Religious and Moral Works.

CHRISTIAN LIFE, its COURSE, its HINDRANCES, and its HELPS; Sermons preached mostly in the Chapel of Rugby School. By the late Rev. THOMAS ARNOLD, D.D. 8vo. 7s. 6d.

CHRISTIAN LIFE, its HOPES, its FEARS, and its CLOSE; Sermons preached mostly in the Chapel of Rugby School. By the late Rev. THOMAS ARNOLD, D.D. 8vo. 7s. 6d.

SERMONS chiefly on the INTERPRETATION of SCRIPTURE. By the late Rev. THOMAS ARNOLD, D.D. 8vo. price 7s. 6d.

SERMONS preached in the Chapel of Rugby School; with an Address before Confirmation. By the late Rev. THOMAS ARNOLD, D.D. Fcp. 8vo. 3s. 6d.

THREE ESSAYS on RELIGION: Nature; the Utility of Religion; Theism. By JOHN STUART MILL. 8vo. price 10s. 6d.

INTRODUCTION to the SCIENCE of RELIGION. Four Lecture delivered at the Royal Institution; with Two Essays on False Analogies an the Philosophy of Mythology. By F. MAX MÜLLER, M.A. Crown 8vo. 10s. 6d.

B 2

SUPERNATURAL RELIGION; an Inquiry into the Reality of Divine Revelation. Fifth Edition, carefully revised, with Eighty Pages of New Preface. 2 vols. 8vo. 24s.

ESSAYS on the **HISTORY of the CHRISTIAN RELIGION.** By JOHN Earl RUSSELL, K.G. Cabinet Edition, revised. Fcp. 8vo. price 3s. 6d.

The NEW BIBLE COMMENTARY, by Bishops and other Clergy of the Anglican Church, critically examined by the Right Rev. J. W. COLENSO, D.D. Bishop of Natal. 8vo. price 25s.

REASONS of FAITH; or, the ORDER of the Christian Argument Developed and Explained. By the Rev. **G. S.** DREW, M.A. Second Edition, revised and enlarged. Fcp. 8vo. price **6s.**

The PRIMITIVE and CATHOLIC FAITH in Relation to the Church of England. By the Rev. B. W. SAVILE, M.A. **Rector** of Shillingford, Exeter ; Author of 'Truth of the Bible' &c. 8vo. price **7s.**

SYNONYMS of the OLD TESTAMENT, their BEARING on CHRIS-TIAN FAITH and PRACTICE. By the Rev. R. B. GIRDLESTONE, **M.A.** 8vo. 15s.

An INTRODUCTION to the THEOLOGY of the CHURCH of ENGLAND, in an Exposition of the Thirty-nine Articles. By the Rev. T. P. BOULTBEE, LL.D. New Edition, Fcp. 8vo. price 6s.

An EXPOSITION of the 39 ARTICLES, Historical and Doctrinal. By E. HAROLD BROWNE, D.D. Lord Bishop of Winchester. New Edit. 8vo. 16s.

The LIFE and EPISTLES of ST. PAUL. By the Rev. W. J. CONYBEARE, M.A., and the Very Rev. J. S. HOWSON, D.D. Dean of Chester :—

LIBRARY EDITION, with all the Original **Illustrations, Maps, Landscapes on** Steel, Woodcuts, &c. 2 vols. 4to. 42s.

INTERMEDIATE EDITION, with a Selection **of Maps, Plates, and** Woodcuts. 2 vols. square crown 8vo. 21s.

STUDENT'S EDITION, revised and **condensed, with 46** Illustrations and Maps. **1 vol.** crown 8vo. price 9s.

COMMENTARY on the EPISTLE to the ROMANS. By the Rev. W. A. O'CONOR, B.A. **Crown 8vo. price 3s. 6d.**

The EPISTLE to the HEBREWS; with Analytical Introduction and Notes. By the Rev. W. A. O'CONOR, B.A. Crown 8vo. price 4s. 6d.

A CRITICAL and GRAMMATICAL COMMENTARY on ST. PAUL'S Epistles. By C. J. ELLICOTT, D.D. Lord Bishop of Gloucester and Bristol. 8vo.

Galatians, Fourth Edition, **8s. 6d.**

Ephesians, Fourth Edition, **8s. 6d.**

Pastoral Epistles, Fourth Edition, **10s. 6d.**

Philippians, Colossians, **and Philemon,** Third Edition, 10s. 6d.

Thessalonians, Third Edition, **7s. 6d.**

HISTORICAL LECTURES on the **LIFE** of **OUR LORD**. By C. J. ELLICOTT, D.D. Bishop of Gloucester and Bristol. Fifth Edition. 8vo. 12s.

EVIDENCE of the **TRUTH** of the **CHRISTIAN RELIGION** derived from the Literal Fulfilment of Prophecy. By ALEXANDER KEITH, D.D. 37th Edition, with Plates, in square 8vo. 12s. 6d.; 39th Edition, in post 8vo. 6s.

HISTORY of ISRAEL. By H. EWALD, late Professor of the Univ. of Göttingen. Translated by J. E. CARPENTER, M.A., with a Preface by RUSSELL MARTINEAU, M.A. 5 vols. 8vo. 63s.

The **ANTIQUITIES of ISRAEL.** By HEINRICH EWALD, late Professor of the University of Göttingen. Translated from the German by HENRY SHAEN SOLLY, M.A. 8vo. price 12s. 6d. [Nearly ready.

The **TREASURY of BIBLE KNOWLEDGE**; being a Dictionary of the Books, Persons, Places, Events, and other matters of which mention is made in Holy Scripture. By Rev. J. AYRE, M.A. With Maps, 16 Plates, and numerous Woodcuts. Fcp. 8vo. price 6s. cloth, or 10s. neatly bound in calf.

LECTURES on the **PENTATEUCH** and the **MOABITE STONE.** By the Right Rev. J. W. COLENSO, D.D. Bishop of Natal. 8vo. 12s.

The **PENTATEUCH** and **BOOK** of **JOSHUA CRITICALLY EXAMINED.** By the Right Rev. J. W. COLENSO, D.D. Bishop of Natal. Crown 8vo. 6s.

SOME QUESTIONS of the DAY. By the Author of 'Amy Herbert.' Crown 8vo. price 2s. 6d.

THOUGHTS for the AGE. By the Author of 'Amy Herbert,' &c. New Edition, revised. Fcp. 8vo. price 3s. 6d.

PASSING THOUGHTS on **RELIGION.** By the Author of 'Amy Herbert.' New Edition. Fcp. 8vo. price 3s. 6d.

The **DOCTRINE** and **PRACTICE** of **CONFESSION** in the **CHURCH of ENGLAND.** By the Rev. W. E. JELF, B.D. sometime Censor of Ch. Ch.; Author of 'Quousque' &c. 8vo. price 7s. 6d.

FASTING COMMUNION, how Binding in England by the Canons. With the Testimony of the Early Fathers. An Historical Essay. By the Rev. H. T. KINGDON, M.A. Second Edition. 8vo. 10s. 6d.

PREPARATION for the HOLY COMMUNION; the Devotions chiefly from the Works of JEREMY TAYLOR. By Miss SEWELL. 32mo. 3s.

LYRA GERMANICA, Hymns translated from the German by Miss C. WINKWORTH. Fcp. 8vo. price 5s.

SPIRITUAL SONGS for the SUNDAYS and HOLIDAYS throughout the Year. By J. S. B. MONSELL, LL.D. Ninth Thousand. Fcp. 8vo. 5s. 18mo. 2s.

ENDEAVOURS after the **CHRISTIAN LIFE**: Discourses. By the Rev. J. MARTINEAU, LL.D. Fifth Edition, carefully revised. Crown 8vo. 7s. 6d.

HYMNS of PRAISE and PRAYER, collected and edited by the Rev. J. MARTINEAU, LL.D. Crown 8vo. 4s. 6d. 32mo. 1s. 6d.

The **TYPES of GENESIS,** briefly considered as revealing the Development of Human Nature. By ANDREW JUKES. Third Edition. Crown 8vo. 7s. 6d.

The **SECOND DEATH** and the **RESTITUTION of ALL THINGS**; with some Preliminary Remarks on the Nature and Inspiration of Holy Scripture. (A Letter to a Friend.) By ANDREW JUKES. Fourth Edition. Crown 8vo. 3s. 6d.

WHATELY'S INTRODUCTORY LESSONS on the CHRISTIAN Evidences. 18mo. 6d.

BISHOP JEREMY TAYLOR'S ENTIRE WORKS. With Life by BISHOP HEBER. Revised and corrected by the Rev. C. P. EDEN. Complete in Ten Volumes, 8vo. cloth, price £5. 5s.

Travels, Voyages, &c.

The INDIAN ALPS, and How we Crossed them: being a Narrative of Two Years' Residence in the Eastern Himalayas, and Two Months' Tour into the Interior, towards Kinchinjunga and Mount Everest. By a Lady PIONEER. With Illustrations from Original Drawings made on the spot by the Authoress. Imperial 8vo. *[Nearly ready.*

TYROL and the TYROLESE; being an Account of the People and the Land, in their Social, Sporting, and Mountaineering Aspects. By W. A. BAILLIE GROHMAN. With numerous Illustrations from Sketches by the Author. Crown 8vo. *[Now ready.*

'The FROSTY CAUCASUS;' An Account of a Walk through Part of the Range, and of an Ascent of Elbruz in the Summer of 1874. By F. C. GROVE. With Eight Illustrations engraved on Wood by E. Whymper, from Photographs taken during the Journey, and a Map. Crown 8vo. price 15s.

A JOURNEY of 1,000 MILES through EGYPT and NUBIA to the SECOND CATARACT of the NILE. Being a Personal Narrative of Four and a Half Months' Life in a Dahabeeyah on the Nile; with some Account of the Discovery and Excavation of a Rock-cut Chamber, Descriptions of the River, the Ruins, and the Desert, the People met, the Places visited, the ways and manners of the Natives, &c. By AMELIA B. EDWARDS. With numerous Illustrations from Drawings by the Authoress, Map, Plans, Facsimiles, &c. Imperial 8vo. *[Nearly ready.*

ITALIAN ALPS; Sketches in the Mountains of Ticino, Lombardy, the Trentino, and Venetia. By DOUGLAS W. FRESHFIELD, Editor of 'The Alpine Journal.' Square crown 8vo. with Maps and Illustrations, price 15s.

HERE and THERE in the ALPS. By the Hon. FREDERICA PLUNKET. With Vignette Title. Post 8vo. 6s. 6d.

REMINISCENCES of FEN and MERE. By J. M. HEATHCOTE. With Maps and numerous Illustrations from Sketches by the Author. 1 vol. 8vo. *[Nearly ready.*

TWO YEARS IN FIJI, a Descriptive Narrative of a Residence in the Fijian Group of Islands; with some Account of the Fortunes of Foreign Settlers and Colonists up to the Time of the British Annexation. By LITTON FORBES, M.D. L.R.C.P. F.R.G.S. late Medical Officer to the German Consulate, Apia, Navigator Islands. Crown 8vo. 8s. 6d.

EIGHT YEARS in CEYLON. By Sir SAMUEL W. BAKER, M.A. F.R.G.S. New Edition, with Illustrations engraved on Wood, by G. Pearson. Crown 8vo. 7s. 6d.

The RIFLE and the HOUND in CEYLON. By Sir SAMUEL W. BAKER, M.A. F.R.G.S. New Edition, with Illustrations engraved on Wood by G. Pearson. Crown 8vo. 7s. 6d.

MEETING the SUN; a Journey all round the World through Egypt, China, Japan, and California. By WILLIAM SIMPSON, F.R.G.S. With 48 Heliotypes and Wood Engravings from Drawings by the Author. Medium 8vo. 24s.

UNTRODDEN PEAKS and UNFREQUENTED VALLEYS; a Midsummer Ramble among the Dolomites. By AMELIA B. EDWARDS. With a Map and 27 Wood Engravings. Medium 8vo. 21s.

The DOLOMITE MOUNTAINS; Excursions through Tyrol, Carinthia, Carniola, and Friuli, 1861-1863. By J. GILBERT and G. C. CHURCHILL, F.R.G.S. With numerous Illustrations. Square crown 8vo. 21s.

The VALLEYS of TIROL; their Traditions and Customs, and how to Visit them. By Miss R. H. BUSK, Author of 'The Folk-Lore of Rome,' &c. With Maps and Frontispiece. Crown 8vo. 12s. 6d.

The ALPINE CLUB MAP of SWITZERLAND, with parts of the Neighbouring Countries, on the Scale of Four Miles to an Inch. Edited by R. C. NICHOLS, F.S.A. F.R.G.S. In Four Sheets, price 42s. or mounted in a case, 52s. 6d. Each Sheet may be had separately, price 12s. or mounted in a case, 15s.

MAP of the CHAIN of MONT BLANC, from an Actual Survey in 1863-1864. By ADAMS-REILLY, F.R.G.S. M.A.C. Published under the Authority of the Alpine Club. In Chromolithography on extra stout drawing-paper 28in. × 17in. price 10s. or mounted on canvas in a folding case, 12s. 6d.

HOW to SEE NORWAY. By Captain J. R. CAMPBELL. With Map and 5 Woodcuts. Fcp. 8vo. price 5s.

GUIDE to the PYRENEES, for the use of Mountaineers. By CHARLES PACKE. With Map and Illustrations. Crown 8vo. 7s. 6d.

The ALPINE GUIDE. By JOHN BALL, M.R.I.A. late President of the Alpine Club. 3 vols. post 8vo. Thoroughly Revised Editions, with Maps and Illustrations:—I. *Western Alps*, 6s. 6d. II. *Central Alps*, 7s. 6d. III. *Eastern Alps*, 10s. 6d. Or in Ten Parts, price 2s. 6d. each.

Introduction on Alpine Travelling in General, and on the Geology of the Alps, price 1s. Each of the Three Volumes or Parts of the *Alpine Guide* may be had with this INTRODUCTION prefixed, price 1s. extra.

VISITS to REMARKABLE PLACES: Old Halls, Battle-Fields, and Stones Illustrative of Striking Passages in English History and Poetry. By WILLIAM HOWITT. 2 vols. square crown 8vo. with Woodcuts, 25s.

Works of *Fiction*.

HIGGLEDY-PIGGLEDY; or, Stories for Everybody and Everybody's Children. By the Right Hon. E. M. KNATCHBULL-HUGESSEN, M.P. With Nine Illustrations from Original Designs by R. Doyle, engraved on Wood by G. Pearson. Crown 8vo. price 6s.

WHISPERS from FAIRYLAND. By the Right Hon. E. H. KNATCH-BULL-HUGESSEN, M.P. With Nine Illustrations from Original Designs engraved on Wood by G. Pearson. Crown 8vo. price 6s.

LADY WILLOUGHBY'S DIARY, 1635—1663; Charles the First, the Protectorate, and the Restoration. Reproduced in the Style of the Period to which the Diary relates. Crown 8vo. price 7s. 6d.

TALES of the TEUTONIC LANDS. By the Rev. G. W. Cox, M.A. and E. H. JONES. Crown 8vo. 10s. 6d.

The FOLK-LORE of ROME, collected by Word of Mouth from the People. By Miss R. H. BUSK, Author of 'Patrañas,' &c. Crown 8vo. 12s. 6d.

NOVELS and TALES. By the Right Hon. B. DISRAELI, M.P. Cabinet Edition, complete in Ten Volumes, crown 8vo. price £3.

LOTHAIR, 6s.	HENRIETTA TEMPLE, 6s.
CONINGSBY, 6s.	CONTARINI FLEMING, &c. 6s.
SYBIL, 6s.	ALROY, IXION, &c. 6s.
TANCRED, 6s.	The YOUNG DUKE, &c. 6s.
VENETIA, 6s.	VIVIAN GREY ,6s.

The MODERN NOVELIST'S LIBRARY. Each Work in crown 8vo. complete in a Single Volume:—

ATHERSTONE PRIORY, 2s. boards ; 2s. 6d. cloth.
MADEMOISELLE MORI, 2s. boards ; 2s. 6d. cloth.
MELVILLE'S GLADIATORS, 2s boards ; 2s. 6d. cloth.
———— GOOD FOR NOTHING, 2s. boards ; 2s. 6d. cloth.
———— HOLMBY HOUSE, 2s. boards ; 2s. 6d. cloth.
———— INTERPRETER, 2s. boards ; 2s. 6d. cloth.
———— KATE COVENTRY, 2s. boards ; 2s. 6d. cloth.
———— QUEEN'S MARIES, 2s. boards ; 2s. 6d. cloth.
———— DIGBY GRAND, 2s. boards ; 2s. 6d. cloth.
———— GENERAL BOUNCE, 2s. boards ; 2s. 6d. cloth.
TROLLOPE'S WARDEN, 1s. 6d. boards ; 2s. cloth.
————BARCHESTER TOWERS, 2s. boards ; 2s. 6d. cloth.
BRAMLEY-MOORE'S SIX SISTERS of the VALLEYS, 2s. boards ; 2s. 6d. cloth.
The BURGOMASTER'S FAMILY, 2s. boards ; 2s. 6d. cloth.

CABINET EDITION of STORIES and TALES by Miss SEWELL:—

AMY HERBERT, 2s. 6d.	IVORS, 2s. 6d.
GERTRUDE, 2s. 6d.	KATHARINE ASHTON, 2s. 6d.
The EARL'S DAUGHTER, 2s. 6d.	MARGARET PERCIVAL, 3s. 6d.
EXPERIENCE of LIFE, 2s. 6d.	LANETON PARSONAGE, 3s. 6d.
CLEVE HALL, 2s. 6d.	URSULA, 3s. 6d.

BECKER'S GALLUS; or, Roman Scenes of the Time of Augustus : with Notes and Excursuses. New Edition. Post 8vo. 7s. 6d.

BECKER'S CHARICLES: a Tale illustrative of Private Life among the Ancient Greeks : with Notes and Excursuses. New Edition. Post 8vo. 7s. 6d.

Poetry and The Drama.

POEMS. By WILLIAM B. SCOTT. I. Ballads and Tales. II. Studies from Nature. III. Sonnets &c. Illustrated by 17 Etchings by L. ALMA TADEMA and WILLIAM B. SCOTT. Crown 8vo. price 15s.

MOORE'S IRISH MELODIES, Maclise's Edition, with 161 Steel Plates from Original Drawings. Super-royal 8vo. 31s. 6d.

Miniature Edition of Moore's Irish Melodies, with Maclise's Designs (as above) reduced in Lithography. Imp. 16mo. 10s. 6d.

BALLADS and LYRICS of OLD FRANCE; with other Poems. By A. LANG, Fellow of Merton College, Oxford. Square fcp. 8vo. price 5s.

MOORE'S LALLA ROOKH. Tenniel's Edition, with 68 Wood Engravings from Original Drawings and other Illustrations. Fcp. 4to. 21s.

SOUTHEY'S POETICAL WORKS, with the Author's last Corrections and copyright Additions. Medium 8vo. with Portrait and Vignette, 14s.

LAYS of ANCIENT ROME; with IVRY and the ARMADA. By the Right Hon. Lord MACAULAY. 16mo. 3s. 6d.

LORD MACAULAY'S LAYS of ANCIENT ROME. With 90 Illustrations on Wood, from the Antique, from Drawings by G. SCHARF. Fcp. 4to. 21s.

Miniature Edition of Lord Macaulay's Lays of Ancient Rome, with the Illustrations (as above) reduced in Lithography. Imp. 16mo. 10s. 6d.

The ÆNEID of VIRGIL Translated into English Verse. By JOHN CONINGTON, M.A. New Edition. Crown 8vo. 9s.

HORATII OPERA. Library Edition, with Marginal References and English Notes. Edited by the Rev. J. E. YONGE. 8vo. 21s.

The LYCIDAS and EPITAPHIUM DAMONIS of MILTON. Edited, with Notes and Introduction (including a Reprint of the rare Latin Version of the Lycidas, by W. Hogg, 1694), by C. S. JERRAM, M.A. Crown 8vo. 2s. 6d.

BOWDLER'S FAMILY SHAKSPEARE, cheaper **Genuine Editions.** Medium 8vo. large type, with 36 WOODCUTS, price 14s. **Cabinet Edition,** with the same ILLUSTRATIONS, 6 vols. fcp. 8vo. price 21s.

POEMS. By JEAN INGELOW. 2 vols. fcp. 8vo. price 10s.
FIRST SERIES, containing 'DIVIDED,' 'The STAR'S MONUMENT,' &c. Sixteenth Thousand. Fcp. 8vo. price 5s.
SECOND SERIES, 'A STORY of DOOM,' 'GLADYS and her ISLAND,' &c. Fifth Thousand. Fcp. 8vo. price 5s.

POEMS by Jean Ingelow. FIRST SERIES, with nearly 100 Illustrations, engraved on Wood by Dalziel Brothers. Fcp. 4to. 21s.

Rural Sports, &c.

DOWN the ROAD; Or, Reminiscences of a Gentleman Coachman. By C. T. S. BIRCH REYNARDSON. Second Edition, with Twelve Coloured Illustrations from Paintings by H. Alken. Medium 8vo. 21s.

The DEAD SHOT; or, Sportsman's Complete Guide: a Treatise on the Use of the Gun, Dog-breaking, Pigeon-shooting, &c. By MARKSMAN. Revised Edition. Fcp. 8vo. with Plates, 5s.

ENCYCLOPÆDIA of RURAL SPORTS; a complete **Account,** Historical, Practical, and Descriptive, of Hunting, Shooting, Fishing, Racing, and all other Rural and Athletic Sports and Pastimes. By D. P. BLAINE. With above 600 Woodcuts (20 from Designs by JOHN LEECH). 8vo. 21s.

The FLY-FISHER'S ENTOMOLOGY. By ALFRED RONALDS. With coloured Representations of the Natural and Artificial Insect. Sixth Edition, with 20 coloured Plates. 8vo. 14s.

A BOOK on ANGLING; a complete Treatise on the Art of Angling in every branch. By FRANCIS FRANCIS. New Edition, with Portrait and 15 other Plates, plain and coloured. Post 8vo. 15s.

WILCOCKS'S SEA-FISHERMAN; comprising the Chief Methods of Hook and Line Fishing, a Glance at Nets, and Remarks on Boats and Boating. New Edition, with 80 Woodcuts. Post 8vo. 12s. 6d.

HORSES and STABLES. By Colonel F. FITZWYGRAM, XV. the King's Hussars. With Twenty-four Plates of Illustrations, containing very numerous Figures engraved on Wood. 8vo. 10s. 6d.

The HORSE'S FOOT, and HOW to KEEP it SOUND. By W. MILES, Esq. Ninth Edition, with Illustrations. Imperial 8vo. 12s. 6d.

A PLAIN TREATISE on HORSE-SHOEING. By W. MILES, Esq. Sixth Edition. Post 8vo. with Illustrations, 2s. 6d.

STABLES and STABLE-FITTINGS. By W. MILES, Esq. Imp. 8vo. with 13 Plates, 15s.

REMARKS on HORSES' TEETH, addressed to Purchasers. By W. MILES, Esq. Post 8vo. 1s. 6d.

The HORSE: with a Treatise on Draught. By WILLIAM YOUATT. New Edition, revised and enlarged. 8vo. with numerous Woodcuts, 12s. 6d.

The DOG. By WILLIAM YOUATT. 8vo. with numerous Woodcuts, 6s.

The DOG in HEALTH and DISEASE. By STONEHENGE. With 70 Wood Engravings. Square crown 8vo. 7s. 6d.

The GREYHOUND. By STONEHENGE. Revised Edition, with 25 Portraits of Greyhounds. Square crown 8vo. 15s.

The OX; his Diseases and their Treatment: with an Essay on Parturition in the Cow. By J. R. DOBSON. Crown 8vo. with Illustrations, 7s. 6d.

Works of Utility and General Information.

The THEORY and PRACTICE of BANKING. By H. D. MACLEOD, M.A. Barrister-at-Law. Third and Cheaper Edition, revised. (In Two Volumes.) VOL. 1. 8vo. price 12s.

M'CULLOCH'S DICTIONARY, Practical, Theoretical, and Historical, of Commerce and Commercial Navigation. New and revised Edition. 8vo. 63s.

The CABINET LAWYER; a Popular Digest of the Laws of England, Civil, Criminal, and Constitutional intended for Practical Use and General Information. Twenty-fifth Edition. Fcp. 8vo. price 9s.

PROTECTION from FIRE and THIEVES. Including the Construction of Locks, Safes, Strong-Room, and Fire-proof Buildings; Burglary and the Means of Preventing it; Fire, its Detection, Prevention, and Extinction; &c. By G. H. CHUBB, Assoc. Inst. C.E. With 32 Woodcuts. Crown 8vo. 5s.

BLACKSTONE ECONOMISED, a Compendium of the Laws of England to the Present time, in Four Books, each embracing the Legal Principles and Practical Information contained in their respective volumes of Blackstone, supplemented by Subsequent Statutory Enactments, Important Legal Decisions, &c. By D. M. AIRD, Barrister-at-Law. Revised Edition. Post 8vo. 7s. 6d.

PEWTNER'S COMPREHENSIVE SPECIFIER; a Guide to the Practical Specification of every kind of Building-Artificers' Work, with Forms of Conditions and Agreements. Edited by W. YOUNG. Crown 8vo. 6s.

COLLIERIES and COLLIERS; a Handbook of the Law and Leading Cases relating thereto. By J. C. FOWLER. Third Edition. Fcp. 8vo. 7s. 6d.

HINTS to MOTHERS on the **MANAGEMENT** of their **HEALTH** during the Period of Pregnancy and in the Lying-in Room. By the late THOMAS BULL, M.D. Fcp. 8vo. 5s.

The **MATERNAL MANAGEMENT of CHILDREN in HEALTH** and Disease. By the late THOMAS BULL, M.D. Fcp. 8vo. 5s.

The **THEORY of the MODERN SCIENTIFIC GAME of WHIST.** By WILLIAM POLE, F.R.S. Fifth Edition, enlarged. Fcp. 8vo. 2s. 6d.

CHESS OPENINGS. By F. W. LONGMAN, Balliol College, Oxford. Second Edition revised. Fcp. 8vo. 2s. 6d.

THREE HUNDRED ORIGINAL CHESS PROBLEMS and STUDIES. By JAMES PIERCE, M.A. and W. T. PIERCE. With numerous Diagrams. Square fcp. 8vo. 7s. 6d. SUPPLEMENT, price 2s. 6d.

A PRACTICAL TREATISE on BREWING; with Formulæ for Public Brewers, and Instructions for Private Families. By W. BLACK. 8vo. 10s. 6d.

MODERN COOKERY for PRIVATE FAMILIES, reduced to a System of Easy Practice in a Series of carefully-tested Receipts. By ELIZA ACTON. Newly revised and enlarged; with 8 Plates and 150 Woodcuts. Fcp. 8vo. 6s.

MAUNDER'S TREASURY of KNOWLEDGE and LIBRARY of Reference; comprising an English Dictionary and Grammar, Universal Gazetteer, Classical Dictionary, Chronology, Law Dictionary, a synopsis of the Peerage useful Tables, &c. Revised Edition. Fcp. 8vo. 6s. cloth, or 10s. calf.

Knowledge for the *Young.*

The **STEPPING-STONE to KNOWLEDGE**; or upwards of 700 Questions and Answers on Miscellaneous Subjects, adapted to the capacity of Infant minds. 18mo. 1s.

SECOND SERIES of the STEPPING-STONE to KNOWLEDGE: Containing upwards of 800 Questions and Answers on Miscellaneous Subjects not contained in the FIRST SERIES. 18mo. 1s.

The **STEPPING-STONE to GEOGRAPHY:** Containing several Hundred Questions and Answers on Geographical Subjects. 18mo. 1s.

The STEPPING-STONE to ENGLISH HISTORY; Questions and Answers on the History of England. 18mo. 1s.

The STEPPING-STONE to BIBLE KNOWLEDGE; Questions and Answers on the Old and New Testaments. 18mo. 1s.

The STEPPING-STONE to BIOGRAPHY; Questions and Answers on the Lives of Eminent Men and Women. 18mo. 1s.

The STEPPING-STONE to IRISH HISTORY: Containing several Hundred Questions and Answers on the History of Ireland. 18mo. 1s.

The STEPPING-STONE to FRENCH HISTORY: Containing several Hundred Questions and Answers on the History of France. 18mo. 1s.

The STEPPING-STONE to ROMAN HISTORY: Containing several Hundred Questions and Answers on the History of Rome. 18mo. 1s.

The STEPPING-STONE to GRECIAN HISTORY: Containing several Hundred Questions and Answers on the History of Greece. 18mo. 1s.

The STEPPING-STONE to ENGLISH GRAMMAR: Containing several Hundred Questions and Answers on English Grammar. 18mo. 1s.

The STEPPING-STONE to FRENCH PRONUNCIATION and CONVERSATION : Containing several Hundred Questions and Answers. 18mo. 1s.

The STEPPING-STONE to ASTRONOMY: Containing several Hundred familiar Questions and Answers on the Earth and the Solar and Stellar Systems. 18mo. 1s.

The STEPPING-STONE to MUSIC: Containing several Hundred Questions on the Science ; also a short History of Music. 18mo. 1s.

The STEPPING-STONE to NATURAL HISTORY: VERTEBRATE OR BACK-BONED ANIMALS. PART I. Mammalia; PART II. Birds, Reptiles, and Fishes. 18mo. 1s. each Part.

THE STEPPING-STONE to ARCHITECTURE; Questions and Answers explaining the Principles and Progress of Architecture from the Earliest Times. With 100 Woodcuts. 18mo. 1s.

INDEX.

Spottiswoode & Co., Printers New-street Square, London.